The Importance of Educational Goals

Education and Learning

Dr. Sharon Campbell-Phillips

 pencil

ISBN 978-93-5458-309-4
© Dr. Sharon Campbell-Phillips 2021
Published in India 2021 by Pencil

A brand of
One Point Six Technologies Pvt. Ltd.
123, Building J2, Shram Seva Premises,
Wadala Truck Terminal, Wadala (E)
Mumbai 400037, Maharashtra, INDIA
E connect@thepencilapp.com
W www.thepencilapp.com

Author biography

My name is Dr. Sharon Campbell-Phillips. I am from Trinidad and Tobago. I am very enthusiastic about community work and the development of others. I am also very passionate about conducting research and writing as it allows me the opportunity to share my knowledge with others and educate them as well as enhance and develop myself.

I am currently employed with the local government of Trinidad and Tobago where I work at the Division of Community Development. This Division is dedicated to developing communities so that persons' standard of living can be enhanced.

My writing career began when I was approached by a classmate from Bangladesh to collaborate and write professionally. I accepted the challenge and we began writing together. When I received my first publication, I was very excited and was motivated to continue writing, I am also a Doctor of Health Sciences.

CONTENTS

Preface

Professionals agree that it's the position of educators to assist beginners set short and long-term desires, as this will assure in addition achievement out of doors the faculty surroundings. Encouraging students to set desires, instructional and non-instructional, is what is lacking in the system. Rookies must be shown the opportunities beforehand, whilst teaching them to be self-pushed and inspired. Teachers must goal at encouraging college students to set milestones for all responsibilities. The manner ought to begin as early as adolescence to permit them to set their very own targets and work closer to getting them to get completed. Goals might also range from home or school sports to network movements, among others.

He explains that during the due route, purpose-placing college students increase several capabilities, including management skills, team constructing, teamwork, duty, and overcoming challenges, which are all critical inside and outside of the faculty. When students are brought to aim setting, they study cut-off dates and managing stress, so one can be applied of their area of labor after faculty. He says teaching college students how to be flexible in all areas is likewise critical. Existence capabilities, or survival skills, cross hand-in-hand with schooling because from my commentary, I've observed that many human beings are in fields that have been now not their choice, however, survival abilities have helped placed meals at the table.

College students have to learn a way to actively concentrate, think, question, and take notes, as well as be capable of pick out their career at any degree. They also need to be given room for conflict as a way to learn how to be accountable. Because the job market is competitive, it's miles important to inspire college students to reap their goals; that is why worldwide college students are preferably higher than those from traditional/local faculties, because they may be introduced to goal placing as early as viable. Students also are influenced by exclusive personalities from distinctive fields; from this, even students that didn't know their talents pick out hobbies. While a pupil is able to set goals, it enables them to be accountable for each motion or step they take.

Having dreams makes learners aware of their moves, efforts, or even their time management talents. Putting desires obligates them to do so, no matter the obstacles that may be in location. As such, it could encourage students to expand vital questioning competencies, new hassle fixing strategies, and higher information of ways to triumph over troubles. Goal placing encourages students to look lower back at previous successes and disasters and compare the regions that need development. As such, it pushes students to address demanding situations head-on and work on their weaknesses for overall success. It additionally helps them realize the techniques that may not be operating for them, for this reason searching for opportunity routes to success.

Purpose setting is essential to the long-time period fulfillment of any scholar. It's difficult for any learner to acquire their goals earlier than knowing how and whilst achieving them. Desires help students to an awareness of the journey to set achievements, because of this they may constantly be prompted with the aid of those desires whenever they feel like giving up. All of it relies upon at the school and hobby of the parents. Ideally, mother and father should strive to offer their kids the high-quality they can with the assets at their disposal; that is the motive why colleges have to have co-curricular activities, for you to cowl such regions which daily scheduled lessons do now not cowl.

Ii is assumed students should be uncovered to as many opportunities as possible to provide them a hazard to excel in areas that can be new to them. It is through such possibilities that hidden talent is located. So programs have to be set with the aid of schools to promote them, inclusive of the junior round square, round square, presidential award schemes, outside and journey, training, debating club, and environmental clubs, amongst others. Colleges have to arrange activities and events wherein successful human beings are invited as motivational or inspirational speakers; this may be a really useful device in helping college students as far as placing desires is worried. Teachers must encourage early steering. He says that through this, college students will discover ways to think seriously.

College students with crucial wondering capabilities have an advantage over the others because they're able to decide what profession is high-quality for them. In truth, they are inside the position to set even extra dreams for themselves and work toward accomplishing them. Depending on the level of a pupil, inviting other college students, specifically those doing the same path with comparable professional dreams, is good. College students can help generate a far richer plan, as opposed to one who's by myself. Also, they should try to find specialists within the institution that best constitute the imaginative and prescient. It's true to associate with as many humans as possible to assist rookies with their desires.

It is vital for educators to teach novices the way to stability their activities, at college and at home. He says this will assist them to spend time wisely. He provides that this will assist learners to avoid recurrence and alternatively check their goals and if they may be running toward their vision. Educators have to intention at coaching rookies the way to be bendy. Careers are continuously changing and that they require new capabilities and new processes. It's proper to keep in mind what's vital to a scholar; as an example, the priorities of a first-term/year student may be specific to the identical scholar two or three years later.

Purpose placing is a procedure and it's good to be flexible continually; parents must be at the forefront to help students acquire their goals. In maximum instances, with regards to more-curricular activities, there are materials needed for one to participate completely; so that they should be inclined to avail the materials. College students, specifically the ones in higher getting to know institutions, should be inclined to alter and adapt to the changes they come upon. that is due to the fact you can actually set goals in primary or secondary school simplest to discover setbacks at a higher degree. It's far believed that instructors and parents should follow up on desires set by means of students as they may emerge as putting unrealistic desires. They should be taught how to set goals and work in the direction of attaining them. Dad and mom ought to act as position models to their youngsters. They have to make sure that anything they gain in existence, however small, is shared by telling their children how they did it. This could encourage kids to work difficult just like their dad and mom.

Introduction

The importance of desires in education should be regarded to all, and studies in education have observed desires to be important for growing pupil success and motivation. Comprehensive meta-analyses have found the effective use of desires to be one of the most effective academic interventions regarded for improving scholar academic success. Having and sharing challenging goals/ intentions with students is a chief circumstance of successful mastering. College students' furnished clean and tough desires significantly outperform peers given easy, vague, or no desires with performance gaps approximating 250% in some research. Moreover, investigations into a hit teaching have constantly found the setting of powerful dreams to be an indicator of superior instructors. The presence of dreams is even more crucial in online and blended getting-to-know settings. Given reduced opportunities for interplay among students and instructors in online courses, there is elevated want for powerful desires to guide and inspire college students. Surveys of online freshmen have discovered that problem expertise instructional goals is a widespread and frequent barrier to academic achievement. And in an analysis of just about 29,000 online scholar questionnaires, researchers observed the elements maximum predictive of student endurance to be clean communique of course dreams and gaining knowledge of results.

Sooner or later, helping students in placing and monitoring getting to know desires is important for supporting the self-regulatory behaviors required of successful online learners. The simplest desires are clear, precise, and challenging. Clear desires provide express success standards and an evaluative widespread that may be used to evaluate learner development. As an instance, the usage of grading rubrics can make assessment expectations obvious to newbies and simply communicate areas in want of development. Unique goals direct attention to aim-relevant statistics and away from purpose-inappropriate behaviors. Goal specificity, for instance, assists learners in spotting vital thoughts in complicated texts and may help instructors cognizance of their comments efficiently. Tough desires present tough however manageable getting to know objectives that energize and motivate freshmen. Constant with Vygostky's idea of the quarter of proximal improvement, powerful getting to know goals should be slightly beyond a scholar's modern-day skills and, as an end result, often require peer or instructor scaffolding to reach first of all. The setting of suitably hard desires requires information on college students' cutting-edge abilities as well as frequent formative exams which can be used to replace academic goals in response to learner development. Further to the characteristics of appropriate desires mentioned above, several contextual factors strongly affect aim effectiveness. Goals are most a hit when there's high learner dedication to accomplishing them. It's crucial to get pupil purchase-in regarding the price of assigned desires and make goal fulfillment individually meaningful for newcomers. A learner's notion in her ability to gain an intention referred to as self-efficacy, also strongly moderates purpose effectiveness. Early possibilities for fulfillment in the pursuit of a tough aim can substantially enhance inexperienced persons' self-assurance in its eventual attainment. Finally, the complexity of a preferred instructional outcome ought to impact the sort of intention setting. If the primary goal is motivating beginners to boom their scalability on a project they already understand, then overall performance dreams (e.g., "enhance your rating by means of five%") are only; but, if the number one subject is supporting college students collect new information then gaining knowledge of goals are most effective.

To date, we've identified the characteristics of good goals as well as numerous essential factors influencing their effectiveness. We now take into account several methods to use this expertise in a normal online and combined getting to know set to promote most useful studying. Growing demanding situations an essential factor of powerful purpose setting is calibrating intention challenge accurately. Numerous techniques for acquiring facts approximately scholar capability may be hired on the internet and blended gaining knowledge of putting. These include diagnostic tests at the graduation of a route, surveys asking college students to rate their familiarity with relevant topics, reviewing pre-needful course syllabi, and frequent formative evaluation activities to pick out styles or gaps in pupil information. Identifying college students' earlier understanding is simplest the first step; however, consistently motivating dreams require common updates to mirror newcomers' growing capabilities. Fostering dedication it's crucial that desires be perceived as significant to students and that there exists a strong learner commitment to accomplishing stated targets. The greater the dedication to achieving learning goals the greater attempt and endurance college students will show in pursuing them. Strategies for increasing learner dedication to goals include making them applicable to college students' lives, explaining why goals are exciting or treasured in their own right, asking college students to make public commitments concerning the fulfillment of dreams, encouraging college students to take part inside the intention-placing system, and connecting desires to college students' pursuits and aspirations. Assisting self-efficacy desires will now not be motivating if beginners do not trust they're conceivable. In reality, if students perceive goals as too tough they'll lessen effort and dedication to avoid the risk of failure. For that reason educators should work to foster high self-efficacy amongst their college students, ensuring newcomers consider goals are viable and that aim fulfillment is inside college students' management. techniques for growing learner self-efficacy consist of presenting possibilities for college kids to revel in early fulfillment (e.g., easy responsibilities or assignments at the beginning of a course to build confidence), sharing examples of past college students who have succeeded and with whom college students can identify, and developing an advantageous studying environment that embraces the educative cost of failure at the same time as emphasizing the incremental nature of know-how acquisition. Dreams will not be motivating if inexperienced persons do now not consider they may be potential. In truth, if students perceive goals as too tough they'll reduce effort and dedication to keep away from the chance of failure.

Where can I research greater approximately desires? Locke and Latham, the foremost professionals in aim placing theory, provide a brilliant introductory precise of the aim-putting literature as well as quick descriptions of its predominant findings. For a radical dialogue of the distinction among mastering and overall performance desires, as well as steerage on while to use each, see the article with the aid of Seijts and Latham (2012). Hattie (2009) affords a beneficial summary of research on the use of dreams in schooling to promote scholar educational success. Imparting remarks maintaining learner motivation and self-efficacy requires common and ongoing comments approximately scholar progress. The extra difficult the purpose, the greater often comments should be furnished. Strategies for increasing learner remarks consist of ordinary formative or low-stakes checking out, requiring college students to submit paper difficult drafts or undertaking proposals previous to very last due dates, and common contact with students to speak about their progress. Additional guidelines along with making students keep learning journals or self-determine their very own work prior to submission can assist teachers to pick out elegance-huge gaining knowledge of difficulties as well as inspire students to interact in treasured self-regulatory mastering behaviors.

Chapter One

The Development of Interests and its Implication

Whether it's a "race to the top" or "no infant left at the back of" or "each pupil succeeds," U.S. academic policies attention on raising college students' overall performance, with a whole lot much less consciousness on sustaining college students' interest. But, when students are interested in an academic subject matter, they may be more likely to visit magnificence, pay attention, become engaged, take more publications, as well as procedure records correctly, and in the long run perform nicely. College students who discover academic hobbies in high school and university are higher prepared for pleasurable careers. Interest is an effective motivational method that energizes mastering and publications academic and professional trajectories. Can guidelines assist teachers to harness this motivation and accordingly assist students to increase interest?

Defining interest

The term interest can describe distinct (although often co-happening) reviews: a man or woman's non-permanent enjoyment of being captivated by an item in addition to extra lasting feelings that the item is exciting and worth further exploration. A hobby is, consequently, both a psychological nation characterized through increased interest, attempt, and affect, skilled in a selected moment (situational hobby), as well as an enduring predisposition to reengage with a particular object or topic through the years (person hobby. This duality no longer simplest highlights the richness of the hobby concept however additionally contributes to the complexity of defining interest precisely. Situational interest combines effective features, including emotions amusement, and exhilaration, with cognitive qualities, such as centered interest and perceived fee, all fostered by using capabilities of the state of affairs. For instance, a student would possibly experience a wonderful lecture approximately tsunamis, end up inquisitive about their energy, interact more inside the class, and respect the subject's private relevance. Thus, being in a state of hobby means that affective reactions, perceived fee, and cognitive functioning intertwine, and that attention and mastering experience effortless. Situational hobby pertains to self-regulation, venture engagement, and patience.

Experiencing situational hobbies can immediately sell learning through growing interest and engagement. A scholar who sees a painting by Monet for the first time in an art records magnificence may be captivated by the bright hues and unusual brushstrokes, and as a result, can pay more attention and interact extra deeply. If that hobby develops into an individual hobby, the student will more likely reengage with the cloth beyond regular time and discover the subject further, consequently, predicts traditional measures of instructional achievement, together with the future course taking and overall performance.

Individual hobby highlights individuals' solid alternatives for unique content. Right here, the on-the-spot experience of hobby reflects a nicely-evolved personal desire to experience and value a selected difficulty or hobby across situations. Man or woman hobby is, therefore, a solid, underlying disposition activated especially in situations. as an instance, college students interested in geophysics might be especially in all likelihood to be in a state of a hobby at some point of a lecture on tsunamis, whether or not the lecture is pleasing or no longer, due to the fact their interest is extra evolved and less depending on situational elements.

How Situational interest will become a person interest

The four-section version of interest development integrates these perspectives and their improvement: specific situations trigger hobby, which can then expand across conditions and through the years to turn out to be extra enduring. First, functions of the surroundings (e.g., novelty, ambiguity, and marvel) catch the character's interest. This situational hobby can last longer, beyond a single situation, if responsibilities seem meaningful and related to (i.e. if the pupil perceives the task as valuable or exciting). Through the years, repeated experiences of caused and maintained situational interest can turn into an emerging man or woman hobby, such that the person seeks possibilities to reengage with the object. For instance, if the pupil who turned into at the start curious about the Monet portray additionally enjoys the teacher's lecture approximately the Impressionist movement after which notices and appreciates the Monet reproductions on show on the dentist's office, the pupil might also decide to Google Monet's artwork and order his biography from the library. Subsequently, this emerging person's interest can grow to be a self-maintaining, well-evolved, man or woman interest (e.g., the scholar visits art museums and majors in artwork history).

Development through those levels calls for a surrounding that supports man or woman pursuit of pastimes. As an instance, a faculty discipline ride to an art museum can foster a pupil's growing hobby in art. As individuals develop through these developmental phases, their connection to the item of hobby turns into greater strong and generalizable. Hobby development starts in a particular state of affairs, however by the point, the one's hobbies are nicely advanced, individuals make aware picks and pursue their interests autonomously. certainly, as hobby deepens throughout those four phases, people turn out to be an increasing number of privy to their very own hobby, as an important part of themselves (e.g., recall themselves Monet fans).

The four-phase version of interest development has implications for teaching practices. First, the version contends that interest develops regularly and that external support (e.g., engaging lectures, school area trips) can foster hobbies. This additionally means that, without external aid, hobbies can pass dormant or maybe be deserted. Second, the model shows that students at extraordinary tiers of interest improvement can also advantage from specific sorts of external support. While college students are unexpected with a subject, instructors may be capable of creating environments that capture their interest (e.g., by starting a chemistry magnificence with an illustration of a chemical response). Whilst college students input a situation with some pre-existing hobby, but, teachers may be capable of preserve those pursuits with interventions to expand their knowledge of the topic and solidify its perceived value. As a consequence, teachers can stimulate college students' developing new interests within the first two stages (triggered and maintained situational hobby), and hold or toughen pastimes for college kids in the second two levels (rising and nicely-evolved man or woman interest). In so doing, instructors can foster students' motivation and success.

Interventions to sell Motivation

Cultivating hobby ought to now not be an afterthought to the everyday mastering scenario: interest is essential to academic success. Interventions to expand college students' interest remember in any educational context, however can be most wished in educational domains that many students do no longer find to begin with thrilling or those domain names in which hobby usually declines over time. For instance, in Center College and high faculty, college students' academic pursuits decline, in particular in science, era, engineering, and arithmetic.

There may be no silver-bullet motivational intervention, and what works for one sort of pupil or classroom context won't generalize (we return up to now later). With that stated, hobby idea informs two intervention techniques:

1. Cause and hold situational interest: offer activities that use structural features (i.e., troubles, demanding situations, surprise) to stimulate attention and engagement for all college students.

2. Build on emerging and nicely advanced character interest: offer content and academic obligations that facilitate connecting instructional subjects with current pursuits.

Triggering students' Situational interest: Structural

capabilities

One way to cause interest is to structure getting to know activities in ways that capture college students' attention. Dewey (1913) argued that educational activities need to awaken and excite the on-the-spot wishes of the person. Berlyne (1970) diagnosed several task features, called collative variables, which affect attention and arousal. In a sequence of studies, he numerous the novelty, complexity, surprisingness, and incongruity of visible stimuli, and observed that each of these collative variables expanded attention, arousal, and hobby. extra broadly, those concepts underlie many interventions meant to promote the situational hobby in educational contexts, which scientists consult with as "triggers for interest." as an instance, different factors brought about situational hobby in a university biology elegance, together with hands-on sports, novelty, wonder, and group work. Similar factors had been vital in ninth-grade biology classes, where novelty proved maximum vital, but desire, physical activity, and social involvement had been additional triggers.

Triggering students' Situational hobby: Context Personalization

Another way to trigger college students' hobbies in a new difficulty is to leverage their current individual interests via offering coaching within the context of those hobbies. For instance, to educate math to a musician, communicate about the mathematical standards inherent in tune. Building content material around existing pursuits is an intuitive approach for educators. To make sure, taking stock of every pupil's hobbies and adjusting the content material, therefore, isn't always without its realistic challenges, especially for teachers of massive classes. Indeed, catering to the private pursuits of a heterogeneous group of students who vary in their pastimes may be tough and time-ingesting.

However, advanced learning technologies that alter content based totally on scholar possibilities can offer feasible and scalable solutions for tailoring guidance to learners' desires and pastimes, as in context personalization. This exercise suits educational duties with characters, items, and subject matters of college students' out-of-faculty interests. For instance, in a physics elegance, a learner interested in severe sports activities might be given a mission that involves sky diving, to learn about gravity and air resistance. Despite content material constraints about what college students are anticipated to analyze, the context of that content can be flexible. Personalized contexts connect new content material to learner's pre-existing personal hobbies. College students given personalized math problems work tougher and carry out better with the maximum reported fine outcomes for college kids suffering from mathematics and among newcomers with a low man or woman hobby inside the content vicinity.

Personalization interventions can be characterized alongside three dimensions: intensity, grain size, and ownership. Intensity refers to the satisfaction of the connections to newbies' present pursuits. Here, interventions range from easy insertions of floor-level facts approximately college students' pastimes (e.g., a fave film) to problematic contextualized responsibilities that relate to college students' pursuits and pastimes. Grain length refers to the dimensions of the reference organization: It differentiates between duties that are tailor-made to the interest of a man or woman learner or corporations of newcomers inclusive of a positive age organization. Here, the intervention relies upon the homogeneity of the elegance and whether or not broad categories of personalization are relevant to a wide target audience or smaller subgroups of college students who might gain from more individualized personalization. Possession refers back to the degree of autonomy in generating personalization. Novel subjects would possibly require help from the instructor or peers to provide ideas for personalization, however, college students can also play a position in personalizing their mastering, and that may create the deepest connections.

For instance, some corporations of college students (native people and Latinos) benefit when the presentation of a science subject matter emphasizes giving lower back to their network, and crucial hobby for these college students. An intervention designed to integrate subjects of giving back to the network in a science direction would be a deep, large-grained personalization intervention as its goals the properly advanced interests of a collection of students. Moreover, this intervention might be carried out with little ownership (e.g., if the instructor gives statistics approximately how technology can be used to deal with network troubles) or with an exquisite deal of possession (e.g., if the instructor responsibilities college students with proposing network outreach sports). What mixture of grain, depth, and possession fine connects with students' existing interests is unclear, however, these principles need to inform the design of personalization interventions.

Triggering and preserving Situational hobby: hassle-based practice

Problem-based gaining knowledge is a tutorial technique that creates a want to resolve a true catch situation. From a hobby concept perspective, problem-primarily based studying presents a mastering environment that may cause and keep situational hobby. First, the hassle presented to students highlights a lack of critical information needed to clear up the hassle, which can cause situational interest. Second, the look for solutions to the problem stimulates interest questions; self-generated questions which can sell the improvement of deeper interest, even as requiring college students to gather and arrange new information approximately the subject that may promote each interest and learning.

Previous research on problem-based getting to know presents insights into a way to create troubles that promote interest. Work with Singaporean college students suggests that fascinating issues (e.g., why the Japanese have been capable to triumph over Singapore all through international war II despite being noticeably outnumbered) may be effective for eliciting situational hobby, but that hobby can also decline once college students find out the solution to the trouble. Consequently, a stimulating problem in and of itself won't be sufficient to promote maintained interest. In a meta-analysis, complicated issues had been greater powerful for promoting students gaining knowledge of than were well-structured troubles. certainly, trouble (climate change) that expanded in complexity as college students discovered more approximately capability solutions, again and again, brought about situational hobby throughout the fifteen-lesson unit, in preference to dropping off as soon as an ability solution become found. Accordingly, complex issues that construct on themselves and constantly lead students to invite additional questions can repeatedly cause situational interest.

Software-value Interventions: Integrating Situational and man or woman hobby processes

Interest concept indicates that every other route to taking pictures and sustaining college students' motivation is helping college students locate which means and value in their guides. Widespread experimental and longitudinal survey research have documented the importance of value-related beliefs, described as perceived usefulness and relevance to the pupil's identity and each quick- and lengthy-time period goals. Whilst students perceive cost in path subjects, they broaden greater interest, work tougher, carry out higher, persist longer, take additional courses, and complete their degree packages. College students who see the cost of a discipline take a look at revel in greater involvement, greater positive assignment attitudes, and greater identity with the domain.

Cost perceptions play a key position in any other prominent theory of motivation: the expectancy-cost principle. According to this idea, humans pick out tough obligations along with persisting in a university physics course if they (a) fee the assignment and (b) count on that they can be triumphant (primarily based on self-ideals). Ideals about the self and beliefs approximately the price of the assignment each predict hobby, course picks, and important preference. Challenge fee includes intrinsic price (the leisure an individual reviews from performing a mission), attainment value (the personal importance of doing properly on a task), and utility value (how useful or applicable the assignment is for the character's modern and future dreams). The intrinsic fee is of path carefully aligned with situational interest, and each intrinsic and attainment value is expecting instructional hobby and patience. Application value, however, is a perfect target for hobby interventions, because it's far from the mission value most amenable to the outside have an impact on.

Intervening to talk about the software of a topic improves motivation. as an instance, convincing parents of the application cost of math and technological know-how for their high college-aged teenagers need to motivate parents to speak to their teenagers approximately their publications, which might promote their young adults' hobby in STEM subjects, and make them take extra non-obligatory math and science publications. Certainly, while utility-value records became communicated to dad and mom (the use of two brochures and an internet site), their teenagers took, on common, an extra semester of math or science of their final years of high faculty, relative to a manipulate institution whose parents did not acquire the application-cost records. A follow-up of those students found that scholars whose mother and father were in the intervention circumstance have been also much more likely to take STEM publications in university and have STEM profession aspirations. Mother and father can promote interest, in addition, to personalize utility-price records on a man or woman foundation. Mother and father understand their young adults' pastimes and can make precise, personal connections in a way that teachers, who work with a couple of students, cannot.

Instructors can, but, harness the strength of deep, particular utility-price connections by way of asking their college students to generate those connections for themselves. To try this requires revising existing path assignments, in addition to infusing new opportunities into the curriculum. Application-fee interventions goal to steer students' perceptions of price by way of the use of writing activities focused on course content (e.g., a homework venture that asks college students to mirror how what they are studying is probably beneficial to their lives). On their very own and in their very own phrases, college students generate connections between direction subjects and their lives; supporting them to respect the value of their coursework and promoting a deeper stage of engagement. The secret's having students actively work to locate the price for themselves. Indeed, self-generated utility-fee connections are greater powerful than externally provided software-fee statistics (as whilst teachers truly inform students that fabric is beneficial) in selling interest and overall performance. A utility-price intervention can assist spark situational hobby in a topic, and it can assist students to join that topic to their pastimes, that may construct on man or woman interest.

The efficacy of the intervention for promoting hobby and performance turned into first established in ninth-grade technology instructions, with the strongest benefits for much less assured college students; the intervention advanced performance for these at-danger students by way of of almost two-thirds of a letter grade, and superior their hobby in science. Furthermore, interest anticipated college students' science-related career plans, suggesting that this simple intervention promotes vital academic consequences.

The Special Case of Introductory publications in higher education

Introductory university guides are ripe with opportunity: right here, students test the waters in specific fields, verify their fit, and gauge their hobby in pursuing majors and careers. However, these guides also gift specific challenges. For instructors, those guides are populated by way of massive, numerous agencies of college students with various tiers of information, hobby, and motivation within the discipline, making it difficult to promote hobby for all students. For students, introductory guides are regularly important gateways to majors and careers, requiring high grades to continue in a subject. Structurally, they're regularly big, impersonal, and overwhelming for college kids who may be new to the college surroundings. Especially amongst first-year college students, introductory courses can be the yardstick through which they degree their suit in college, not just in a specific area. for this reason, for many college students, introductory courses present high-strain exams in their academic belonging in a specific discipline and college greater normally, and these pressures are exacerbated for sure corporations of at-threat college students (e.g., first-technology and underrepresented minority students) who are much more likely to doubt their belonging in college, come to be disengaged in massive-lecture courses, or each.

What are the logistics of implementing an interest intervention in a big introductory magnificence? The use of collative elements (novelty, marvel, humor) can take hold of college students' attention, however also can appear gimmicky and incorrectly rub university students. In comparison, context personalization interventions meet character students wherein they're and create interest in course subjects through affiliation to their specific private pastimes. at the beginning look, the logistics of context personalization may not appear possible in a big-lecture putting. As coursework actions online, however, advances in adaptive mastering technologies may additionally help university professors individualize some educational sports. Further, problem-based mastering techniques may be perfect for middle faculty or high faculty instruction, however are not as easily applied in massive-lecture publications. These strategies are probably usefully carried out in smaller laboratory sections, which permit extra flexibility.

The utility-price intervention is properly perfect for introductory college guides. as an instance, in introductory undergraduate psychology lessons, using quick application-value writing assignments promoted hobby for college kids who had been performing poorly within the magnificence, relative to a management organization that wrote summaries of route material. indeed, the utility-cost intervention is bendy, can attain college students at varying ranges of hobby, and can even assist underrepresented students to connect what they are studying to their particular set of pursuits and values, with the potential to close chronic achievement gaps. As a case in point, a utility-fee intervention carried out in a massive introductory biology direction (with 3 brief writing assignments during the semester) become powerful for all college students and specifically for students who tended to war the maximum within the course: first-era underrepresented minority college students. These students carried out about half a grade factor higher within the intervention circumstance than inside the control circumstance. Similarly, they have become greater engaged inside the software-fee mission, writing longer essays notwithstanding identical period requirements. The software-cost intervention is a crucial device, especially for undergraduate teachers, to effect pupil success with far-achieving fantastic advantages.

One size suits a few

No hobby intervention is one length suits all. Thinking about college students' pre-current hobbies and degree of competence for a given subject matter is vital. Indeed, a few interest triggers merely distract students who already have a properly developed interest in a topic, whereas those same triggers promote situational hobby for college kids in the earlier levels of interest. As an example, visually stimulating, catchy features together with including shade, numerous fonts, and shiny photos to math responsibilities better situational hobby for college students who have been low in man or woman interest, but had a poor effect for college kids who had greater evolved hobby in math.

On the whole, utility-fee interventions frequently improve motivation for all students and the blessings are often biggest for the most at-risk college students. Yet, college students who experience extra competence from time to time advantage extra from the maximum direct application-value communications. The manner that application price is communicated also differentially influences students in specific phases of hobby development. Directly communicated utility value is most useful for college kids with well-evolved pursuits, but self-generated application price is more effective for those who are to start with low interest. These nuances should inform the choice of an intervention, which requires thinking about the specific dreams of the educator, the academic setting, and the needs of the scholars.

Hobby matters in educational coverage

With the passage of each student Succeeds Act (ESSA) in December 2015 (U.S. branch of education, 2015), extra autonomy is granted to the neighborhood and state companies to set instructional evaluation standards. What is more, the ESSA prioritizes the use of evidence-based instructional interventions. The time is consequently ripe to remember the contribution of hobby principle to new and current okay-twelve and better education guidelines, accreditation standards, and teacher licensure necessities. Teacher training, incentivizing, and responsibility guidelines each may additionally contribute to a greater engaged mastering revel in for our state's pupil frame, as follows.

To get to an area where student motivation is a valued procedure and final results, rules ought to inform the schooling of our next technology of educators. Country-wide accreditation forums (e.g., Council for the Accreditation of Educator practice), country accrediting corporations, and instructor licensing structures would possibly need to take into account tighter alignment with classes discovered from motivational technology after they set trainer coaching policies and standards. One feasible coverage action is the pro-lively design of teacher coaching applications primarily based on the principles of hobby theory and the interventions that cause and preserve college students' situational interest or build on their rising and well-evolved character pastimes. For instance, instructor guidance policy should mandate publications on how to compare and undertake interest interventions in curricular, co-curricular, and even extracurricular efforts. One promising course is to put in force a middle trainer-education path, and continuing training courses, on student hobby development methods. This type of route ought to emphasize one-of-a-kind styles of hobby-triggering structural capabilities strategies for context personalization strategies for trouble-primarily based education strategies for top-rated communication of application-cost facts and ultimate implementation of software-price interventions. any such path might always emphasize how interest triggers foster connections and deeper processing, in addition, to lay out the science in the back of how struggling and at-threat college students can enjoy the one-of-a-kind kinds of interest interventions.

Teacher education regulations and practices are beneficial best insofar as they translate to movement within the schoolroom, which indicates incentivizing the layout and adoption of interest interventions and worthwhile schools for the downstream benefits in their efforts towards enhancing student motivation. Getting down into the weeds of creating educational possibilities that sell and preserve students' hobbies or facilitate application-cost connections is time-consuming and requires careful attention to intervention implementation information. Various evaluation policies should reward educators who use evidence-primarily based motivational technological know-how to inform their curricula and educational methods, for instance, using imparting expert development budget, developing organizational coaching awards, and other meritorious reputation for such efforts.

Subsequently, policies need to cross beyond strict performance requirements and don't forget multiple signs of scholar fulfillment that encompass pupil hobby. The subsequent step is revising current guidelines that already preserve directors and teachers answerable for student learning, and expanding those policies to include fostering interest. This can start, as an example, by using obligatory inclusion of rankings of the degree of interest in, or application of, path content in pupil and peer reviews of coaching which are factored into annual college reviews and merchandising choices. Different options are to create guidelines that require colleges to outline the software fee of their path content, include interest interventions as a preferred requirement for faculty process applicants, and mandate that advertising and retention dossiers include proof of efforts closer to enhancing scholar motivation. Such responsibility guidelines might set a brand new norm for the vital position of scholar hobby in education.

The effect of scholar interest and trainer effectiveness

Studying is a pastime that college-age children engage in daily. For some, it's far a joy, whilst for others, a war. Instructors have to discover approaches to cope with the huge variety of reading abilities and differentiate their training to house all talent levels. Similar to these varying ability ranges, students have special backgrounds, motivation tiers, and pursuits. With the creation of the not unusual middle standards into English Language Arts lecture rooms throughout the state, each instructor and student are faced with extra demanding situations. One such assignment is determining which texts to select and the way to use them correctly inside the classroom. With the notably latest advent of common core, there's a pressure to now not best encompass, however to awareness on, non-fiction texts, which may be challenging for college students who face up to analyzing even if given texts which might be of a high hobby. The studies on this have a look at is meant to expose the link between scholar comprehension and writing capacity, and the style (fiction or nonfiction) of the guiding text, as well as the impact of the instructor's effectiveness. Without clean know-how of how precise texts affect student motivation, it is tough for instructors to devise instructions and units that their college students will respond to. There can be a sizeable quantity of guesswork and ineffective use of time, which isn't always a green way of reaching all college students, nor is it ideal for instructors who want to plot-relevant and precious classes. on occasion instructors are restricted by directives from the school or curriculum in terms of what styles of texts they'll choose; as such, it is to their advantage to be aware of how a style affects scholar overall performance so that they'll tailor their training to maximize scholar gaining knowledge of. Whilst students aren't invested in their getting to know, they're not as in all likelihood to be engaged. Loss of student engagement influences not most effective their mastering, however the studying of others in the study room; they're greater inclined to fulfillment.

The effect of pupil hobby and instructor effectiveness

Few things are greater irritating than making plans for a lesson that fails to interact with college students. Whilst it's far inevitable that such instructions happen every so often - and those classes can even provide valuable opportunities for reflection and teachers could make higher use in their time via understanding the hobbies in their college students beforehand. They can learn about their college students' hobbies in a variety of approaches through the usage of pupil questionnaires, rating scales, or interviews. Further to being aware of the needs and hobbies of their college students, teachers have to now not forget about the importance of their dating with their students-which does no longer always implies it must be described by way of students "liking" their instructors. It truly way that for most efficient studying to arise there must be mutual appreciation. Based on personal enjoyment, it's miles less difficult to reach suffering students whilst a trusting courting has been installed. The principal question that drives this research venture is how student engagement and relationship with the evaluator impact pupil performance. The studies became collected while running with two center faculty college students at some point of guided reading periods. To help me answer my studies query, I presented the students with a series of studying passages so one can collect pupil work samples and make observations-two that would be taken into consideration high hobby, and two that might be taken into consideration low-interest. I also created and accrued questionnaires from the students, one about their pastimes, the other to their emotions approximately me as a teacher. My findings confirmed a measurable benefit in pupil scores on written responses to high hobby passages in comparison to low-interest passages. The work the students finished for the excessive interest passages was thorough and much greater evolved than the work that they finished for low-hobby passages. Further, there was a clean increase in focus and motivation even as running on high-interest passages. These findings call for teachers to consider student hobbies when making education plans.

The effect of pupil interest and trainer effectiveness
Pupil motivation and the fulfillment they locate whilst fully engaged is important to creating getting to know meaningful, applicable, and lifelong. Theoretical Framework the foundation of this examination is primarily based on the word "literacy," which may suggest different things to exclusive humans. My definition of literacy is the potential to study, realize, talk, and make meaningful connections between text and language. Literacy is verbal and non-verbal, oral and written, social and cultural. Its definition is continuously changing and evolving. Gee defines literacy as "fluent manipulate of the secondary discourse". Literacy is the use of language, thinking, and acting that enables people to become aware of a selected organization. This definition can be prolonged into the study room when college students are expected to use language in a particular manner that identifies them as part of a set of their peers. Whilst examining literacy and the way it pertains to scholar mastering, it's far essential to be familiar with the theories surrounding the problem.
The sociocultural principle defines the pupil as an

energetic member of a continuously converting community of newcomers in which knowledge constructs and is constructed through large cultural systems. In terms of its significance for instructors, their study room will become that network whilst the scholars are in faculty. children want to be able to narrate and hook up with what they may be studying, in addition to one another and the bigger world, that's in particular crucial for instructors to recall when choosing suitable and relevant texts for their students. They want so that it will make connections to what they examine. They will need steering in doing this, mainly suffering readers. The sociocultural concept shifts the point of interest in the study room from being teacher-targeted to being student-focused. When instructors pick out texts with little to no pupil enter or consideration, they're already commencing at a disadvantage. After they do not recall the desires of their college students as individuals and as a community, they may be setting their college students at a drawback, and now not mining their complete capacity.

The effect of scholar interest and trainer effectiveness

Using gaining perception into the factors that motivate students, teachers can use that knowledge to guide, foster, and encourage a network of focused and successful newcomers. Proof suggests that youngsters acquire language in culturally precise methods, which's supported via the socio-cultural concept of literacy acquisition. Every scholar will gather language at domestic in a different way. Instructors must take into account this aspect, considering a few children will acquire language via the analyzing of several books and others will research via oral language on their own. Students' way of acquiring literacy will impact their hobbies as well as their talents. any other idea which could provide further assistance for this have a look at is the social constructionism idea, which states that an infant's identity in literacy-based events is impacted through his or her surroundings. The identification of the reader is without delay associated with the stories the child has with literacy. Consequently, the feelings of the kid and the trainer about the kid will impact the literacy experience. That is in which the effectiveness of the teacher turns into an aspect in pupil overall performance. Whilst an instructor engages and motivates college students, they may be more likely to want to take part in sports and display their competencies. Trainer effectiveness and the position of the teacher are critical in figuring out scholar success. Assessment and assessment of this aspect of getting to know will assist me to move forward in my coaching profession. Student achievement has such a lot of factors, but that is one which we, as educators, have control over.

The effect of pupil hobby and trainer effectiveness

The research question for the reason that literacy is a social practice and getting to know takes place for the duration of social interplay, this motion research task asks, how does pupil interest inside the text and instructor effectiveness impact his or her overall performance in duties related to the text? the following action research examine will discover the position of student interest and motivation on overall performance in college. Student school performance is a place extensively researched and documented. It spans age, grade stage, potential, and geography. Countless studies have been accomplished to decide elements that influence student fulfillment; lots has additionally been achieved to establish why students fail and what can be accomplished to treatment the state of affairs. This evaluation will discover the studies and theories which have come earlier than and which shape its foundation. The socio-cultural principle, mainly, performs an essential function within the studies and conclusions in this area. Further, as an exploration into this subject matter advanced, three tendencies emerged. A long time of students within the studies ranged from pre-kindergarten to undergraduate degree, however, the trends transcended age, gender, race, and socio-monetary reputation. The first, and most full-size to this examine, is that scholar hobby impacts motivation and achievement. The second is that a student's relationship with his or her trainer is a thing in student success. Subsequently, intention placing becomes discovered to be influential in scholar motivation and academic behaviors.

Several types of research had been executed that positively correlate scholar hobby with instructional overall performance. Several of the examples that assist this idea are primarily based specifically on interest in literature, even though a few studies may be generalized throughout content material areas. In a -twelve months have a look at middle school students, researchers found that self-decided on texts increased the readers' high-quality feelings approximately analyzing and progressed fulfillment ratings?

The impact of pupil hobby and trainer effectiveness

The lecturers provided college students with time to study, preference in e-book selection, and possibilities for reader response. This study was unique to non-fiction texts, which's considerable, given the common core requirements push for integrating greater expository texts into the schoolroom. Know-how, why students chose the books they did, will help educators motivate students. The take a look at observed that self-choice turned into critical whilst attempting to inspire students to examine and that non-fiction may be just as motivating as fiction. The significance of student interest was a key get rid of from that examination, and that is a critical component for teachers to do not forget, although no longer just with middle faculty students. In Hargrove's (2005) look at younger students, the same fashion will be visible. The study became encouraged via one teacher's frustration while faced with excessive capacity however underachieving college students. The two male second-graders who participated in the observation were given two one-of-a-kind assignments: one trainer-led, the alternative student-directed. Hargrove tested the consequences of this instructor's study and decided that the scholar-directed undertaking changed into successful, ensuing in expanded energy and output. The instructor-led mission showed the same effects that led to the teacher's initial frustration and motivation to start the examination inside the first location. The instructor considered students as individuals and took their pastimes and personalities into attention when developing the task. It may be concluded, then, that both studies reaffirm the reality that pupil interest is a factor in motivation and fulfillment. Pupil interest spans age levels, however additionally geography. The research above has been carried out in urban settings. However, the value and importance of student hobbies are not limited to specific regions. Hardr, Sullivan, and Crowson (2009) carried out a have a look at students, grades nine to twelve in a rural high college. College students had been given questionnaires that examined scholar self-perceptions, goal orientations, interest (because it pertained to success), and achievement as to the school of entirety it related.

The impact of student hobby and instructor effectiveness

The researchers observed that once college students saw cost and relevance in what they had been learning and the way it can assist acquire their goals, they had been more likely to have elevated interest, positioned the fourth attempt, and graduate going on to post-secondary opportunities. Further, the extra ready they felt approximately their abilities, the more likely they were to commit to endured have a look at and training. Consequently, the interest those college students felt in their learning had a great impact on their feelings of fulfillment, and, in the long run, their overall performance. Students must view their studying stories as genuine and significant. College students are ways more likely to place forth effort once they understand why they may be doing a venture. The impact and effect of college students' intrinsic motivation are vital for teachers to bear in mind whilst supplying statistics in their classrooms. Many researchers could believe the assertion that student engagement increases while college students find the undertaking hard, balanced, applicable, and below their manipulation. They decided this in their examination by asking students to song their educational sports in the course of the direction of the school day and document how they felt in the course of the one's activities. Students felt maximum engaged when participating in a collection pastime or discussion as opposed to paying attention to a lecture. They concluded that based totally on Csikszentmihalyi's (1997) go with the flow concept, awareness, interest, and amusement in an activity must all be a gift. All the research above guide the argument that scholar hobby performs a key function in pupil success. Interest is important for persevering with motivation and learning. Researchers located that venture and delight in challenging final touch will encourage college students and interact their interest. Therefore, instructors should increase sports which can be tough and applicable, and additionally deliver students some control of their studying.

The impact of pupil interest and teacher effectiveness
 A tool that instructors can use to assist them with growing such sports is a student survey, which includes the one hired via Diaz-Rubin (1996). Since instructors need to first be aware of scholar pursuits if you want to provide them with suitable and effective materials, a survey or questionnaire is one way to acquire that information. Such focus on the part of the teacher will assist college students to turn into unbiased readers and make connections to actual international. To that cease, Diaz-Rubin created a survey for which the sole reason become to decide to study topic alternatives of excessive faculty college

students. College students pronounced wanting to study subjects that allowed them to "escape"–i.e., humor and fable. They also expressed a hobby in gangs/crime, which can be related to the media's portrayal of it and college students' exposure to the romanticism of that lifestyle. Instructors can inspire college students with thrilling substances and a survey like this allows them to decide what those interests are. Whilst college students are allowed to make an analyzing selection based totally on their pursuits, it is much more likely that a better degree of comprehension will arise. Like Hargrove (2005), Diaz-Rubin concurs that choice prompted by using scholar hobby is a successful way to have interaction with college students. By way of tuning into student hobbies, teachers can promote literacy. Without motivation, students are in reality much less engaged and much less probable to be successful. Teachers must be privy to their college students' interests and capitalize on them whenever possible. They can decide interest through scholarly hobby surveys, interviews, verbal remarks, and statements. Student hobby and engagement isn't always constantly an easy thing to be expecting, nor is it static. Due to the fact, students are continuously changing and growing, educators must be aware of how those changes affect the students. Some researchers explored the feelings and behaviors that correlate with engagement and disaffection in the study room. College students in fourth to seventh grade and their instructors finished self-report questionnaires. The examination discovered that students had been extraordinarily engaged early on, but engagement declined within the transition to Center College.

The impact of student hobby and instructor effectiveness

Fees of disengagement have been proportional to preliminary ranges of engagement. College students and teachers determined that boredom becomes a massive thing in disengagement. Trainer guide performed a big role in the dynamics of engagement. trainer get right to entry to the results of the observation may also assist teachers to discern which motivational helps they may install place to first-rate gain their students. Skinner et al. located that scholar engagement declined as they get older. Therefore, educators need to be both be prepared to reach college students in any respect grade levels or ought to take preventative measures. College students often suggest their engagement thru certain behaviors, and while instructors understand those behaviors and the emotions at the back of them, they can first-rate address the issue. As an instructor, it's important to recognize those symptoms (each high quality and poor) and either toughen or remedy the state of affairs. Marks (2010) purported that three factors influence scholar engagement and getting to know: private background and orientation toward faculty, college projects, and problem dependents. She looked at twenty-four faculties' present process restructuring, specifically grades five, eight, and ten. Students completed surveys about their attitudes, behaviors, and reviews, their fashionable faculty revel in, and their personal/own family history. She became capable of drawing numerous conclusions from her look. First, like Skinner et al., scholar engagement decreased as grade level multiplied; high college students stated the least positive orientation towards colleges. By way of evaluation, emotions of being supported in the schoolroom had been maximum amongst elementary faculty students. The challenge to remember did have an impact on reports of authentic work (that is, students feel that the work is hard and relevant). Success students had been more engaged, but students who suggested feeling alienated have been much less so (Marks). These findings tie into the studies completed by Zepke and Leach (2010), whose conclusions challenged teachers to offer their college students real-international reports and actual mastering opportunities.

The impact of student hobby and teacher effectiveness

Marks; that fun and hardsports are much more likely to inspire student engagement. When college students have a few semblances of manipulating over their mastering, they may be much more likely to be engaged and obtain educational fulfillment. Many researchers help this declare with the conclusions of their observation. They found that locus of manage, hobby in schooling, and self-efficacy are all elements in predicting instructional achievement. The locus of management refers to a character's notion of what causes achievement. It may be internal, wherein the pupil believes fulfillment is due to non-public effort and ability and is more likely to work difficult. Students who believe in an outside locus of management will characteristic their success to good fortune or destiny, and may not put forth as a good deal effort. More widespread to this review are the consequences that analyzed scholar hobby in schooling. Similar to Diaz-Rubin's (1996) study, the researchers discovered gaining knowledge becomes intrinsic praise when interest is an element. When teachers recognize signs of both engagement and disaffection, they can make the word of what college students are doing during that point and then use that fact while reflecting upon the lesson. Without a doubt pupil engagement isn't always the handiest element to affect pupil performance and conduct—there are numerous factors over which instructors have little or no control. However, through awareness and commentary, teachers can observe rising tendencies and patterns, to assist them when planning classes and selecting materials. Based totally on the studies outlined above, it is reasonable to conclude that scholar hobby is an important factor in scholar success. As huge a role as pupil interest plays, however, we cannot forget about the importance of other factors that still contribute to scholar fulfillment and the way they may be all entwined. Pupil hobby can be linked to their investment in what is going on in the study room. Here we have a look at the significance of instructors' academic methods and their effect on pupil fulfillment. Several types of research assist the hyperlink among the real forms of obligations students are asked to carry out and their ability to efficiently complete those responsibilities.

The effect of student interest and instructor effectiveness

Dai and Wand (2006) gave university undergraduates rating scales, narrative and expository texts, and corresponding a couple of of-preference questions. Topics finished the obligations after which rated their hobby stage for each piece. The consequences of the have a look at confirmed that scholars carried out higher duties that piqued their interests, which helps the idea that what the reader brings to the reading enjoy will influence both the methods and results (goals/techniques used and comprehension/hobby). The take a look at reaffirms the fact that educators need to bear in mind many factors that impact pupil motivation, comprehension, and performance. Similarly, Connor (2009) finished a case look at wherein records were accrued from self-reviews of college students writing extended essays. Students had been allowed to choose their subjects, the notion being that this will increase their engagement. The outcomes found that a better percentage of students pronounced being engaged. Teachers searching at these records can conclude that scholar choice does boom motivation and engagement. In a try to outline greater particularly what instructors can do to boom pupil funding, Zepke and Leach (2010) performed a have a look at that sifted through earlier studies and then proposed ten motion steps for increasing scholar engagement. Zepke and Leach outline student engagement as "students' cognitive investment in, active participation in an emotional dedication to their learning". They searched databases to synthesize research that explores student engagement and fulfillment and drew their very own conclusions. Zepke and Leach then synthesized the conclusions into movement steps for educators. Essentially they recommended instructors to encourage students, provide them a risk to work autonomously in addition to with friends, and be approachable, prepared, and sensitive to pupil desires. in addition, they ought to create a laugh and hard academic experiences, even as also encouraging range and offering help services (orientation, mentoring).

The effect of student hobby and trainer effectiveness

Teachers need to help students domesticate social and cultural capital to expand a feel of belonging and shape relationships with others. Instructors can adapt, modify, individualize, and increase upon those action steps of their school room to boom pupil engagement. Dai and Wand (2006) would agree that such steps will lead to elevated scholar motivation, overall performance, and fulfillment. The key right here is spotting the position that educators play in determining student outcomes. While they cannot be expected to govern what occurs outside of the lecture room, it stays their obligation to take the important steps to recognize and deal with the desires of their students inside the lecture room. Without that cognizance, possibilities for pupil success and engagement may be minimized or neglected totally. As noted in advance, these findings are regularly interrelated, with certain studies specializing in one predominant idea, at the same time as additionally addressing different issues. Training is a discipline that requires professionals to discover and grow to be acquainted with a mess of things as a way to high-quality serve their college students, which brings us to the following trend that emerged: the effect of trainer-student relationships on scholar success. The relationship among students and instructors is a Key thing in student success teachers, especially within the essential grades, spends a sizable part of a given day with their students. It stands to cause that they have an effect on student achievement and failure, which include, however now not limited to, grades and exams. Studies have observed that student relationships with their instructors can be a predictor for the extent of fulfillment that students experience. The instructor is mainly answerable for developing the school room surroundings. It has therefore concluded that schoolroom surroundings primarily based on nice social relationships that still encourage the personal empowerment of its students will foster elevated motivation and gaining knowledge.

The effect of student interest and trainer effectiveness

A forty-item questionnaire changed into given to two hundred pre-service, secondary, or simple instructors. Their responses yielded the following suppositions: teacher attitude (whether tremendous or defeatist) will affect his or her classroom surroundings. management can help foster superb classroom surroundings, however, it is greater tough with the constraints of duty and takes a look at ratings which have turn out to be such a focal point in current years. Pre-service teachers could advantage from precise education in the way to create this form of environment. If the aim is scholar achievement, then the advent of surroundings wherein students sense secure and inspired can have a positive impact on their performance. Teachers are responsible for doing this, however, with the emphasis on check rankings and student performance created via APPR and different kingdom and country-wide mandates, they will sense pressured to the cognizance of other regions-the ones genuinely being assessed. In the end, the advent of a superb studying environment may have brief and long-time period blessings that would additionally meet the demands of management and kingdom requirements.

Nichols (2007) have a look at also supports the idea that

scholar-instructor relationships are a key component in scholar engagement and closing achievement. It is agreed that teachers affect the lecture room surroundings and their impact on students. Their examination located that there's a correlation between teachers' scores of war and closeness with students' academic abilities. based totally on surveys and observations, they determined that scholars who had poor relationships in preschool favored school much less by way of first grade, based totally on the styles that were established from information analysis. Poor emotions caused much less engagement inside the schoolroom. The research observed and some researchers could agree that teachers need to be aware that their mind, emotions, and interaction with college students are all factors in students' engagement, and, in the long run, scholar fulfillment. Additionally, closer monitoring and remark of trainer-scholar relationships could have enough money more possibilities for scholar success.

The impact of student hobby and teacher effectiveness

Like Nichols's have a look at, Pianta and Stuhlman's conclusions show that the environment that teachers create is vitally critical to pupil fulfillment. Others might agree that scholars' achievement in school is impacted through the emotional weather of their classrooms. They surveyed sixty-three instructors and a couple of,000 college students in 90 fifth and sixth grade ELA lecture rooms, amassing data via lecture room observations, report cards, and student reviews. The school rooms have been assessed for emotional support, school room agency, and educational support. They found that characteristics of lecture rooms with an incredibly advantageous emotional weather covered: experience of connectedness and belonging, enjoyment, enthusiasm, and admiration for self and others. Students in these lecture rooms have interaction in extra getting to know and have fewer behavioral troubles. Teachers in these school rooms are conscious of the academic, social, and emotional wishes of their college students, and additionally, help them hassle-resolve. All of those traits led to more instructional success.

The take-away for teachers is that students who experience a connection to their teacher engage greater and have expanded academic achievement. While this studying weather disappears, so does the student engagement. Instructors are answerable for growing and maintaining study room surroundings that engage students and creates fine emotional weather. It is also found that significant and authentic instruction takes region extra successfully in a study room that emotionally engages the students. When students have nice relationships with their instructors early on, it can be a hallmark of later pupil success. Swanson, and others located this to be real based on a survey of 266 students, dad and mom, and instructors. They also administered the scholar-instructor dating Scale and looked at pupil document cards. They concluded that after mother and father and teachers are aware of how they affect college students, the result may be positive interventions and, in the end, student achievement.

The impact of student interest and trainer effectiveness

College students who engage in the effort are much more

likely to interact with teachers definitely and accomplish educational responsibilities. As a trainer, it is vital to notice that after there are so many different factors that affect a toddler's performance in faculty, it's essential to build a high-quality dating between scholar and instructor. Some factors are outdoor of the school's control, however, an instructor can control sure elements of what a toddler is uncovered to in the walls of the classroom. Those choices can have a long-lasting impact on the scholar's college performance. Further, many researchers followed a set of college students from kindergarten to eighth grade. Students and teachers had been given screening measures and questionnaires. Numerous developments were located: in simple years, teachers suggested fewer conflicts with women than boys; women acquired more "tremendous habits" feedback than boys normal. Usually, early trainer-scholar relationships had been dependable predictors of student instructional and conduct patterns through eighth grade.

The effects of the take a look at help their declaration that the instructor-pupil dating is crucial in predicting scholar outcomes. Low negativity rankings in kindergarten caused fewer behavioral troubles in later years. But, college students who had early behavioral issues but have been able to expand relationships with instructors have been much less probably to have persevered with behavior issues. Teachers can finish that their dating with a student is a vital aspect in that toddler's achievement in college, even if it isn't necessarily educational. While students have a superb courting with an instructor, they'll be extra invested in faculty, main to accelerated motivation and attempt. When searching at the massive picture of scholar motivation and performance, this relationship cannot be ignored. Every other aspect in the trainer-baby dating is the figure. Because it has been installed that the connection between the instructor and scholar is important for success, the role of the figure on this equation ought to additionally be taken into consideration and researchers blanketed discern comments in making their determinations.

The effect of student interest and teacher effectiveness

Some other observe showed that showed how relationships among teachers, parents, and college students component into scholar success and feelings of school-relatedness. A pattern of first-grade college students changed into given the Woodcock-Johnson III fulfillment checks. In addition, Hughes and Kwok analyzed trainer reports, administered a trainer relationship stock, allotted a questionnaire of instructor-figure relationships, and conducted scholar interviews. They determined that pupil fulfillment extended while students and parents sense supported through teachers. They also reasoned that "social relatedness is crucial to kids' engagement and educational fulfillment". The take look at emphasized the importance of growing high-quality domestic-faculty relationships. We ought to take into account that students' perceptions of their instructors can have an effect on their overall performance, and instructor perceptions of their students can have an effect on their view of the scholars' performance. Normally, pupil engagement and motivation may also grow when they and their mother and father experience supported using the instructor. Scholar perception can go beyond their views of the trainer; it may increase to different sports within the schoolroom. The various studies demonstrated that students' likes and dislikes in terms of coaching that they have experienced will influence their perceptions of the mastering environment, learning, and overall performance.

The study turned into performed with older students, ranging in age from eighteen to twenty. Questionnaires and standardized checks were used to achieve information. In line with the results of the study, many elements influenced students' likes and dislikes concerning guidance. In this have a look at, there were five academic organizations, all being taught the same direction however with special methods: one turned into lecture-primarily based; the alternative four have been pupil-activated. They were assessed in four specific approaches (more than one desire test, portfolio case research, and peer tests.

The impact of scholar hobby and instructor effectiveness

Their perceptions of the direction had been amassed via of entirety of a questionnaire (using a five-point scale). Students' notion of mastering changed into equal among lecture-primarily based and student-activated. Feedback approximately the lecture-primarily based turned into in most cases high-quality, at the same time as the four scholar-activated techniques have been greater ambiguous and numerous. The aim for teachers is "matching students' instructional choice and teaching" which will offer an "instructional putting that is conducive to mastering." This group of college students genuinely favored a lecture-based coaching fashion. The obligation of the lecture room instructor, regardless of the age of the students, is to evaluate college students' mastering patterns and plan the transport of preparation for that reason. The statistics amassed in this have a look at is also supported by the research because they each put the onus at the trainer to evaluate the wishes of the scholars inside the lecture room after which provide coaching is enticing and applicable. There might be instances whilst that is a daunting undertaking for teachers. There are numerous contributing elements to the occasions that occur throughout an afternoon. This concept becomes examined in an examination completed using Jackson and Lunenburg (2010), who surveyed a collection of center school teachers. The academics rated themselves and their colleges about instructional excellence, developmental responsiveness, social equity, and organizational structures. in step with the effects of the measures, there was variability in instructor behaviors, ideas, and strategies, learning environments, services available, instructional techniques used assets to be had (Jackson and Lunenburg). The takeaway from this look is that faculties themselves may additionally vary in what they could provide students. But, as became discovered, the instructor is steady, and therefore in a role to create those tremendous surroundings for college students. There can be times whilst teachers are confined through the budget, sources, and demands; the task is to find methods to create a lecture room environment this is nonetheless authentic, and tough.

The effect of pupil interest and trainer effectiveness
Instructors can try this by way of placing targets,

implementing educational techniques (note-taking, questioning, image organizers), and looking for support from management in which essential and suitable. The act of building a court between student and trainer is multi-faceted, complex, and notably critical to pupil success, fulfillment, and perceptions. Those research continue to guide the declaration that the relationship between the pupil and teacher is an essential one, no matter differences in age, grade, gender, and problem remember. Intention setting is a key aspect in student success the final fashion that emerged after reading the articles changed into the necessity of scholar desires to instructional success. Developing and assembly targets are predicted within the submit-college international. It makes sense that students might locate purpose creation to be helpful and intention final touch to be enjoyable. Researchers addressed the outcomes of age as opposed to education on reading engagement and studying activities. Their examination became constructed from records accrued from high college students. They applied self-reviews to gather records on student motivation and goals as they pertained especially to studying. They also gathered self-reports from instructors in regards to the faculty's said dreams for its students. Their look at located that there's a wonderful impact of education on scholar performance dreams. In records collected from the lecturers, however, there has been a disconnection between school-said desires (private improvement, social capabilities, cognitive, and information acquisition), and the student-stated dreams, most of which have been cognitive. When you consider that many schools do now not presently well known or reward fulfillment of dreams which are non-cognitive, students might not see them as critical and may decrease their attempt in the one's regions. Educators need to be conscious that it's far important that goals be regular in their advent, implementation, and evaluation. Lack of follow-through can result in students being less invested in desires–especially when they do now not see any effect or effect.

The impact of pupil interest and teacher effectiveness
When students can take possession of their work and notice their development, they may be much more likely to make investments inside the work. Martin (2007) determined that understanding college students' strengths and needs after which supporting them create focused dreams will help them correctly attain those desires. This investment will occur itself in student motivation and fulfillment. Cao and Nietfield (2007) also posit that there may be dating between students' gaining knowledge of goals, performance dreams, study techniques, and performance. Their research sought to prove this via a take a look at undergraduate college students; students set desires at the beginning of a fourteen-week path after which were given reflection time and substances after every test, all through which they might pick to regulate their dreams. Researchers and students assessed the effectiveness of sure types of studying techniques. After students created gaining knowledge of and performance desires and assessed them after the path, they have been requested to describe take a look at strategies they used. Some students had changed them over the 14-week course with a purpose to higher meet their overall performance and studying dreams, which confirmed that students have

been cognizant of their progress and willing to alternate elements in their behaviors. Examples of taking a look at techniques have been flashcards, looking for help, enterprise, and reviewing elegant notes. Factors of this look at may be adapted to help college students set dreams in any schoolroom and any content material place. Permitting students' reflection after test feedback may be helpful for college kids to evaluate their achievement and make any modifications wished. Remarks are vital, and fostering a relationship with a scholar that permits for dialogue and mirrored image may be an issue in student success. Motivation and expectations of self-play an important function within the use of examining techniques and educational overall performance. Like the observation that turned into collaboration shows that there are reasons students may not reach their desires and that student needs ought to be carefully monitored. Comments and reflection are key components in assisting students to realize fulfillment, mainly because it pertains to intention-setting.

The impact of pupil interest and instructor effectiveness

Many researchers also support the concept that student self-expectation is essential to the goal of entirety. Their speculation became that the relationship between man and woman-oriented fulfillment motivations has a fine correlation with social-orientated fulfillment motivation. The two aren't together special and students will try to meet their desires as well as the desires of others. To check this, they gave a questionnaire to excessive college students. Primarily based on their answers, the scholars had been not simplest concerned with their private desires;

they wanted to advantage social approval via assembly the desires of others, along with instructors. This examination can provide instructors with insight approximately the way to help college students set their desires; a greater wonderful technique may additionally yield higher effects (in place of goals beginning "I will no longer", set goals that being with "I can". The look at reinforces literacy is social, as asserted by using the socio-cultural principle. Students want to gain success no longer only for their gain, but for the sake of others. Lecture room instructors can help them set those goals, which might also increase their probabilities for achievement.

This has a look at also supports the idea that constructing that relationship among the pupil and the teacher will foster fulfillment. One cannot get away from the truth of scholar tests and the function they play in a student's day-by-day existence. Pupil perceptions may be accountable for their reactions to high school. Others help this concept and felt that it turned into crucial to apprehend character perceptions of classroom assessments due to the fact they're the ones that scholars encounter maximum often. They performed a case look at where they asked college students in three high faculty social research classes to fee twelve exams. Brookhart and Durkin based their study on the framework that "each scholar's notion of the significance and value of the assigned mission and each student's notion of his or her potential to perform this particular venture affect attempt".

The impact of pupil hobby and teacher effectiveness
This observes ties in with the work of Diaz-Rubin in phrases of the significance of interest on motivation. For

this take a look at, surveys that have been given before and after every one of the twelve tests. Pre-surveys assessed their perceived ability to complete the assignment while publishing surveys measured perceived attempts primarily based on scales. Brookhart and Durkin discovered that one-of-a-kind exams yielded different degrees of student attempt. Based on feedback, one of their conclusions changed into that institution performance assessments can also boom pupil effort in comparison to individual assessments. Teachers must bear in mind, then, that students may go harder when they should be accountable to a person else. Others additionally believed that there is a courting between social impacts and student fulfillment (especially grades). To determine the validity of that declaration, secondary college students were given a survey that requested them to assume again to after they got their exceptional or worst marks after which fee the subsequent for its influence on the one's grades: capability, attempt, mission difficulty, luck, own family, instructor, and friends. A rating of one indicated "no effect" even as a score of four denoted a "huge have an impact on." college students attributed their high marks to their effort and ability and their low marks to venture difficulty. They attributed good fortune extra often to excessive marks than low marks. Most significantly to the reference to Brookhart and Durkins's (2003) examine, the researchers observed that scholars had a high-quality view of social effect: college students additionally attributed their excellent marks to pals, instructors, and own family. Those discoveries lead us to the truth that scholarly notion can be effective affect achievement and failure as properly. Students place which means and significance on factors like teachers and peers, in addition to their capability and attempt. There are elements outside of an educator's manipulate, but this takes a look at suggests that there are some that are within it (motivating college students, task difficulty) that scholars see as influential of their fulfillment.

The impact of pupil hobby and teacher effectiveness

Whilst concluding pupil motivation, teachers have to understand that numerous factors have an impact on scholar conduct and performance. The two that they have got manipulate over are the materials they select and the manner they gift the one's substances to the students. In doing so, they're influencing other factors consisting of their relationship with the scholars and the students' improvement of instructional dreams. However, the number one activity of the teacher has to be to choose texts that inspire students to interact in mastering. When this is not viable, possibly because of reasons beyond the control of the individual instructor-the effectiveness of the coaching fashion has to attempt to atone for the restrictions of the substances being taught.

Chapter Two

Steps to Success and Academic Goal Implementation

Putting and for attaining professional desires

Purpose placing is the procedure of organizing preferred results that guide and direct behaviors. Goals contribute to the improvement of the experience of motive and challenge this is a necessary aspect in being an achievement inside the professional global. Priorities, determination, and goals are significant foundations for the motivation of employees that could result in collective accomplishment even in trying times. While these dreams could affect employee performance, it's far vital to take into consideration the specific needs of various tasks that could affect the degree and the route of the consequences. I've several professional desires, the primary being advancing into a managerial or administrative position in my contemporary place of business, which I've lately done. In addition, I have every other goal of obtaining employment in a supervisory, managerial or administrative role in an employer ideally inside the clinical field. In the meantime, I can focus on my first intention in my cutting-edge place of employment. I frequently prevent and ponder accomplishing desires and objectives. It's vital to be encouraged and chronic in striving to obtain my goals and goals until I without a doubt reach them. How a whole lot you need your desires and objectives determines the power of your motivation.

Setting and accomplishing dreams

A person needs to obtain certain dreams in a single's life earlier than you can call a success. Fulfillment is to obtain dreams, you have got set. I've set sure desires I would like to attain in my lifetime. Some of those dreams are private even as others are professional. My expert desires in life are to discover the right activity that makes me satisfied, get a good education, find a task that makes enough cash for me to assist my circle of relatives, and assist humans. Dreams it is very crucial for me to acquire an amazing education. Maximum task fields require a decent education. If I do not have an education I would not be capable of feature well in the work area and I might now not apprehend what to do.

I consider attending school at the college of Phoenix I can have greater task possibilities, multiplied income strength, and getting to know opportunities, increase my perspective, career coaching, and most significantly attaining a lifelong dream of acquiring a college diploma. I am an antique and considering becoming a new pupil at the University of Phoenix; that is in which some of my dreams start. the primary aim is to wait for a college to permit me to earn a diploma at the same time as running a complete-time job I understand I'm within the right region due to the fact I take one class every five weeks that is what I need. It is lots simple to use your strength to the elegance. My second aim is to get an education with a view to permit me to get a task or a higher process. It'll also give me task safety even though it could not essentially be on the same process however it's going to permit me the safety of knowing that once I decide to move on I do now not need to worry approximately what sort of profits I can be earning. With my degree, there are numerous exceptional possibilities for me. My third aim to be efficient in using computer literacy while attending the college of Phoenix. This could permit me to expand my abilities for the latest corporate in the USA. I also have a purpose to develop my perspective even as attending the University of Phoenix online. It has given me a risk to earn a diploma in surroundings that has human beings from distinctive religions, cultures, races, and social state of affairs that all have the one not unusual intention of getting a university diploma.

To measure the effect of intention setting on reading fulfillment, scholar overall performance at the studying section of the national assessment has been analyzed while students had been in fourth and 5th grades. statistics from the 2014 nation analyzing assessment, while the chosen college students had been in fourth grade and did now not participate in aim putting, were in comparison with facts from the 2015 state reading evaluation, whilst these same college students have been in fifth grade and participated in goal setting. McNemar's exchange check evaluation turned into used to decide if a sizable distinction existed between the analyzing growths performed in fourth grade as compared to analyzing growth completed in fifth grade. Consequences of the students collaborating within the look at, sixty nine% made ok growth after intention placing usage compared to handiest 60% previous to the implementation of aim setting. Especially, McNemar's check consequences indicated that a great distinction existed inside the analyzing growth overall performance while evaluating the reading increase for the months' duration. In 2014, 60.4% of the scholars were classified as making adequate growth, while 68.6% acquired the designation in 2015. discussion purpose setting in Carter County before leading students inside the method of writing effective dreams, it's far vital that teachers are knowledgeable of the technique. Like students, teachers must enjoy the one-of-a-kind intention sorts, components, and steps required to effectively mentor others toward attaining person dreams. Begin by asking instructors to pick a dependent on a colleague to serve as a mastering associate. Letting adults decide on their companion will make teachers extra at ease at some point in a studying manner. partners will work together in the course of the orientation said that excessive-stakes accountability has instructors and directors across the country attempting to find confirmed strategies to ensure persistent improvement. Additionally, organizing approaches that sell shared management and duty for pupil success is of super hobby to educators. Moreover, motivating college students to perform at excessive ranges has to turn out to be more and harder. Jenkins (1994) advocates that many students' greatest troubles in faculty are associated with irresponsibility, no longer incapacity.

The results of this complacent outlook and shortage of motivation are ways of accomplishing and necessitates a new path so as for faculties to reach their goals. For the faculties in Carter County, Kentucky, a rural district of approximately 5,000 college students, goal placing has been verified to be the solution. Over the past two years, the lecturers and college students in Carter County were utilizing intention placing. As a result, the district has proven high-quality increase on now not simplest country assessments, but additionally on nearby tests. Additionally, the range of students meeting benchmarks for university and professional readiness has elevated drastically. The method has supplied college students and instructors with a focus that has more suitable scholar performance. Goal placing described goal placing as described in lecture room instruction that Works, is the process of setting up a route for getting to know clarifies that at the same time as intention placing can cause pupil motivation and higher educational success, without a doubt mentioning a goal does no longer mechanically benefit college students. But, if carried out successfully, intention putting can impact the studying presentation section to train every different through the distinctive steps of intention setting. Then, in the same manner, that we explicitly teach children by connecting new studying with earlier expertise, begin teachers' practice of purpose placing using deciding on a topic that they are acquainted with which includes weight loss. Allow teachers to report their present-day weight and their preferred weight on paper. Subsequent, talk about the extraordinary types of activities that they can do to assist them in reaching their installed perfect weight. Then, ask individuals to decide a timeline for accomplishing their purpose. It's critical to realize that a few teachers could have a much larger range among their modern weight and their favored weight, pushing the intention date beforehand for a few people. Subsequently, set updates for progress monitoring so that the teacher companions can discuss development towards achieving the goal and revisions of sports if necessary.

This exercise will enable instructors to better relate to the worries and possible misconceptions that scholars can have when they start the procedure. It's far crucial to offer teachers with possibilities to end up proficient in every step of intention setting before an introduction, and the approach to college students gives a common language and a uniform procedure during the faculty. College students have to be taught to document their goals on paper for you to refer lower back to it at some point in the studying system. The documentation needs to consist of a place for the specific purpose, the anticipated date for accomplishment, activities to be applied to obtain the intention, development monitoring notes, and a place for each student and instructor's signatures. Having students sign the intention form will increase the level of responsibility and further confirms the expectancy that the instructor has for the scholar.

Set dreams which might be particular, measurable, practicable, sensible, and time touchy. So as for college students to view goals as meaningful, they need to have a clear knowledge of what specific goal(s) they're aspiring to accomplish. There are more than one alternatives for developing effective student boom goals. First, desires may be set for man or woman getting to know targets as in the following instance. A second choice for placing scholar academic increase goals is to awareness on an entire examination. 2. Expand a course of action. As stated earlier, genuinely writing down an intention does now not affect pupil mastering. It's the activities that the pupil will participate in at some point of the gaining knowledge of the system which can influence pupil success. In collaboration with the instructor, the scholar will need to brainstorm one-of-a-kind possibilities beyond middle coaching that could grow success. Many do now not suggest writing commonplace movements consisting of paying higher interest in magnificence, attempting tougher, or turning in all assignments; these are things that must be a part of the same old expectations for all students. Activities need to be meaningful and provide getting-to-know opportunities with a purpose to decorate the scholar's understanding and information within the precise vicinity. One example to keep in mind is encouraging the student to spend a minimum of one hour for two evenings in line with a week on a studies-based laptop application designed to offer enrichment inside the specific area of awareness. Another other concept is to have the scholar decide to afterschool tutoring or enrichment for an exact wide variety of times according to week. It's vital to don't forget when growing activities to make certain that they're precise to the child's intention and that there's a way of duty. If the responsibility piece is missing from the activity, the likelihood of the scholar genuinely finishing the hobby decreases. Adding accountability to some conventional sports takes a little creativity, however, it's miles well worth the attempt. Take the following instance: A baby sets a goal of scoring 95% on the imminent social research exam and decides on a plan of action that includes analyzing for a half-hour each day. I assume we can all agree that reading for thirty minutes each day for the test might be an extraordinary hobby for any student.

However, there is the opportunity that the child will now not comply with via with the commission due to the lack of responsibility. Having a discern or dad or mum sign a pupil-generated form every night verifying the amount of time spent analyzing provides accountability, increasing the chance that the pastime will take vicinity. 3. Monitor progress regularly. The 1/3 step in scholar aim implementation is arguably the maximum vital. Monitoring the effect that planned sports have on student achievement is vital. This step calls for the instructor to screen the development that the scholar is making toward reaching mounted desires. This method in addition allows the instructor to assess their instructional practices to determine effectiveness. Additionally, as scholar possession is an important piece in aim putting, development tracking presents a device to make certain that students cost and personal they're getting to know. Development monitoring allows for this shape with the aid of immersing students inside the implementation of a self-developed desires-based action plan this is evaluated systematically. A simple technique to reveal a student intends to create a trajectory with small intervening time dreams along the way. For instance, if a pupil is presently reading sixty phrases in step with a minute and has set an intention to study one hundred words consistent with minute, setting up target factors alongside the manner will assist to display progress and provide a motivational guide. If after one month of goal implementation the student increases fluency to eighty words according to minute, the student and teacher will understand that the unique strategies are operating. Similarly, figuring out that their efforts are generating effects will encourage college students and teachers to acquire even higher ranges of fulfillment. 4. Have good time successes; even the small ones. We have all heard the age-old adage that "achievement breeds fulfillment," and as it seems, there's validity inside the proverb. As students realize fulfillment in achieving their dreams, accomplishments must be celebrated. Spotting the efforts of students will encourage them to try for extra achievement as well as inspire teachers of their quest to help all college students be successful. I lately visited a neighborhood excessive school in which college students have been taking a placement assessment that measured their abilities in math. If college students reached an established benchmark at the evaluation, they might now not be required to take a remedial math path in college.

The students shared a number of the rigorous work they had completed to put together for the assessment. Purpose documentation indicated extensive work that has been finished for numerous weeks which include attending tutoring periods after school. It became apparent that those students have been devoted to their aim of a successful outcome on the assessment. The assessment became computer-primarily based and outcomes had been straight away discovered to students. The maximum of the students had been a hit and met the specified benchmark. The birthday party for these college students began right away with the whole lot from tears to excessive fives. Three students, however, we're no longer celebrating; the students felt defeated as that they had no longer reached the required benchmark. Knowing the importance of celebrating even the small things, the trainer serving because the mentor for the three students approached the students with a grin telling them of the outstanding development that had been made. She talked about the one-of-a-kind activities they had been a success at finishing and what kind of boom that they had proven. While she completed together with her communication, the frowns become smiles and the students' defeated attitudes were determined. Even as those students did no longer understand complete achievement in their intention, they'd advanced, and that becomes a purpose to rejoice. To similarly emphasize the spirit of celebration, all college students have been for my part diagnosed for his or her dedication. At the same time as those college students did no longer understand complete achievement in their goal, they'd stepped forward, and that changed into cause to rejoice. To similarly emphasize the spirit of celebration, all college students were in my opinion diagnosed for completing the activities outlined in their aim documentation at some stage in a school-wide meeting. This popularity ceremony, which recognized effort, bolstered the significance of trying your great although the favored outcome isn't fully realized. The power of aim putting has been studied for decades. Setting desires continues for college students centered on preferred results and provides a clear direction for achievement. The important thing to organizing goals that produce consequences is making them particular, measurable, practicable, applicable, and time touchy. Moreover, desires should be supported by a particular plan of action that outlines the stairs to be taken to maximize success. Monitoring the development of the plan guarantees that activities being utilized are producing the preferred effects. Ultimately, celebrating the development made by way of students reinforces the significance of effort and acknowledges improvements.

Goals are powerful, particular statements about your

intentions. They're encouraged with the aid of plans, goals, and desires, powered via subject and maintained via commitment. When it comes to university studies we recognize that successful students automatically set potential academic dreams. Intention setting focuses the thoughts; forces you to be unique, and requires which you discover ways to prioritize, control sometimes, and commit to finishing responsibilities

During the route of your research, you may stumble upon procrastination, low motivation, ill fitness, personal issues, tension, despair, and self-doubt. In reality, many troubles can get in the way of your non-public and academic development. However, making use of the fundamental techniques of setting up sensible dreams, prioritizing responsibilities, and placing doable timeframes may be very beneficial in getting you returned heading in the right direction. Correctly achieving your dreams will make contributions undoubtedly for your sense of effectiveness as a scholar, boost your confidence, and encourage you to keep attaining.

Blueprint for weekly goal setting

- Step 1

Devote a fixed time each week to loosen up in a quiet putting and consider the take a look at desires you would love to obtain over the approaching week.

- Step 2

Write dreams down as they come to you. Once completed, rewrite them so as of precedence, e.g. a) ought to do b) critical, and c) less important. Make certain that your goals are specific, conceivable, and measurable, and time-restricted.

- Step three

Smash down massive goals into smaller, extra potential tasks that may be performed in quick time frames. Growing day by day 'To Do' lists is an exquisite way of doing this.

- Step 4:

Time manipulates your desires by putting conceivable time limits. This focuses your interest, attention, and innovative energies. Make sure which you simplest work on one intention at a time and move off each goal from your listing as you complete it. Use a diary to assist organize some time.

- Step five:

Evaluate your development closer to your dreams frequently and definitely. Adopt a fantastic, positive attitude and remember your progress in terms of what you have got carried out, in preference to how a good deal is left to do. Use superb self-speak and phrases of encouragement to keep achieving.

- Step 6

Dedication, persistence, and self-control are the values upon which the success of your dreams relaxed. Clear up to in no way ever give up, even whilst you hit setbacks. Recollect, quitters in no way win and winners never cease.

- Step 7

Reward yourself frequently to rejoice you're a hit achievement along the way. This can permit you to have breaks and experience intervals of positivity even as you work.

Quotable rates

'Subject is the bridge between goals and accomplishment.' Jim Rohn

'You can't hit a six in case you don't step as much as a bat, you cannot paint a canvas if you do not select up a broom, and also you cannot obtain your dreams in case you do not strive. Our desires can handiest be reached via an automobile of a plan, wherein we should fervently trust, and upon which we ought to vigorously act. There is a no different direction to fulfillment.' — Stephen A. Brennan

'The maximum vital aspect about motivation is aim putting. You must always have a goal.' — Francie Larrieu Smith

The clever method to intention fulfillment

* Particular

Be very clean approximately what it's far which you want to gain. This reduces indecision and increases your ability to understand the sub-goals you need to acquire your intention. as an instance, an intention of: 'study physics today' may be made more unique with the aid of mentioning 'study chapter 5 of my physics textbook, write questions within the margin of textual content.

* Measurable

Your intention has to be tangible sufficient so that whilst you are via you have clear proof that you've completed the undertaking. It feels right to peer something there finished in front of you, indicating a job properly performed.

As equally important, you may be able to show to yourself that you have been a success and your time wasn't wasted. Without such proof, the stop result of an aim inclusive of 'study bankruptcy' cannot be reliably assessed. Did you recognize what you read whilst you checked out the pages?

A smarter purpose could be: 'study chapter 3, then jot down a summary of the primary factors from reminiscence.' The precise might imply that you examine the chapter and understood what you study. Producing tangible evidence like this requires active reading in your component. Studies time and again unearths that lively take a look at produces superior getting to know and retention.

- Plausible/ideal

Your aim must be set so that you can attain it inside a particular length. If the intention is simply too huge or too worried to acquire within an inexpensive time frame, then destroy it down into greater potential responsibilities. You know fine your strengths and weaknesses and might use this information to maximize your chances of achievement.

- Realistic

Set goals that are realistic and capable of being accomplished by you with the sources available to you. Keep away from making plans matters if you are not going to observe through. It's far better to devise only a few matters and achieve success in preference to plenty of things and fail. Success breeds fulfillment! Begin small with the tasks you place, revel in the joys of assembly your purpose, and steadily increase the quantity of work that you set yourself. Putting desires that account for each minute of the day is unrealistic. Unplanned activities will crop up and interrupt your schedule. As a substitute, a component in bendy time to deal with unexpected interruptions. In case you don't use it for trouble fixing, end early and use it to reward yourself for an activity properly achieved.

• Time frame

Commit clear timeframes to work to your aim, e.g., between 9 am and 10:00 am. Lengthy intervals without a destroy cause fatigue, distraction, and loss of enthusiasm. Break huge goals into smaller, greater manageable chunks and have small breaks frequently.

Whilst analyzing, the average interest span lasts around forty to forty-five minutes earlier than attention wanes. So, plan to work in brief, sharp, lively bursts to maintain powerful purpose fulfillment.

Putting and accomplishing dreams

A few humans are goal-oriented and appear to easily make choices that cause achieving their desires, at the same time as others seem just to "go along with the flow" and take delivery of what existence gives them. At the same time as the latter might also sound pleasantly comfortable, moving via existence without goals may not lead anywhere at all. The reality which you're in college now shows you have already got the important intention to finish your university application.

An intention is a result we intend to reach primarily via our movements. Matters we do can also pass us closer to or farther away from that result. Analyzing actions us closer to success in a hard direction, even as snoozing via the final exam may also absolutely save you from accomplishing that purpose. That's fairly apparent in a severe case, but still, numerous college students don't attain their aim of graduating. The trouble can be a loss of commitment to the goal, however frequently college students have conflicting dreams. One manner to save you troubles is to reflect on consideration on all of your desires and priorities and to analyze methods to manage a while, your research, and your social life to fine attain your dreams. Don't forget these four college students:

To help his widowed mom, Juan went to work full time after excessive college but now, some years later, he's disenchanted with the types of jobs he has been capable of getting and has begun taking computer programming courses within the nighttime. He's often worn out after work, but, and his mother would like him to spend extra time at home. Every so often he cuts elegance to stay domestic and spend time together with her.

In her senior yr of college, Becky has simply been elected president of her sorority and is excited about making plans for a first-rate community provider assignment. She is aware of the need to be spending greater time on her senior thesis, but she feels her community project may additionally advantage the contacts that could assist her to discover a better activity after commencement. Besides, the sorority undertaking is lots greater amusing, and she's taking part in the esteem of her function. Although she doesn't do well on her thesis, she's positive she'll pass.

After an easy time in excessive faculty, James is surprised his university classes are so tough. He's were given sufficient time to take a look at his first-year guides, however, he also has quite a few buddies and amusing things to do. Now and again he's surprised to look up from his PC to see it in the middle of the night already, and he hasn't begun analyzing that chapter yet. In which does the time go? When he's pressured, however, he can't examine properly, so he tells himself he'll stand up early and study the chapter before class, and then he turns back to his computer to look who's online.

Carla turned into successful in slicing again her hours at work to provide her greater time for her engineering lessons, however, it's difficult for her to get a good deal of analysis performed at home. Her husband has been awesome approximately looking after their young daughter, but he can't do everything, and currently, he's been hinting more approximately asking her sister to babysit so that the two of them can go out inside the evening the manner they used to. Currently, whilst she's had to take a look at on a weekend, he leaves along with his pals, and she finally ends up spending the day along with her daughter and no longer getting a lot of studying performed.

What do those very specific college students have is not unusual? Each has dreams that battle in a single or greater approach. Everyone wishes to develop strategies to meet their other dreams without threatening their instructional fulfillment. And they all have time control troubles to work via three due to the fact they sense they don't have sufficient time to do the whole lot they want or want to do and one due to the fact even though he has enough time, he needs to discover ways to manage it more effectively. For all four of them, motivation and attitude will be vital as they expand strategies to gain their dreams.
All of it starts with setting desires and thinking about

priorities. As you reflect on consideration of your desires, consider greater than just being a student. You're additionally a person with man or woman wishes and desires, hopes and dreams, plans and schemes. Your long-term desires likely include commencement and a career however might also involve social relationships with others, romantic courting, own family, interests or other sports, where and how you stay, and so forth. Whilst you are a scholar you could now not be actively pursuing all of your desires with identical fervor, but they stay goals and are nevertheless vital in your life.

Goals additionally range in terms of time. The quick-time period desires attention on today and the following couple of days and perhaps weeks. Midterm desires involve plans for this college yr and the time you intend to remain in college. Lengthy-term desires can also start with graduating college and everything you want to show up thereafter. Often your long-term desires (e.g., the type of career you need) guide your midterm dreams (getting the right education for that profession), and your quick-term desires (which include doing nicely on an examination) come to be steps for attaining one's large dreams. thinking about your goals in this way facilitates you to recognize how even the little stuff you do each day can hold you transferring in the direction of your maximum important lengthy-time period goals.

Write out your goals; you ought to write them down because the act of finding the fine words to describe your desires enables you to suspect greater in reality about them.

Follow these suggestions:

- Desires should be practical. It's appropriate to dream

and to protect yourself, however, your goals ought to relate to your private strengths and skills.

• Desires ought to be unique. Don't write, "I turn into a superb musician"; as an alternative, write, "I can end my tune diploma and be employed in a symphony orchestra."

• Desires need to have a time body. You won't sense very encouraged if your purpose is vague "to finish college sooner or later." if you're sensible and particular to your goals, you need to also be able to challenge a time frame for accomplishing the aim.

• You ought to need to reach the intention. We're willing to work tough to attain dreams we certainly care about, however, we're likely to surrender whilst we come upon limitations if we don't experience strongly about an aim. In case you're doing something simplest due to the fact your dad and mom or a person else want you to, then it's now not your very own private intention and you may have a few extra questioning to do approximately your existence.

Considering your desires gets you began, however, it's additionally essential to think about priorities. We regularly use the phrase "priorities" to consult how vital something is to us. We might assume, this is a truly critical intention, and this is much less crucial. Do this experiment: go lower back to the desires you wrote in pastime and notice if you can rank every goal as a (top precedence), (middle priority), or three (lowest priority).

It sounds clean, however, do you experience secure doing that? Maybe you gave priority 1 to passing your courses and a priority to playing your guitar. So what does that imply—which you in no way play guitar again, or at least not whilst in college? On every occasion you have got an hour free between class and work, you need to look at it because that's the better priority? What about all your different dreams do you need to forget about the whole thing that's not a priority? And what occurs when you have to pick out amongst unique dreams that are both number one priorities?

In truth, priorities don't work pretty that way. It doesn't make quite a few feel to try to rank desires as usually more or less vital. The query of priority is surely a query of what's greater vital at a specific time. It's far crucial to do well in your training, but it's also crucial to have a social lifestyle and enjoy your time off from studying. You shouldn't have to pick among the two, besides at any given time. Priorities usually involve time: what's maximum essential to do right now. As we'll see later, time management is often a way to juggle priorities so that you can meet all your goals.

While you manage a while properly, you ought not to forget about a few desires completely so one can meet other dreams. In other words, you don't should surrender your lifestyle whilst you check in for college, however, you can need to work on managing your existence extra correctly. But time control works handiest when you're dedicated to your goals. Attitude and motivation are very essential. If you haven't but advanced a mindset for the fulfillment, all of the time control abilities inside the international received preserve you focused and stimulated to prevail.

An attitude for achievement

What's your mindset right now? What started running through your mind as you saw the "An attitude for fulfillment" heading? Were you groaning to your self-announcing "No, no longer the mindset component again" Or, at the alternative severe, maybe you had been wondering, "this is incredible! Now I'm about to research the entirety I need to get thru college without a hassle!" those are two attitude extremes, one terrible and skeptical, the opposite high-quality and hopeful. Most college students are someplace in among, however, everybody has a mindset of one sort or another.

The entirety human beings do and how they do it starts with mindset. One student receives up with the alarm clock and cheerfully prepares for the day, making plans to study for a couple of hours between classes, move to go for walks later, and see a pal at dinner. any other pupil oversleeps after partying too past due last night time, decides to pass his first elegance, come what may receive thru later training fueled with the aid of fast food and power drinks at the same time as dreading the following day's exam, and straight away accepts a friend's concept to go out this night in preference to reading. Each student may want to have identical situations, lessons, finances, and academic instruction. There could be simply one large difference but it's the only that subjects.

Right here are some traits related to a superb attitude
- Enthusiasm for and leisure of everyday sports
- Acceptance of obligation for one's moves and feeling properly about achievement
- Normally upbeat temper and high-quality feelings, cheerfulness with others, and pleasure with oneself
- Motivation to get the activity finished
- Flexibility to make adjustments when needed

- Capability to make productive, powerful use of time

 Right here are some characteristics associated with a poor attitude
- Frequent complaining
- Blaming others for something that is going incorrect
- Frequently experiencing poor emotions: anger, despair, resentment
- Lack of motivation for work or studies
- Hesitant to exchange or are looking for improvement
- Unproductive use of time, procrastination

We commenced this bankruptcy speaking approximately dreams, due to the fact people's desires and priorities have a huge effect on their mindset. Someone who truly desires to achieve university is higher motivated and may develop an extra advantageous mindset to succeed. But what if you are committed to succeeding in university however nevertheless sense type of dubious or involved or even down on yourself what can you do then? Can human beings genuinely exchange their attitude? Aren't human beings just "naturally" fantastic or terrible or something?

At the same time as attitude is motivated by way of one's persona, upbringing, and beyond stories, there is no "attitude gene" that makes you one manner or some other. It's not as simple as taking a tablet, however, mindset may be modified. in case you're devoted to your goals, you can learn to regulate your mindset. The following are some things you may start doing.

Be more upbeat with yourself

We all have conversations with ourselves. I might do badly on a check, and that I begin thinking things like, "I'm just not clever sufficient" or "That teacher is so hard no person ought to skip that check." The problem whilst we talk to ourselves in this manner is that we listen and we begin believing what we're listening to. Consider what you've been announcing to yourself because of your first day at college. Have you ever been poor or making excuses, maybe due to the fact you're terrified of not succeeding? You're smart enough otherwise you wouldn't be here. Even in case, you did poorly on a take a look at, you could turn that around into a more tremendous mindset via taking responsibility. "Good enough, I goofed off an excessive amount of once I ought to be reading. I learned my lesson, now it's time to buckle down and observe for the subsequent test. I'm going to ace this one!" hear yourself saying that sufficient and guess what you soon find out you could be successful even in your toughest training.

Choose Whom You Spend Time With

We all recognize bad and tremendous human beings. Once in a while, it's a laugh to hang out with a person with a bad attitude, particularly if their sarcasm is humorous. And if we've simply failed a take a look at it, we would experience being with a person else who also blames the teacher or "the machine" for anything that goes incorrect. As they say, distress loves corporation. However, often being with terrible humans is one of the highest quality methods to live negative yourself. You now not handiest pay attention your self-speak making excuses and blaming others and setting yourself down, however you hear different human beings announcing it, too. After a while, you're convinced it's real. You've developed a bad attitude that sets you up for failure.

University offers a super possibility to make new buddies. Friendships and other social relationships are important to all humans and perhaps to college students most of all, because of the stresses of college and the changes you're possibly experiencing. Later chapters on this eBook have some recommendations for making new pals and getting actively concerned about campus lifestyles, in case you're now not already there, and most vital, try to pick pals with a fantastic attitude. It's more a laugh to be with individuals who are upbeat and enjoying existence, people whom you recognize and who, like you, are devoted to their studies and are influenced. A high-quality mindset can genuinely be contagious.

Overcome Resistance to exchange

At the same time as it's true that most of the people are extra cozy while their state of affairs is not continually changing, many kinds of trade are correct and should be welcomed. College is a huge change from high school or running. Accepting that truth helps you be extra fantastic approximately the differences. Sure, you have to take a look at more, and the instructions are more difficult. You'll be operating more and have less time on your private lifestyles. But living on those differences most effective reinforces a poor mindset. Look instead on the superb changes: the thrilling and interesting humans you're assembling, the training you're getting with a purpose to lead to a shiny destiny, and the mental challenges and stimulation you're feeling every day.

Step one may be virtually to look at yourself succeeding in your new existence. Visualize yourself as a scholar taking manipulate, taking part in lessons, analyzing correctly, and getting precise grades. This book will help you try this in many approaches. it all begins with the proper mindset.

Overcome Fears

One of the most common fears of university students is the worry of failure or no longer being capable of making the grade. All of us recognize that lifestyles aren't all roses and that we're now not going to be triumphant at the whole lot we strive for. All people report some form of failure at some time and all and sundry has fears. The query is what you do approximately it.

Once more, think about your goals. You've enrolled in university for true motives, and also you've already shown your dedication with the aid of coming this a long way. If you nevertheless have any fear of failure, turn it around and use it in a high-quality way. If you're afraid you can now not do nicely on an upcoming exam, don't mope around—sit down and schedule instances to begin analyzing properly in advance of time. It's in most cases a count of mindset adjustment.

Live focused and stimulated

Ok, you've got a high-quality mindset. However you've got a whole lot of studying for training to do this night, a take a look at tomorrow, and a paper due the following day. Perhaps you're a touch bored with one in every of your reading assignments. Perhaps you'd as a substitute play a computer sport. Uh oh, now what? Attitude can alternate at nearly any second. One minute you're enthusiastically beginning a category mission, after which maybe a friend drops with the aid of and abruptly all you want to do is near the books and loosen up some time, hold out with pals.

One of the characteristics of successful human beings is accepting that lifestyles are full of interruptions and exchange and making plans for it. Staying focused does not suggest you become a humdrum character who does not anything but go to elegance and study all of the time. You just need to make a plan.

Making plans in advance is the unmarried quality manner to live focused and prompted to reach your desires. Don't wait till the night time before an examination. in case you recognize you have got a major examination in five days, start with the aid of reviewing the material and determining what number of hours of examination you want. Then time table the one's hours spread out over the following couple of days at times while you are maximum alert and least likely to be distracted. Permit time for different sports, too, to praise yourself for a successful analysis. Then when the exam comes, you're cozy, the fabric, you're in an awesome mood and assured, and you do well.

Making plans is usually a relying on managing some time nicely, as we'll see later. Right here are some different tips for staying centered and prompted:

• In case you're now not feeling prompted, consider the consequences of your dreams, now not simply the desires themselves. If simply considering completing college doesn't sound all that thrilling, then assume as a substitute approximately the extremely good, high-paying career that comes afterward and the matters you could do with that earnings.

• Say it aloud to yourself or a pal with a high-quality mindset: "I'm going to take a look at now for any other hour before I take a ruin and that I'm getting an A on that to take a look at tomorrow!" It's wonderful how saying something aloud places commitment in it and affirms that it may be true.

• Keep in mind your successes, even small successes. As you start a mission or approach studying for a test, think about your beyond success on a one-of-a-kind mission or test. Don't forget how desirable it feels to succeed. Recognize you can be successful again.

• Awareness on the right here and now. For some human beings, looking beforehand to goals, or to whatever else, may also lead to daydreaming that keeps them from that specialize in what they need to do right now. Don't worry approximately what you're doing the day after today or subsequent week or month. In case your mind maintains drifting off, but, you may need to reward or maybe trick yourself to cognizance on the here and now. As an instance, if you couldn't forestall thinking about the snack you're going to have when you finish studying in a pair of hours, exchange the plan. Inform yourself you'll take a smash in twenty minutes if you want it however most effective if you without a doubt work nicely first.

• If you simply can't attend in on what you should be doing because the mission seems too massive and daunting, break the undertaking into smaller, practicable pieces. Don't start off wondering, "I want to observe the subsequent 4 hours," however assume, "I'll spend the subsequent thirty minutes going via my elegance notes from the remaining three weeks and figure out what subjects I need to spend extra time on." It's lots easier to live centered when you're sitting down for thirty minutes at a time.

• By no means, ever multitask even as reading! You might imagine that you could screen email and send textual content messages at the same time as analyzing, however, in fact, these other activities lower the first-rate of your analyzing.

• Imitate successful people. Does a friend constantly seem better capable of stay with analyzing or work till they get it finished? What are they doing that you're now not? All of us analyze from watching others, and we can accelerate that method by deliberately the use of the equal techniques we see operating with others. Visualize your self-analyzing within the same way and getting that identical high grade on the take a look at or paper.

• Separate yourself from unsuccessful human beings. This is the flip aspect of imitating a hit human beings. If a roommate or a pal is usually disposing of matters until the ultimate minute or is distracted with other hobbies and activities, inform yourself how distinctive you are. When you listen to different students complaining about how hard a category is or bragging about not studying or attending class, visualize yourself as no longer being like them at all.

• Praise yourself whilst you complete a substantial task but handiest when you are executed. A few humans seem capable of stay centered most effective when there's a reward waiting.

• Whilst a few humans work harder for the reward, others are prompted more with the aid of the price of failing. At the same time as some human beings are nearly paralyzed by using tension, others are moved by using their worry to acquire their excellent.

• Get the vital things executed first. We'll speak

approximately coping with your educational planner and to-do lists later in the chapter, however, for now, to live centered and encouraged, concentrate on the matters that count maximum. You're about to sit down to read a chapter in an e-book you're no longer plenty playing, and also you abruptly be aware of some clothing piled up on a chair. "I without a doubt have to ease up this vicinity," you believe you studied. "And I'd higher get my laundry done earlier than I run out of factors to wear." Don't try to idiot yourself into feeling you're undertaking something through doing laundry as opposed to analyzing. Stay centered!

Community for success

Making friends with human beings with effective attitudes, not handiest helps you maintain a high-quality mindset yourself, but it receives you started out networking with different students in ways that will help you succeed.

Did you have a look at alone or with pals in excessive faculty? Because college training is generally tons extra challenging, many university students find out they do better and discover it a good deal more exciting, if they study with different college students taking the same course. This might imply organizing an examination institution or just getting collectively with a pal to study fabric earlier than a take a look at it. It's correct to start thinking proper away approximately networking with different college students in your lessons.

In case you take into account yourself an unbiased man or woman and like studying and doing initiatives on your very own rather than with others, suppose for a minute approximately how most of the people function in their careers and professions, what the enterprise global is like.

Most work these days is performed through groups or individuals operating together collaboratively. Very few jobs involve a person continually being and running alone. The extra you discover ways to study and work with different college students now, the more abilities you're mastering for a successful career.

Analyzing with other students has immediate blessings. You can quiz each different to help make sure that everybody is aware of the path material; in case you're now not clean about something, someone else can assist educate it to you. You could read and respond to every other's writing and different work. You can divide up the work into organizational projects. And through it all, you can regularly have extra amusing than if you had been doing it to your very own.

Studying collectively is also an extraordinary manner to begin networking; a subject we'll talk about greater in the coming chapters. Networking has many capability blessings on your future. College students who feel they're a part of a community on campus are greater motivated and more a hit in college.

Tips for fulfillment to stay influenced

• Hold your eyes to your lengthy-term dreams whilst running toward instant goals.

• Keep your priorities directly- but also keep time for fun.

• Work on retaining your mindset tremendous.

• Preserve the enterprise of fantastic human beings; imitate successful human beings.

• Don't permit past conduct to drag you down.

• Plan in advance to avoid last-minute pressures.

- Focus on your achievement.
- Spoil huge initiatives down into smaller responsibilities or stages.
- Praise yourself for completing significant responsibilities.
- Keep away from multitasking.
- Network with other college students; form a examine group.

Problem fixing: when setbacks take place

Even if you have clear goals and are inspired and centered to gain the ones, issues once in a while show up. Be given that they may take place because unavoidably they do for everybody. The difference between people who prevail using fixing the hassle and shifting on and those who get pissed off and surrender is in part mindset and in part revel in and understanding the way to cope when a problem occurs.

Lots of different types of setbacks might also occur while you're in university, simply as to everybody in lifestyles. Right here are some examples:

- A financial disaster
- An illness or harm
- A disaster concerning the circle of relatives participants or cherished ones
- Pressure related to frequently feeling you don't have enough time
- Strain associated with courting issues

A few things show up that we cannot save you consisting of a few varieties of infection, dropping one's activity due to a business slowdown, or crises regarding the circle of relatives contributors. However many different varieties of issues can be prevented or made less probable to arise. You could take control of your price range and keep away from most economic problems commonplace amongst university students. You may discover ways to build successful social relationships and get alongside higher with your teachers, with other college students, and in private relationships. You can analyze time control strategies to make sure you operate it slow successfully for studying. maximum of the chapters on this e-book additionally provide take a look at tips and recommendations to help you do properly to your lessons with effective studying, observe-taking, test-taking, and writing talents for training. Stopping the problems that typically hold college students from succeeding is tons of what this book is all approximately.

Not all problems may be averted. Infection or a monetary problem can considerably set one again, specifically whilst you're on a decent schedule and price range. Other problems, consisting of a social or dating difficulty or an educational problem in a sure class, can be extra complicated and no longer without difficulty prevented. What then?

First, work to remedy the on the spot hassle

1.   Live encouraged and centered. Don't allow frustration, tension, or other bad emotions to make the problem worse than it already is.

2.   Analyze the hassle to remember all possible answers. A surprising monetary setback doesn't mechanically imply you need to drop out of school, no longer whilst alternatives along with pupil loans, much less luxurious living preparations, or different feasible answers can be to be had. Failing a midterm exam doesn't automatically

imply you're going to fail the direction, no longer when you make an effort to determine what went incorrect, work along with your teacher and others on an improved observation plan, and use higher techniques to put together for the subsequent check.

3.   Are searching for help whilst you want to. None of us receives thru life on our own, and it's not a sign of a weak spot to look your instructional consultant or a college counselor if you have a hassle.

4.   When you've developed a plan for resolving the hassle, work to comply with through. If it's going to take some time before the problem is solved, music your development in smaller steps so that you can see you are succeeding. Each day will pass you one step towards placing it behind you.

Once you've solved a problem, make sure to avoid it once more within the destiny

1.   be sincere with yourself: how did you contribute to the hassle? Once in a while, it's obvious: a pupil who drank closely at a party the night before a huge check failed the examination due to the fact he became so hungover he couldn't think instantly. From time to time the source of the trouble is not as obvious but might also emerge as clearer the extra you consider it. some other scholar did a whole lot of partying all through the period however studied all day earlier than the large check and become well rested and clearheaded at taking a look at the time however nonetheless did poorly; he may not but have found out properly examine capabilities. Any other student has frequent colds and different moderate ailments that keep him from doing his pleasant: how a whole lot higher would

he sense if he ate well, got plenty of exercises, and slept enough each night? in case you don't explore the elements that led to the hassle, it's much more likely to occur again.

2.   Take duty to your existence and your role in what happens to you. in advance we pointed out people with poor attitudes, who're usually blaming others, destiny, or "the system" for his or their troubles. It's no coincidence that they hold on having troubles. Unless you want to keep having troubles, don't maintain blaming others.

3.   Taking obligation doesn't imply being down on yourself. Failing at something doesn't imply you're a failure. All of us fail at something, sometimes. Modify your mindset so you're equipped to get back on the right track and sense glad that you'll never make that mistake again!

4.   Make a plan. you would possibly still have a hassle on that next massive take a look at in case you don't make a powerful look at the plan and keep on with it. You may need to alternate your behavior in some manner, which includes mastering time control techniques.

Techniques for educational success: the usage of your strengths

Recognize your strengths

It's human nature to need accurate weaknesses. But understanding your strengths and the way to use them efficiently may have a far extra full-size impact on achievement and well-being. So how will you reframe your thinking?

According to Deb Levy, the sphere of fine psychology offers much beneficial equipment. One, in particular, assists you to gauge your strengths and weaknesses. The test ranks customers' character strengths from strongest to weakest, making an allowance for a goal view into where you excel and in which you may need work. Once you recognize what your strengths are, you can play to them. But it's also critical to recognize that sometimes strengths want to be tempered. Each energy if overused turns into a deficit. For instance, a person who ranks rather a in humor may run the danger of making an insensitive or inappropriate comment that would damage relationships. Creating a plan to strengthen weaknesses while remaining aware of strengths may be a first-rate method to make sure now not just instructional success, however personal success.

Set specific desires

Reaching your desires depends closely on how properly you can manage some time. Levy recommends making a concern pie that maps out the way you'll divide it slowly over the path of a semester. "While you say yes to become a scholar, you have got to say no to different things," she says. "So purpose-putting requires a strategic plan for the semester. Students who do higher in preferred are the ones who take time to devise." Your precedence pie must reflect all of your personal, professional, and academic endeavors. For example, Your priority pie must consist of no longer just instructions and your workday, however additionally a time for your own family, reading and homework, and self-care like going to the health club or getting an ordinary massage.

Prioritize happiness

Feeling good approximately what you're doing and why you're doing it's far the satisfactory manner to make sure achievement. In keeping with Levy, happiness often results in achievement, however, an achievement on its personal might not lead to happiness. As such, prioritizing your wellbeing is the important thing to achieving your desires. Well-being consists of tremendous emotions, engagement, which means, and achievement. Via the nature of being in college people are already prioritizing nicely-being. They're getting engaged, working on accomplishments. Aside from making time for yourself, you could practice building positivity. One exercise that Levy recommends is writing down 3 suitable matters at the end of every day. These can be stuff you're proud of, stuff you're grateful for, or matters that simply deliver a smile for your face. Studying subjects that deliver your lifestyle's reason or which means also can be beneficial. People who join that means to their desires are more inspired.

Be resilient

Regardless of a good plan, boundaries will get up. How nicely you cope with the ones boundaries depends on your attitude.

In resilience training, Levy frequently refers back to the work of psychologist Carol Dweck. Her research identifies fundamental mindsets: constant and increase. Constant mindsets view errors or setbacks as insurmountable. Growth mindsets view them as possibilities for effective change. If you lean towards a set mindset, the good news is that it's not everlasting. no one falls into one attitude 100 percentage of the time. Training your brain to look for opportunities where you once noticed a roadblock is feasible.

"Give yourself permission to be human," Levy says. "Predict you're going to make errors." One manner to build resilience is with the aid of making ready for boundaries with implementation intentions, which can be if-then plans designed to assist human beings to obtain desires. For instance, "If I can't get the financial useful resource I want, then I can reallocate cash from my excursion or enjoyment budgets." Putting those intentions gives you a default answer that allows you to keep on with your plan without having to deliberate or make a snap decision.

Make time to recover

Instead of warding off stress altogether, Levy recommends placing apart time to mentally and bodily recover. As a scholar, you may on occasion fall into a "stretch zone," wherein you're extending yourself to the house for specific duties. Durations of stress can be high quality and motivating if they enlarge your notion of what's possible. But it could result in persistent strain when you don't construct in time to recover. Viewing your eight hours of sleep each night time as sacrosanct can cross a protracted way closer to staving off persistent stress. So earlier than you pull every other all-nighter, reflect on consideration on the outcomes it may have on you tomorrow. Taking breaks, putting apart time for meals, and playing pastime can help gasoline you and maintain you on course to obtain your goals

Ten keys to achievement in lifestyles

Do you need to recognize what leads one man or woman to attain fulfillment in lifestyles over some other? After doing plenty of research on achievement in lifestyles, researchers came up with ten keys to fulfillment in existence. Something your desires, these ten keys were identified as essential to achieving hit effects.

What's fulfillment in life?

Earlier than we explore these ten keys to achievement in lifestyles, it's vital to have readability to your definition of fulfillment. To succeed method to accomplish an aim. in case you don't know what you're aiming for, you'll by no means know while you've succeeded.

Having "achievement in lifestyles" can look very otherwise for everyone, relying on your particular desires. It's essential to choose dreams that in particular pass you closer to the destiny you have in thoughts for yourself. If are supposed to be a yoga teacher, you'd possibly be upset in existence as an "a success" funding banker.

Most people would define fulfillment in life as which include a few degrees of happiness. So don't neglect dreams so one can guide a happier life. Prioritizing relationships, bodily health, protection, contributing to others, and innovative expression have been proven to enhance emotions of happiness. Something your goals, these keys are the gear, habits, or pathways that will help you to acquire achievement, however, you define it.

- Make a plan

The first actual secret is making plans for success. This means having a clear photograph of what a successful life looks like to you and setting together with a nicely defined plan to get you to that life. Making plans nicely begins with identifying what you need and writing it down in detail. This is the inspiration for your plan. From there, set up the goals, grade by grade, so one can get you to this life.

- Prepare for the surprising

Most of the best-laid plans were derailed by using a single misstep. It's no accident we chose this as the second of the ten keys to fulfillment in existence. Making ready for the sudden can make the distinction between your plans finishing in failure or succeeding notwithstanding a bump in the road. So how do you put together for the surprising? Begin with the aid of making a list of factors that could go incorrect on your plan. Then create workarounds and backups for each potential hassle. Even when I'm driving in a direction I understand nicely, I generally hold my GPS up and walking to assist me to navigate visitors' jams, creation, or ignored turns.

- Expand properly habits

You may have massive goals, great dreams, and nonetheless fail. Achievement calls for turning knowledge into action. It means, again and again, taking action closer to your dreams. Repeated actions end up habits. And after you shape the proper behavior, you create momentum. Growing structures in your life as you're forming good habits can help you to stay on the right track. You can construct systems by grouping accurate habits collectively. Having a device in the vicinity can keep you from having to make decisions on the fly or maintain music of doing all your goal-orientated responsibilities one by one. As an alternative, you observe an intentional day-by-day pattern that moves you toward your dreams with much less strain. This has the added benefits of lowering strain and liberating your interest to cognizance at the matters that virtually require extra mind power.

- Prioritize your dreams

As you create your structures and placed your excellent conduct into exercise, you'll in all likelihood find there isn't enough time in every day to work towards each goal. Prioritizing goals will assist you to figure out which things your to do first or spend greater time on. In case you're no longer certain a way to prioritize desires, it could help to apply a few techniques like a numerical ranking system or the Eisenhower Matrix. Prioritizing your goals additionally means no longer letting things that never even made your list get in front of pursuing what did. In other phrases, don't permit speaking to a telemarketer to derail your plan to smooth the house.

- Study out of your mistakes

They say "the road to success is paved with failure." What they don't say, is that every piece of failure on that street probably looks different than the opposite. Success most in all likelihood came by using manner of trying (and failing) many exceptional ways. Sure, you may fail your manner to success, however nearly never via making the equal mistake time and again. Failure is a part of the technique of becoming successful if you make it a teacher. Mastering and growing after failure make it beneficial. As an example, recall a runner. Every race a runner loses, they'll be shifting ahead. If they build up power and try new strolling techniques, they'll probably see development.

They may flow up from 5th area to 3rd place to second. Even though they aren't first, each race is part of the method of achievement, moving them in the direction of getting the first area.

- Try distinct strategies

The street to fulfillment isn't straight. There are stops and starts, turns and detours. All people who say they've got the precise path to fulfillment for you are probably mendacious. as the (creepy) pronouncing goes, "There are multiple manners to pores and skin a cat." Heck, there's more than one way to get the means of that announcing across. Permit's make up a more recent extra puppy-friendly one. "There are multiple ways to peel a banana." Any manner you put it, there's a couple of ways to do — pretty much the whole lot. So, if at first, you don't prevail, strive any other way. Try a brand new approach. Come at your goal from a new attitude, at a specific time, with a different person. There may want to be many effective techniques. You simply need to locate the proper one. The handiest way to discover it's far to hold converting and maintain trying until you discover one that works.

- Take clever risks

As you try out unique strategies, you could locate that you're trying something entirely new. It might feel frightening. Admittedly, taking risks is intimidating, but taking clever risks can have big payoffs. Taking a clever or calculated hazard means learning potential results and determining what your possibilities of fulfillment are and if the payoff is worth risking the damage that would be performed. It takes time to develop suitable threat-taking talents. You can have some painful screw-ups as you determine a way to take calculated risks in lifestyles. It's high-quality to start out taking small dangers. As you get better at it, you'll possibly turn out to be greater relaxed. But don't let your comfort be the most effective deciding element. Often, taking a threat is the simplest manner to attain success.

- Examine from the professionals

While it's genuine that there is nobody direction to success, lots may be found out from analyzing different successful humans. Even higher is to be mentored or to have a look at once underneath someone. Recorded records don't usually catch all of the information and nuances. Begin with doing some studies and take a look at successful folks who did something within the identical realm of what you are striving to acquire. Want to innovate? Examine innovators. Want to be an exceptional painter? Look at Van Gogh, Monet, and Picasso. Want to very own a eating place? Learn from a person who is aware of cooking and business. Watch what they do, take notes, and ask questions.

- Grasp how to say no

I suppose our culture undervalues the significance of announcing no. it can be uncomfortable. If you concentrate on interviews with a success people, you'll probably hear them communicate about turning down excellent possibilities they knew aren't right for them. Studying how to say no is a critical key to fulfillment in lifestyles. Successful humans say no all the time. Saying no means understanding yourself, your limitations, and being capable of deciding what's worth a while and power. Announcing no to the incorrect thing leaves space to mention sure to the proper aspect. It leaves room for the proper possibility.

- Spend money on relationships

At the same time as pronouncing, "it's not what you know it's who" can also overstate the importance of relationships to achievement, it's truly now not without advantage. Mainly, investing in relationships is pretty valuable. Human beings are made to be in-network. The blessings of being in a safe and inspiring community go past success in any individual region of existence.

There are many styles of relationships that could enhance your possibilities of achievement in existence. For example, the connection you want most can be a chum who has no "connections," but helps you while instances are tough. Perhaps the connection you want is with a competitor, a person to task you and maintain you sharp. Particularly pursue a mentoring courting, that could lead to networking possibilities and invaluable recommendation. We understand that the shortage of those relationships may be the most important hole between aged out foster young people and achievement.

- What makes someone a success in life?

These keys to success in existence are not all or nothing. Odds are, the more you have, the higher you'll do as you try to determine the way to attain success in existence. And all of these keys or equipment can be acquired and advanced via anyone with enough time and grit. It also bears bringing up that a successful life isn't always all approximately pursuing achievement. It isn't consumed my delusions of grandeur. Some of your most effective and most significant moments will appear amid failure and defeat. a number of the exceptional recollections may be made within the mundane. These are precious too. Truly, fulfillment in life additionally way developing the ability to be thankful and to discover the nuggets of beauty in much less glamorous times.

• A successful college students have desires

Succeeding in college is alternatively like succeeding in existence. It's truly plenty more approximately you than it's far approximately university. So the maximum essential vicinity to start is to recall why you're here, what topics to you, and what you expect to get out of it. Even when you have already an idea about those questions, it's proper to reaffirm your commitment to your plan as we start to don't forget what's surely worried in being a university pupil. Permit's test successful pupil have dreams.

College students who have long time life and professional goals see university as one step in the direction of accomplishing their dreams. This will set a cause and a path for college students. it can increase students' everyday and semester-to-semester motivation due to the fact they see that every path is a part of an extra complete a good way to assist them within the destiny. This will additionally help with patience, with preserving at it while things are difficult. There could be demanding situations throughout your university career. There may be times you experience giving up or you just don't feel like going to elegance, studying your textbook, or writing that paper. Having that reason, that long-term purpose can help to decide to transport past that assignment and hold going. We name this resiliency.

Goals assist you to put priorities and stay motivated and

committed to your college success. Placing a long time goal generally results in setting medium and quick-term desires. Those are practical goals related to being a student that can help you make higher choices when considering your selections of the way to spend some time. Putting priorities with shorter-term desires assist you to see what you need to do subsequent. Running thru goals allows you to sense more on top of things and can lessen strain. Attitude is the largest element determining fulfillment in university. Work to live fantastically and surround yourself with fantastic humans and also you'll discover you are influenced to perform the sports that will help you reach your publications.

Aim placing

An aim is a result we intend to attain basically thru our very own actions. Things we do may additionally move us towards or farther away from that result. Analyzing moves us toward achievement in a difficult route, even as sleeping thru the final examination may also completely save you from reaching that intention. That's fairly apparent in a severe case, yet nonetheless, quite a few university college students don't reach their purpose of graduating. The hassle can be a loss of commitment to the aim, however regularly students have conflicting dreams. One manner to prevent problems is to consider all your dreams and priorities and to learn methods to control some time, your studies, and your social existence to quality attain your desires. It all starts with putting dreams and considering priorities.

As you think about your very own dreams, reflect on

consideration of more than just being a scholar. You're also a person with character needs and goals, hopes, and dreams, plans, and schemes. Your lengthy-term desires probably consist of commencement and a profession however can also contain social relationships with others, a romantic courting, own family, interests or other activities, wherein and the way you live, and so on. Even as you're a scholar, you could now not be actively pursuing all your goals with identical fervor, but they stay goals and are nevertheless critical for your existence.

Desires also range in phrases of time.

•	Quick-time period goals attention on these days and the next few days and possibly weeks.

•	Midterm goals contain plans for this school for 12 months and the time you intend to remain in college.

•	Long-time period dreams may begin with graduating from university and the entirety you want to manifest thereafter.

Frequently your lengthy-time period goals (e.g., the kind of profession you want) guide your midterm dreams (getting the right education for that profession), and your brief period goals (such as doing nicely on an examination) turn out to be steps for reaching those large dreams. thinking about your desires in this manner helps you realize how even the little belongings you do each day can keep you shifting toward your maximum essential lengthy-term dreams.

Write out your desires

You ought to write them down because the act of locating the quality words to explain your desires help you watched greater surely about them. Comply with those hints:

- Dreams ought to be realistic. It's good to dream and to task yourself, but your dreams have to relate to your strengths and abilities.
- Desires should be unique. Don't write, "I will become an excellent musician;" as an alternative, write, "I will finish my track degree and be hired in a symphony orchestra."
- Desires must have a time body. You won't sense very inspired in case your intention is vague "to complete college in the future." if you're sensible and precise in your desires, you ought to additionally be able to mission a time frame for accomplishing the intention.
- You should want to reach the aim. We're willing to work difficult to reach desires we surely care approximately, however we're possibly to surrender while we encounter boundaries if we don't sense strongly about an aim. If you're doing something most effective due to the fact your parents or someone else wants you to, then it's now not your private purpose and you may have a few more wondering to do approximately your life.

Mindset

The whole thing humans do and how they do it begins with mindset. One student gets up with the alarm clock and cheerfully prepares for the day, making plans to have a look at it for a couple of hours between instructions move to stroll later, and spot a pal at dinner. Every other student oversleeps after partying too late remaining night time, decides to skip his first magnificence, come what may receive thru later training fueled through rapid food and strength drinks even as dreading tomorrow's exam and right away accepts a chum's inspiration to exit this night in preference to studying.

Both students ought to have equal conditions, lessons, price range, and academic practice. There could be just one great difference but it's the only that matters. Here are some characteristics related to a tremendous mindset:

- Enthusiasm for and amusement of daily sports
- Attractiveness of obligation for one's moves and feeling suitable about fulfillment
- Generally upbeat temper and fantastic feelings, cheerfulness with others, and delight with oneself
- Motivation to get the task done
- Flexibility to make modifications while wished
- Capability to make efficient, powerful use of time

And here are a few characteristics related to a poor mindset:

- Frequent complaining
- Blaming others for whatever that goes incorrect
- Regularly experiencing terrible feelings: anger, frustration, resentment
- Loss of motivation for work or research
- Hesitant to trade or are trying to find development
- Unproductive use of time, procrastination

Live targeted and stimulated

You've were given a fantastic attitude. However, you've got a variety of reading for training to do this night, a check day after today, and a paper due the following day. Perhaps you're a little uninterested in considered one of your studying assignments. Perhaps you'd rather play a PC game. Mindset can exchange at almost any second. One minute you're enthusiastically starting a category undertaking, and then maybe a chum drops by using, and unexpectedly all you need to do is near the books and relax sometimes, dangle out with pals. One of the characteristics of successful human beings is accepting that lifestyles are full of interruptions and exchange and planning for it. Staying focused does now not mean you come to be a run-of-the-mill person who does nothing however visit the class and have a look at it all the time. You just want to make a plan.

Plan beforehand

Making plans ahead is the single satisfactory way to live centered and motivated to attain your desires. Don't wait until the nighttime earlier than an exam. If you understand you have got a chief examination in five days, start with the aid of reviewing the fabric and figuring out how many hours of look at you want. Then agenda those hours unfold out over the following few days at times when you are most alert and least in all likelihood to be distracted. Allow time for different activities, too, to reward yourself for successful studying. Then while the exam comes, you're comfy, you understand the fabric, you're in a good mood and assured, and you do well. Making plans is usually a count number of managing some time well.

Here are some different recommendations for staying centered and prompted

• In case you're not feeling prompted, consider the results of your dreams, now not just the dreams themselves. If simply considering finishing college doesn't sound all that interesting, then think rather approximately the amazing, excessive-paying career that comes afterward and the things you may do with that earnings.

- Take into account your successes, even small successes. As you begin an assignment or technique reading for a take a look at, consider your past fulfillment on a one-of-a-kind mission or check. Don't forget how appropriate it feels to succeed. Recognize you can be successful once more.

- Get the crucial things executed first. Remains targeted, motivated, and concentrate on the things that be counted most. You're about to sit down to examine a bankruptcy in an e-book you're now not a good deal enjoying, and also you be aware of a few pieces of clothing piled up on a chair. "I in reality must clean up this vicinity," you suspect. "And I'd better get my laundry done before I run out of factors to put on." Don't try to idiot yourself into feeling you're engaging in something by using doing laundry as opposed to studying. Live targeted!

- In case you simply can't focus on what you should be doing because the project seems too huge and daunting, destroy the project into smaller, workable portions. Don't start out thinking, "I want to have a look at the subsequent four hours," however think, "I'll spend the subsequent thirty minutes going thru my magnificence notes from the last three weeks and discern out what subjects I need to spend more time on." It's plenty less difficult to live targeted whilst you're sitting down for thirty minutes at a time.

- Imitate successful human beings. Does a friend constantly appear higher capable of stick with studying or work till they get it accomplished? What are they doing which you're no longer? All of us examine from looking at others, and we can accelerate that technique by deliberately the usage of the equal strategies we see operating with others. Visualize yourself reading in the same manner and getting that identical excessive grade on the test or paper.

• Separate yourself from unsuccessful human beings. This is the turn facet of imitating successful people. If a roommate or a friend is always casting off things until the ultimate minute or is distracted with other interests and sports, tell yourself how special you are. While you listen to other college students complaining approximately how tough a class is or bragging approximately not studying or attending magnificence, visualize yourself as now not being like them at all.

• Reward yourself when you complete a vast undertaking, however simplest when you are executed. Some humans appear capable of stay focused most effectively when there's praise waiting.

Thinking about your goals gets you commenced, but it's also important to reflect on consideration on priorities. We often use the word "priorities" to refer to how important something is to us. We would suppose, that is a sincerely vital goal, and this is less important. Do that experiment: move back to the desires you wrote and spot if you could rank every goal as a

1. Pinnacle precedence
2. Middle priority
3. Lowest priority

It sounds smooth, however, do you certainly sense secure doing that? Perhaps you gave priority 1 to passing your publications and priority three to playing your guitar. So what does that mean that you in no way play guitar again, or at least now not even as in college? Every time you have an hour free between elegance and work, you need to observe because's the higher priority? What about all of your other dreams, do you need to forget about the entirety that's no longer a concern 1? And what takes place when you have to choose among one-of-a-kind desires which can be each no 1 priorities?

Priorities don't work quite that way. It doesn't make quite a few feel to try to rank goals is continually greater or much less crucial. The question of priority is truly a query of what's greater crucial at a selected time. It's critical to do properly to your lessons, however, it's also crucial to have a social life and experience your time off from reading. You shouldn't need to select among the two besides at any given time.

Priorities constantly contain time: what is maximum critical to do proper now. As we'll see later, time management is mostly a manner to juggle priorities so you can meet all of your desires. Whilst you manage it slow nicely, you ought not forget about some dreams completely a good way to meet other dreams. In different words, you don't need to give up your life while you sign up for university however you may want to work on dealing with your life more efficaciously. But time management works only when you're committed to your dreams. Mindset and motivation are very crucial. If you haven't yet evolved a mindset for the fulfillment, all of the time management talents within the global gained maintain you centered and encouraged to be successful.

Chapter Three

The Importance of Goals in Education

Intention putting is essential to lengthy-time period success. Despite everything, it's tough to get to a favored destination earlier than you have clearly described wherein that destination is. Goals assist college students to awareness upon the journey to a group of set achievements, meaning they allocate their resources and time more efficaciously and can get admission to motivation for the duration of times when they'll experience like giving up.

From an academic perspective, desires enhance performance using ensuring Cadets stay chargeable for their failures and successes, propelling themselves ahead through a selection of small achievements designed to interrupt down a larger purpose. What's extra, placing and attaining dreams interprets to feelings of success and self-belief for college students, which in turn ends in extra self-assurance and productivity.

Goals hold students transferring ahead

Writing a specific aim right into a calendar or journal gives students something to work and plan toward. Whilst written down, these goals shape an outside representation of inner desires to get a higher grade, development with sporting talents, or acquire a new rank. They are a constant reminder of what that scholar desires to accomplish. Aim setting even fuels ambition and self-belief via encouraging willpower through difficult durations and imparting a sense of pride while fulfillment sooner or later arrives.

Without set desires, students can go with the flow from one vicinity of lifestyles to the following, achieving accomplishments and doing their first-rate. Setting up an aim creates a feel of readability and correlation among the technique of running tough and engaging in something full-size. Because of this, Cadets access the motivational power that they want to work thru periods in which cognizance might also start to wane.

Goals break down Insurmountable Mountains

Maximum teens have large dreams that may appear not possible to perform at the beginning. It's smooth for students to feel discouraged when they're staring at a destiny that seems too big to achieve. But, proper intention placing can break one's large, more intimidating aspirations down into practicable stepping stones. not most effective does making plans in the direction of smaller desires make it easier to formulate a plan of how one achievement can lead to some other, however, studies show that reaching smaller milestones gives more ranges of contentment and motivation.

Students may be advocated to work toward a quick-time period and lengthy-term goals that interconnect, giving them extra focus on what they have to be spending power and time toward. Through the pursuit of those smaller desires, Cadets learn extra about themselves — their competencies, weaknesses, and what they want to accomplish.

Desires keep college students accountable

Having dreams makes Cadets accountable for their moves, their efforts, or even their time control capabilities. Putting a goal obligates a character to take action, no matter the obstacles that may be in the area. As such, it could encourage students to expand critical wondering abilities, new hassle fixing strategies, and a better knowledge of how to overcome problems.

What's greater, the duty of purpose setting encourages college students to appearance lower back over their preceding successes and disasters, evaluating regions they need to enhance. As such, it pushes them to tackle challenges head-on and work on their weaknesses so that they can produce better probabilities of standard success. It may also assist Cadets to recognize techniques that may not be operating for them so that they will are trying to find out opportunity routes to fulfillment.

Desires make college students want to be higher

There are various experimental and correlational studies displaying that putting desires increases fulfillment quotes in almost each putting, including education. Part of the motive for this is that putting goals pushes young adults to articulate the things they want out of lifestyles so that they stay more consciously.

Without goals, college students challenge themselves to default or a natural set of actions that might be there to keep them feeling secure and secure, without presenting any possibility for increase. With dreams, Cadets can find out extra approximately themselves and work in the direction of becoming satisfactory versions of themselves.

In other words, dreams allow students to tap into their inner capacity by giving them goals to strive towards. These targets make young adults project into new conditions, new contexts, and new demanding situations that location them right away inside the proper role for boom and improvement.

Goals put together college students for maturity

Through purpose putting, college students study that hard work and appropriate habits nearly are the keys to achievement. Because of this, they find out a stage of admiration for the determination and determination required to reap further crucial goals in life. Not best is goal placing important for supporting students get greater out of their educational studies, but it also way that they will keep to apply the equal competencies in the destiny to apply for an excessive-ranking task or achieve a new promotion

The real goals of education

"Training isn't always prepared for life; education is life itself."

~ John Dewey

After I watch youngsters walk into the construction on their first day of college, I reflect on consideration on what I want them to be like after they walk out on their remaining day. I also think about what I want them to be like on the day I come across them within the supermarket 10 or two decades later. Over the direction of three a long time looking kid's walk into my colleges, I have decided that I want them to

• Be lifelong learners

- Be passionate
- Be ready to take dangers
- Be capable of trouble-clear up and think critically
- Be able to take a look at things otherwise
- be capable of work independently and with others
- Be innovative
- Care and need to present returned to their community
- Persevere
- Have integrity and self-admire
- Have the ethical braveness
- Be capable of using the world around them nicely
- Communicate properly, write nicely, study nicely, and work nicely with numbers
- Surely experience their lifestyles and their work.

To me, these are the real dreams of education

I need college students to learn to use the resources around them. I need them to examine something or see something they are interested in and observe upon it. I want them to have an idea after which get at the smartphone and call human beings they can talk to approximately it, or pick out up an e-book and examine extra approximately it, or take a seat down and write about it. When I imagine certainly one of my students as a person, I believe someone who is a thinker and a doer, and who follows his or her passions. I see an adult who is sturdy sufficient to get up and communicate for what she or he wishes and believes, and who cares approximately himself or herself and the world. A person who understands himself or herself and knows getting to know will take the important steps to be successful. Creativity, passion, courage, and perseverance are the non-public features I want to peer in my graduates. I need them to stumble upon matters they have visible every day and observe them in an entirely new way. I need them to feel good about themselves and be exact, honest human beings within the manner they live their lives. And, catchphrase or now not, I need my college students to score high on the "tests of emotional IQ" that lifestyles will necessarily throw at them time and again.

Finally, I want my college students to get together with and respect others. A person once requested me, "what's the maximum important component a school does?" I spoke back that everything I believe about the actual dreams of education isn't always viable if the children in the college do not care approximately and cannot get together with each other or with the humans they meet outdoor of school. I agree that this is at the heart of what we suggest while we speak about celebrating and respecting range, and it's far from the heart of what makes a faculty and a society work.

while a kid leaves my college, I need her to have the fundamental existence abilities to be able to help her get along inside the adult global, like knowing a way to act in a meeting or the way to keep her existence and work prepared. primary stuff that too many schools neglect about of their rush to cram in three sciences, social research, math, and so on, but I additionally want her to be the kind of person who will hold constructing on what she got in my school, who will preserve developing capabilities, maintain learning, preserve growing. Every folk, if we stay to be simply seventy years antique, spends the best nine percent of our lives in faculty. Considering that the alternative ninety-one percentage is spent "available," then the only sincerely sizable element schooling can do in assisting us to grow to be continuous, lifelong freshmen. Newcomers who learn without textbooks and exams, without licensed instructors and standardized curricula. Freshmen who like to study. To me, that is the last aim of training.

In 1999, the faculty board in Howard County, Maryland, removed two criteria from its authentic policy on figuring out high faculty college students' grades. You understand that neither of them had been standardized tests. No, they had been, and that I quote, "originality" and "initiative." this College Board decided that the characteristics of a pupil's work have been not important. They determined this due to the fact, they said, it's far "not possible" to measure how hard a student tries or if a scholar's work is unique. What they have been definitely announcing, and what manner too many college boards are now announcing, is that this: If it cannot be measured easily, then we cannot care about it, we cannot teach it, and we certainly cannot decide if a child has learned it. Take originality and initiative completely from your academic desires and just teach to the take a look at. It makes me scream.

Ernest L. Boyer, the renowned schooling professional and then-president of the Carnegie Foundation for the advancement of coaching, as soon gave a speech entitled "Making the Connections." In it, he said (superbly),

I know how idealistic it could sound, however, it's miles my urgent hope that inside the century ahead students within the nation's faculties can be judged not with the aid of their overall performance on an unmarried take a look at, however by way of the excellent of their lives. I desire that students within the classrooms of the following day might be encouraged to be creative, not conforming, and discover ways to cooperate instead of competing.

Boyer stated this in 1993. He died years later, after an extended war with most cancers. Boyer knew that schools have been headed in the wrong route and he made that clear by pronouncing that his desire was "idealistic." it is so sad to me that if he had been here today, he would not best see how idealistic this hope nonetheless is, however how ways we've got long gone in view that then in the precise opposite direction.

I don't forget in the eighth grade, my science instructor had us do those posters that he placed up everywhere in the college. Although it wasn't exactly a take a look at, it becomes a primary mission, and all of us knew our grade relied on it. So there those posters have been, hung everywhere in the partitions and that they have been lovely, and the teacher appeared excellent to his boss and co-workers, and he in all likelihood felt pretty true approximately himself, too. I suppose this becomes the first time I found out how a great deal of my training become the total bull. I knew I hadn't discovered something about what became on those posters, which includes my personal. And the trainer just hung them up. We slightly pointed out the posters, we made no connection with them to anything else, and he in no way went any deeper with the getting to know than that very last project. My classmates and I had definitely copied pix and phrases out of the encyclopedia, and for that, we not only passed the check of poster making but were additionally assumed to have gained the predetermined "set of knowledge" for that area. In no way mind that none of us had found out very a great deal approximately technology, let alone approximately initiative or originality. We did precisely what the "test" required us to do and nothing extra and so did the teacher.

These days, checks as meaningless as that take a look at of poster making are figuring out the dreams of education. Assessments are dictating what we as a society preserve valuable in our young humans. Our addiction to testing is blinding us to what we accept as true within our hearts is the important training our children ought to study.

If we labored backward, and idea first approximately the sort of person we respect, we might no longer name traits that might be measured on a couple of of-preference tests. No unmarried size or tool can get at what's sincerely crucial in any region of studying. And the cutting-edge push for one to take a look at that every child has to skip to move to the next grade or graduate makes the complete state of affairs even sadder.

What we need to look at is the kid in pursuit of understanding, and no longer knowledge in pursuit of the kid. With their awareness on cease consequences, too many colleges and education policymakers forget about how plenty the method affects how a child takes in knowledge after which makes use of it. Too many forget how intrinsic motivation and choice are to studying. a lot of our whole approach to schooling inside the USA cheats kids out of the risk to end up lifelong novices.

I want students so that they can find the records they need, which allows them to go through the process of locating gaining knowledge. And the key is that they may be influenced to do it. I care greater that a scholar is happy to go deeper in her exploration of the history of girls in her native country than I do about that scholar's potential to answer every query on a standardized U.S. history test. I care manner extra about supporting children discover ways to follow expertise than I do about offering them with know-how and finding out if they have memorized sufficient of the information to spit them returned at me. Maximum faculties simply give out the knowledge and then take a look at it. They explain photosynthesis and then ask the child to spit lower back photosynthesis. In among, no photosynthesis-like method came about the interior that kid! He did not take in that knowledge after which go to the library to locate more books approximately photosynthesis, name a nearby greenhouse to go see how it works, or talk to a scientist who researches flora. And he simply did not grow at all in between receiving the knowledge and being tested on it. He took it in and spit it right back out and the records and himself, unchanged.

So what is getting to know?

How will we realize if our kids have become lifelong beginners? I supply a variety of speeches around the United States to those who stroll into the room thinking they know what it means to be a knowledgeable man or woman. They're ready to research from me approximately how to train, but they feel pretty assured that they know what a knowledgeable person looks like. After which I show them that famous scene from the film My Cousin Vinny. You understand the one I am talking about approximately. Marisa Tomei is at the stand proving to the jury that it couldn't probable had been the defendants' car that left the tire tracks determined at the scene. She spews out all sorts of records and theories and historic information about automobiles to demonstrate her case. She generalizes, she pulls things together, and he or she teaches what she is aware of to the courtroom. It's an exquisite scene. And then I forestall the tape and ask the audience if they might recall her to be "a knowledgeable character." If I see that there are nevertheless individuals who assume, "properly, but she's a hairdresser, so she cannot simply be knowledgeable," I sometimes ask them, "If she had the identical know-how about and ardor for cars, but became a physician rather than a hairdresser, might we take into account her knowledgeable then?" Of direction we might.

No matter who you are, if you can arise and be obsessed with something and inform others approximately what, and you then are displaying that you are knowledgeable about that subject matter. that is what an exhibition is: it is kids getting up and talking passionately about an e-book they have read, a paper they've written, drawings they have made, or even what they recognize approximately auto mechanics. It's a way for students to have conversations about the matters they have found out. Exhibitions are the high-quality way to measure learning due to the fact they positioned the kids right inside the midst of their getting to know, which makes a lot more sense than asking them to sit down quietly for an hour and fill in take a look at bubbles with a pencil. And due to the fact exhibitions are interactive, they propel the kids to need to analyze more. **That is what matters.**

I don't forget one time while I was taking a set of eighth-graders on a trip. The conductor became truly having amusing speaking with them and listening to them about their plans for the experience. The kids instructed him about the research they'd completed and the selections they had made together. Then the teacher conductor advised them he wanted to find out how smart they were. So he started out quizzing them on kingdom capitals. It's so sad to me that when the whole lot he had discovered approximately them, their unique personalities and skills and after seeing how passionate they were about learning, he still desired to recognize if they were absolutely "smart youngsters and he, like such a lot of, and notion memorization takes a look at changed into the way to decide that.

Some other instance that I exploit to show human beings what gaining knowledge of clearly is a phase of a videotape on math and science learning referred to as a personal universe. The video was produced by way of the Harvard-Smithsonian Center for Astrophysics and shows these types of short interviews with Harvard college students, school, and alumni on graduation day. Most of them look so "educated" of their caps and robes and flowing academic robes. After which the interviewer asks them considered one of the questions: "What causes the seasons?" or "What causes the stages of the moon?"

Twenty-one of the twenty-three randomly selected Harvard oldsters to provide the wrong solution. What is more, their wrong solutions reveal the same misconceptions about these things that the solutions of grade-schoolers do. Then the interviewees are requested to listing all the technical instructions they've taken over time, both at Harvard or in high school. after I display this video to audiences, I say, "Come on, they have got taken every sort of technological know-how route possible and handed each one in all them and accomplished this and that, however, they cannot use it on something as fundamental because the change of seasons!?" because of their Harvard diplomas, these grads are going to turn out to be a number of the most powerful human beings in our international, but what sort of power is it whilst you cannot apply the expertise that the diploma stands for? Elliot Washor, the co-founder of The Met and The big photograph organization, points out that this says loads approximately how too many schools view gaining knowledge of. He relates it to what we're doing at the Met and our large image colleges in this manner: "They say understanding is power. We are saying using expertise is strength."

My point is that gaining knowledge is about going beyond the know-how given to you in a category or an e-book or at a museum. Getting to know is personal. It occurs one on one, it takes place in small corporations, it occurs alone. Certain, a conference, a speaker, a lecture is motivating but the real gaining knowledge of takes place after. It is what you do with it, how you combine it, how you communicate with your family, pals, and classmates about it. That is what gaining knowledge of is. As referred to by psychology and education professional Seymour Sarason reminded us recently, it's just like psychotherapists' notion that patients don't get higher at some point of the hour, however between the hours.

I am not suggesting we throw out the whole lot faculties do now or everything the ones Harvard kids learned. I'm suggesting that we appear more deeply at what we define as learning and be honest and attempt different things and spot what works. Getting to know is ready gaining knowledge of the way to suppose.

Tom Magliozzi, from countrywide Public Radio's popular show automobile talk, has plenty to mention about what gaining knowledge of clearly is within the e-book he and his brother wrote, In Our Humble Opinion. One in all my favored components is while Tom, a man with a Ph.D. in chemical engineering from MIT, says this:

It appears to me that faculties mainly train children how to take assessments (a skill one hardly ever uses in real lifestyles unless one is a contestant on a quiz display). Elementary college prepares youngsters for junior excessive; junior high prepares them for excessive college. So, the aim if we can name it that of colleges is to prepare children for extra faculty.

Psychologist Robert J. Sternberg has written about the dichotomy between his "real international" achievement and the problem he had reading psychology in college. Here is a quote from him that reminds us that, even in higher education, there is often a large breakup between what we are taught and anticipated to research, and what is truly essential "out there":

Gaining knowledge isn't always approximately memorizing. Gaining knowledge of is set being aware. Mindfulness is an idea I found out about a while lower back, and it certainly makes feel to me as something we're seeking to broaden in our college students at the Met. Ellen Langer is a professor of psychology at Harvard and the author of the books Mindfulness and The power of conscious getting to know. In those books, she talks approximately how cultivating mindfulness is assisting human beings to recognize that the arena is complete of thrilling possibilities for getting to know and that the arena will continually look one-of-a-kind from distinct views. Our education gadget has to see developing conscious rookies as its goal. Novices who are aware of all that surrounds them and all this is interior them tend to be extra alert and a hit than individuals who aren't.

Too often, we train people such things as, "there may be a proper manner and an incorrect manner to do the whole thing, regardless of the instances." What we must be teaching them is a way to suppose flexibly, to bear in mind all of the specific possibilities of each scenario, and not near themselves off from statistics that might assist them.

For example, any person likes tennis. While they used to be more youthful, they would have gone to a tennis camp and were taught the way to hold a racket when they served. One day I was looking at the U.S. Open, and I found out that now not one of the players correctly held the racket.

The hassle comes with the way we study. We're not often taught conditionally: "This might be an excellent grip for you." usually, we are taught: "this is the proper grip." Being mindful—using imagination and creativity to examine what works exceptional for you is what makes the distinction between an average participant and a champ.

Coaching is listening, learning is talking

~ Message painted on a Met consultant's truck with the aid of his students

Once I lay out my imagination and prescient of the actual desires of education in an orderly-looking listing, I fear about what human beings, instructors especially, will do with it. I worry about what they will interpret it to intend approximately coaching. I don't trust that you could separate coaching from learning. Please don't study my listing and say, "adequate, I agree that these are the matters kids have to study, so now permit's set out a rigid factor-via-point curriculum that may be taught to a class of twenty-five college students." To me, the act of being an instructor is to recognize these goals of education, knowledge of how learning works, and figuring out the way to observe all this to each scholar, one by one. I realize that it'd be pretty easy for a person to take the desires I consider in and contort them so that they match properly and without problems right into a lecture-based totally curriculum designed to be assessed with a standardized, more than one-preference check. However, being a teacher and building a device of training, for that depends is ready taking these desires and developing the best feasible surroundings for helping kids and getting to know them. It isn't always approximately taking those desires and locating a manner to shape them into the traditional strategies of training.

here's an instance of the way educators can miss the point: Some folks trust that studying to be an ethical man or woman is the maximum critical goal of training, and most of these curricula have been evolved around teaching ethical individuals. There are textbooks with "moral struggle situations" that sound good on paper, however, may also have nothing to do with wherein a selected kid is at right now. Then there are a couple of of-desire assessments to assess whether or not the kid is aware of what is moral and what is not. Morality is that this large, arms-on, actual-global problem and properly-intentioned faculties are taking the scholars' arms and global right out of the equation.

Just having the proper goals isn't the solution. It's the way you reach one's dreams; the act of coaching that is so important. another instance: If we say that each scholar inside the US have to recognize democracy, which I assume all of us agree on, most of the people suppose, "ok, well, children find out about democracy by using studying the charter and speaking approximately the way it becomes evolved, and so forth." yes, that is very cool stuff to recognize. But while they may be getting to know this stuff, maximum kids aren't making one democracy-stimulated choice all through their years of training.

Most children either are not allowed to or do not consider they have got proper to make decisions about whatever full-size at some point of the years they are in faculty. So, to me, if we're seeking to educate children about the significance of democracy and being accurate citizens and approximately balloting and all that comes with it, we surely should be giving children the possibilities to make real choices and take actual obligation for what goes on around them. They ought to simply be voting, not simply talking about it.

The act of being an instructor is the act of taking the dreams I've described and then using your skills and love for kids to determine a way to create a pleasant environment to help your students attain their one's goals. At the equal time, you have to understand that each child approaches getting to know in a man or woman manner and could meet those goals in that person manner. And every child is coming to you with his private luggage that could need to be worked via earlier than he may even begin to research what you are attempting to train him. The trainer's role is to locate what that manner is for every child. Teaching will become identifying how to see and listen to every youngster, one child at a time so that the kid can reach the goals for himself or herself. It's far about locating the proper relationship between the student and the adult, the relationship that works properly for both of them. And, most significantly, coaching can't take place in a vacuum. The community and the kid's circle of relatives need to be blanketed in every manner possible. Dad and mom are the scholar's first and maximum critical teachers and that they cannot, and need to now not, be unnoticed of the schooling equation no longer even when there are "experts" around.

w\Within the early Nineteen Seventies, the government had been setting pupil teachers in colleges with "open school rooms." those schools have been motivated by using a big motion within the '60s that started having kids doing initiatives in small corporations became a better set-up for studying than the traditional lecture layout. One of the scholar-teachers, a younger, idealistic female, made a declaration someday and stated, "this is awesome, however, whilst am I truly going to learn how to train?" She was standing there in interesting, wealthy studying surroundings, however, she couldn't see it as it didn't shape her idea of what coaching turned into, which was status up in the front of the room, looking out at quiet rows of faces, and pouring knowledge into them.

Coaching is so much greater than we ever idea it'd be
~ A Met guide, after his first twelve months
Alas, to most people, coaching is the giving of

understanding. What are you going to tell the students? What's your knowledge? But teaching is truly approximately bringing out what is already inner people. On the Met, we've got completely redefined coaching. We've even changed the name from "teacher" to "consultant" to symbolize how we're breaking the stereotypes surrounding the career. Our instructors aren't givers of understanding, however, adults who inspire the scholars to locate their very own passions and their very own methods of learning and who offer aid alongside the manner. No longer by being a charismatic lecturer, however by way of being a splendid coach, role model, motivator, consultant, and, sure, instructor. now not by way of displaying college students wherein to find the know-how inside the textbook, but by using assisting them to find the know-how within the real global. Now not with the aid of giving youngsters the solutions, however by using brainstorming with them about a way to clear up the problems. now not through telling college students what they ought to examine, however with the aid of letting them select their very own books, based totally on what they may be interested in. not through getting students to write papers that meet a positive set of the schoolroom, college, or country requirements, however via running with them one-on-one to revise their papers till they experience appropriate about what they have written and it meets their standards. On the Met, advisors are a vital part of an environment that lets in college students the liberty to discover themselves with the guide and motivation of inspiring adults. This, to me, is precisely what a faculty have to be.

While we rent instructors at the Met, we do it in this

sincerely democratic way, with all of the workforce and a few students worried about the decision-making. Our primary standards for brand new instructors are that they love and are committed to children and that they are lifelong rookies. While I am interviewing a person, many requested themselves, is this someone who can be a role model to a child thru his or her very own exhilaration approximately getting to know? in addition, they try to see how they interact with youngsters. Are they relating to them and respecting them? If I get a danger to take a look at applicants in a coaching context, lots of them are greater interested by wherein their attention is and how top the lesson is: Are they more inquisitive about the content material or the sound of their voice than they are within the children sitting right in front of them?

We have lots of individuals who can train what they understand, however very few who can teach their capability to study. While a teacher loves kids, is enthusiastic about the act of teaching, and is a learner himself or herself, that is when the first-class teaching occurs whether or not it's in his or her "location of know-how" or no longer. I as soon as had an instructor who taught a class at the Bible, not as a spiritual work but as a bit of literature, and she had in no way virtually studied it before. She informed me later that, in the course of that class, she was the first-class trainer she had ever been because she turned into on the same degree with her students, she was experiencing it considering the primary time proper together with them. This meant she wasn't saying such things as, "take a look at the metaphors in here and compare them," but became asking questions that she didn't realize the solutions to, like, "What will we reflect on consideration on this passage as compared to this one?" It was very thrilling for her and very invigorating for her students.

All over again, I had a home economics instructor who needed to train math to a small organization of students who had been suffering. She changed into no longer excellent at math. Some may say, "Oh, no, a good way to in no way work," but it became a number of her most terrific teaching. I'd watch her sitting with the ones six ladies, and they would be identifying the one's problems together. She turned cozy with the scholars understanding that she didn't recognize the whole lot. She turned into comfortable with the idea that she became not just there as a query answerer, but as a position model who could display children a way to discover the answers. She wasn't yelling at them about why they didn't understand it; she did not get impatient with their lack of knowledge. She without a doubt went thru the mastering revel in with them. And that they went through it together with her.

This is not to mention that teachers shouldn't understand the content. The greater knowledge you have, the less difficult it could be to examine greater due to the fact you know which questions to ask. However, I trust that know-how also can get within the way every so often. It's excellent for instructors to have depth in a certain region, as long as they don't simply hand it over. They must use that deep information to help their students discover the gaining knowledge of on their personal. Teaching and mastering are approximately hassled fixing. Education is the method by means that you put teachers and beginners inside the first-class feasible surroundings for them to try this together. And the best possible surroundings are one where people feel safe, supported, and respected, and wherein youngsters and adults are excited and obsessed with gaining knowledge.

The goals of schooling

No infant Left at the back of (NCLB) holds all basic colleges, no matter scholar traits, liable for reaching proficient pupil ratings in studying and math. using demanding that faculties record success for racial, ethnic, and monetary subgroups, the duty system targets to polish a light on schools that "depart children in the back of."

In the beginning look, this technique appears reasonable. but few who debate the details of implementation have considered how this responsibility machine has begun to shift how we consider what schools need to do. With the aid of basing sanctions entirely on math and analyzing rankings, the law creates incentives to limit or in a few instances to dispose of completely time spent on other vital curricular targets. This reorientation of education disproportionately impacts low-profits and minority kids, so fulfillment gaps can also in reality widen in areas for which schools aren't now being held responsible.

The shift in curricular insurance is also at odds with the consensus approximately the dreams of public schooling to which people historically have subscribed. Extra relatively, it's also starkly at odds with the apparent intentions of College Board participants and kingdom legislators, who are liable for enforcing the coverage, and with the intentions of the public whom those leaders constitute. we can speak the proof about these intentions later in this article. For now, allow us to start via documenting the intention displacement inspired through NCLB.

The federal authorities' periodic country-wide survey of instructors demonstrates the curricular shifts. In 1991, teachers in grades one to four spent a mean of 33% of their lecture room instructional time on reading. By way of 2004, studying turned into ingesting 36% of instructional time. For math, common weekly time went from 15% to 17%. Meanwhile, time for social research and science decreased. Since 1991, academic time spent on social studies went from nine% to eight%, and time spent on technological know-how went from 8% to 7%.

These reputedly small common changes mask a disproportionate impact on the maximum disadvantaged students. The Council for basic schooling surveyed college principals in numerous states within the fall of 2003 and discovered that principals in faculties with high proportions of minorities were much more likely to have reduced time for records, civics, geography, the arts, and foreign languages so that they may dedicate greater time to math and analyzing. In New York, as an example, twice as many principals in high-minority schools mentioned such curricular shifts as did principals in mostly white colleges. In high-minority standard faculties, 38% of principals mentioned lowering the time devoted to social studies (normally meaning history), but in low-minority schools, only 17% mentioned reducing such time.

A 2005 survey through the center on schooling policy (CEP) found that ninety seven% of excessive-poverty districts had new minimum-time necessities for studying, at the same time as handiest fifty five% of low-poverty districts had them. The CEP had formerly located that, in which districts had adopted such minimal-time guidelines, approximately half had reduced social research, forty-three% had decreased artwork and song, and 27% had reduced physical education.

Thus, although NCLB goals to slender the success gap in math and analyzing, its accidental consequence is to widen the distance in different curricular regions. This is how one former teacher describes her modified lecture room sports: From the revel in of being a basic faculty instructor at a low-acting city college in la, John said that the pressure became so severe that we had to expose how every single lesson we taught connected to a well-known that became going to be examined. This supposed that artwork, tune, and even technology and social research were not a priority and have been hardly ever taught. We have been pressured to spend ninety percent of the instructional time on studying and math. This made coaching dull for me and was a huge part of why he determined to leave the profession.

These distortions did not begin with NCLB. They evolved steadily inside the 1990s as states carried out comparable duty policies. A 2001 evaluation by using researchers at the University of Colorado observed high-quality results of better math and reading requirements, however, those gains have been offset by using losses in different regions, in particular in sports that developed citizenship, social duty, and cooperative conduct. One Colorado trainer mentioned:

Our district has told us to awareness of analyzing, writing, and mathematics, he said. Inside the beyond he had hatched out baby chicks within the lecture room as part of a technology unit. He didn't have time to do that. He had dissected frame elements, and that he didn't have time to do that. We don't take as many area journeys. We don't do community outreach like we used to, like journeying the nursing home or cleaning up the park because we had followed a park and that turned into our process to maintain it clean. Properly, we don't have time for that anymore.

Some from outside the world of education have expressed challenge approximately those tendencies. In testimony before a U.S. Senate committee, the historian David McCullough discovered, "because of No baby Left in the back of, unfortunately, records are being put on the back burner or taken off the stove altogether in lots of or maximum faculties, in want of math or studying.

O'Connor now co-chairs a "campaign for the Civic challenge of faculties," which laments that, below NCLB, "as civic studying has been brushed aside, society has left out an essential cause of American schooling, setting the health of our democracy at risk and U.S. Senator Robert Byrd (D-W. Va.) Has reacted to the inadequate attention civics gets in public faculties using effectively sponsoring regulation requiring that each educational institution in the kingdom train approximately the federal charter every September seventeenth. It can hardly ever be taken into consideration an affordable solution to have Congress mandate particular days of instruction for each of the many schooling goals now being deemphasized beneath the testing strain of NCLB.

The growing national diabetes epidemic also shows how accountability for math and reading on my own can exacerbate inequity in other important elements of schooling. On average, blacks are 60% more likely to have diabetes than whites of comparable age. (The prevalence of the disorder is even better for Mexican Americans and Puerto Ricans. One purpose of this epidemic, although now not the best one, is the decline in physical interest amongst younger people, especially minority youths. This, in turn, consequences in part from the substitution of more take a look at instruction in math and studying for health club instructions. Black essential school children are 50% much more likely to be overweight than their white peers, even as white youngsters are twice as probably as black kids to participate in prepared day-by-day bodily activity.

In 2004, the centers for ailment manage cited that 20% of black youngsters in primary faculties were obese, in comparison to fourteen% of white essential-schoolers. now not notably, forty-seven% of whites in fourth to eighth grades (the years of NCLB testing) participate in prepared day-by-day physical activity, at the same time as simply 24% of blacks achieve this. Eleven Meanwhile, 18% of black high college students and 12% of white high college students are overweight.12 From 2001 to 2003, as academic requirements had been raised and excessive college goes out exams developed, the proportion of white high faculty students collaborating in daily physical training become unchanged, but the percentage of blacks collaborating in the day by day bodily training declined extensively.

It's clear that black students, whose instructional overall performance, on common, decreases and who've been enrolled, on common, in fewer academic publications, are more likely to be laid low with multiplied instructional requirements. But due to the fact, black students are less in all likelihood to have opportunities to take part in inside and out-of-college sports activities, they also are extra dependent on ok bodily schooling packages in school to protect their health. universal, thinking about each in- and out-of-faculty exercising, the CDC determined that, in 2003, 65% of white excessive college students participated in a sufficient amount of strenuous physical interest (along with playing basketball or soccer, going for walks, swimming laps, bicycling speedy, dancing fast, or carrying out similar aerobic sports) for appropriate fitness, whilst only 55% of black high college students did so.

NCLB's position in distorting the curriculum isn't unrecognized via folks who promoted and hold to guide the regulation. Therefore, a few can be having second thoughts. Robert Schwartz, for example, changed into the founding president of gain, Inc., the joint enterprise/governors' organization that was largely answerable for the trying out and responsibility demands that culminated in NCLB. He now writes:

The goal of equipping all college students with a strong foundation of educational knowledge and talents is leading to an undue narrowing of curricular choices and a reduction within the kinds of gaining knowledge of possibilities for academically at-chance college students which are most possibly to interact and encourage them to take college critically. That is a painful acknowledgment from someone who considers himself a constitution member of the standards motion.

But other NCLB supporters take pride in how the curriculum has been reshaped by way of testing, however the loss of interest to crucial, however non-tested, subjects. Responding to a report with the aid of the Thomas B.

Fordham foundation displaying how NCLB's focus on math and studying has led schools to decrease the time committed to a science practice, Secretary of schooling Margaret Spellings boasted, "I'm a what-receives-measured-gets-accomplished type of gal," and claimed that the answer turned into to check science as nicely. But, at the same time as science checks are to be brought to NCLB in 2007-08, faculties will no longer be held accountable for the outcomes. Even within the not going occasion that exams created for informational functions simplest would serve as incentives to redirect teaching time back to technology, the Spellings approach says nothing about the many other regions of know-how and behavioral developments which are being dropped from curricula via colleges held accountable simplest for math and reading.

A historical perspective

The cutting-edge overemphasis on fundamental instructional talents is a historic aberration. All through American history, we have held a greater expansive set of desires for our public faculties. Whilst the Founders endorsed the need for public training, their motives were usually political. Studying to examine turned into much less important than, and handiest a method closer to, helping citizens make smart political choices. Records coaching become a notion to educate students' appropriate judgment, allowing them to analyze from prior generations' mistakes and successes and inspiring them to develop such individual tendencies as honesty, integrity, and compassion. The Founders had absolute confidence that schools may want to produce students who exhibited these trends, and it might in no way have occurred to them that coaching in studying and arithmetic by myself could guarantee appropriate citizenship.

In 1749 Benjamin Franklin proposed that Pennsylvania establish a public faculty that ought to, he said, area as tons emphasis on bodily as on intellectual health because "exercising invigorates the soul as well as the frame." As for lecturers, Franklin idea records specifically essential, because "questions of right and wrong, justice and injustice, will certainly stand up" as students debate historic troubles "in conversation and writing." college students, Franklin insisted, ought to also read newspapers and talk modern controversies, thereby developing their logic and reasoning.

George Washington's dreams for public faculties were also political and ethical. In his first message to Congress, he recommended public faculties that could teach college students "to value their very own rights" and "to distinguish between oppression and the vital exercise of lawful authority." His farewell address warned that, due to the fact public opinion affects coverage in a democracy, "it's far important that public opinion has to be enlightened" by faculties that teach virtue and morality. He wanted to go even further, but his speechwriter (Alexander Hamilton) reduce from the farewell cope with a plea for a countrywide public university that would encourage tolerance of range, bringing collectively students of various backgrounds to reveal to them there may be no foundation for their "jealousies and prejudices."

Thomas Jefferson, the Founder most customarily connected with schooling in the public thoughts, thought popular public schooling needed commonly to put together citizens to workout smart judgment. He desired not what we now call "civics training", getting to know how authorities works, how bills are surpassed, how long a President's period is, and so on. as an alternative, Jefferson concept schools should prepare voters to assume critically about candidates and their positions and then choose accurately. In the direction of the end of his existence, he proposed a public schooling machine for the kingdom of Virginia:

to present to every citizen the facts he wishes for the transaction of his enterprise; to permit him to calculate for himself, and to specific and hold his thoughts, his contracts and debts in writing; to enhance, with the aid of studying, his morals and colleges; to understand his obligations to his neighbors and US, and to discharge with competence the functions confided to him by either; to understand his rights; to exercise with order and justice the ones he retains, to choose with discretion the fiduciary of those he delegates; and to observe their behavior with diligence, with candor and judgment; and in general, to observe with intelligence and faithfulness all the social relations underneath which he will be placed.

As the 19th century improved, the earliest labor unions insisted that public faculties sell social reform. Looking forward to through almost two centuries our cutting-edge duty rules, union leaders of the time feared that public colleges for the bad would encompass only fundamental studying and arithmetic and no longer the extra essential highbrow improvement that would empower the working elegance.

In 1830, a workingmen's committee examined Pennsylvania's city public schools, which primarily served the terrible while wealthy kids attended personal colleges.

The committee denounced the city schools for education that "extends no in addition than a tolerable scalability in analyzing, writing, and mathematics." The committee delivered: "There can be no actual liberty without a huge diffusion of real intelligence. Training, as opposed to being restrained as in our public poor faculties, to a simple acquaintance with words and ciphers, ought to have a tendency, as some distance as viable, to the production of a just disposition, virtuous habits, and a rational self-governing character." Equality, the committee concluded, is but "an empty shadow" if terrible children don't get an "equal schooling inside the habits, inside the manners, and the feelings of the community."

In 1837, Horace Mann was elected secretary of the newly created Massachusetts Board of education and thereafter wrote twelve annual reviews to inspire aid for public faculties. One document harassed the significance of coaching vocal songs. Some others, following Mann's visit to Europe, concluded that popular primary training in reading and mathematics did no longer on my own ensure democratic values. Prussian students have been literate, in any case, however, supported autocracy. Mann concluded that faculties in a democracy could not be held answerable for academics by myself however have to inculcate democratic moral and political values so that literacy would no longer be misused. In his last record, Mann articulated a listing of goals for education that blanketed health and physical schooling, intellectual (instructional) schooling, political training, moral schooling, and spiritual training (via which he intended coaching the moral principles on which all religions agreed).

As education elevated within the early 1900s, the federal Bureau of education commissioned a 1918 record, the Cardinal concepts of Secondary schooling. even though a few present-day academic historians have popularized the perception that the Cardinal ideas turned American training far from instructional abilities, that is an exaggeration. In truth, the commission that produced the file asserted that "much of the electricity of the basic college is nicely devoted to teaching positive fundamental techniques, consisting of reading, writing, arithmetical computations, and the elements of oral and written expression" and that the secondary school has to be committed to the software of these tactics. But the document argued that instructional abilities had been no longer sufficient; it continued in the culture of the Founders and educators like Horace Mann through urging a balanced approach to the goals of training.

As its first intention, the fee listed physical activity for students, preparation in non-public hygiene, and education in public health. Its second purpose turned into educational talents. 0.33 turned into education for the conventional family division of labor among men and women. Fourth changed into vocational training, along with the choice of jobs suitable to every student's skills and pursuits, as well as upkeep of suitable relationships with fellow people.

Just like the Founders, the fee emphasized in its fifth aim the want for civic education: coaching to participate in the community, metropolis or metropolis, kingdom, and nation. The Cardinal principles record dedicated greater area to civic training than to another aim, stressing that colleges should educate "precise judgment" in political matters and that students can learn democratic conduct only if school rooms and faculties are run with the aid of democratic methods. Even the examination of literature should "kindle social ideals."

The sixth intention was "worthy use of leisure," or student appreciation of literature, artwork, and song. And ultimate, the seventh purpose, moral character, was described as paramount in a democratic society. It covered growing a feel of private duty, initiative, and the "spirit of service."

 many years later, the country-wide training association (NEA), then a quasi-governmental group that protected now not only teachers, however, all specialists and policymakers in training, became considering how public schools should reply to the incredible depression. Its 1938 report, written via a federal training professional, set forth what is known as the "social-economic dreams" of Yankee education.

Echoing Horace Mann's reflections following his go to Prussia, the NEA file proclaimed: "The safety of democracy will now not be confident simply by way of making training established"; in different phrases, without a doubt by way of making all individuals literate. "The venture isn't as smooth as that. The dictatorships [Germany, Italy, Japan, and the Soviet Union] have prevalent training and use this very approach to prevent the spread of democratic doctrines and institutions." teaching democratic values and habits had to be an explicit cognizance of faculties and couldn't be assumed to waft mechanically from proficiency in studying and math. The essential capacity to differentiate among demagogues and statesmen "demands the capability to examine appropriately, to prepare statistics, to weigh evidence, and to split reality from falsehood." colleges, it went on, have to additionally develop college students' morality: justice and fair dealing, honesty, truthfulness, renovation of organization understandings, right admire for authority, tolerance and admire for others, habits of cooperation, and work conduct consisting of enterprise and self-control, at the side of endurance and physical strength.

The document argued that college time for social research needs to be elevated and have to consist of room for an extensive historical past in social and economic records, as well as ongoing dialogue of current affairs. "Excellent coaching demands that pupils be habituated in weighing the evidence on all aspects of a query," it said. Schools ought to additionally broaden a commitment to promote social welfare and beliefs of racial equality. Faculty-backed extracurricular and network sports might be the best approaches to attaining these goals, the document stated.

Prefiguring our modern-day dilemmas, the 1938 report went directly to warn: most of the standardized checking out devices and written examinations used in colleges today offer largely with records. There must be a miles extra issue with the improvement of attitudes, interests, ideals, and conduct. To recognition tests completely on the acquisition and retention of data might also apprehend targets of training which might be especially unimportant. Measuring the outcomes of education needs to be increasingly more concerned with such questions as these: Are the youngsters developing in their capability to work together for a commonplace stop? Do they show more skill in accumulating and weighing proof? Are they learning to be fair and tolerant in conditions in which conflicts stand up? Are they sympathetic within the presence of struggling and indignant in the presence of injustice? Do they display extra problem approximately questions of civic, social, and financial importance? Are they using their spending cash wisely? Are they becoming greater skillful in performing some useful kind of work? Are they greater sincere, extra dependable, extra temperate, and greater humane? Are they locating happiness of their present own family lifestyles? Are they dwelling by the guidelines of fitness? Are they acquiring abilities in the usage of all the essential equipment of studying? Are they curious about the natural global around them? Do they appreciate, each to the fullest diploma possible, their rich inheritance in artwork, literature, and tune? Do they recoil at being led around by their prejudices?

This huge consensus that faculties need to be responsible for extra than just the primary skills was additionally supported by the conservative economist Milton Friedman, who in 1955 first referred to as for vouchers to allow any scholar to attend any public or private school. However in contrast to today's privatization advocates (who declare him as their highbrow father), Friedman special that schools taking part in his plan should meet minimum goals established through the general public. He distinguished among results that completely advantage students themselves (in better income) and outcomes that benefit the community, for which all schools need to be responsible. Friedman wrote, "A stable and democratic society is not possible without giant attractiveness of a few not unusual set of values and a minimum degree of literacy and understanding on the part of maximum citizens." In basic college, "the three R's cowl maximum of the ground," but secondary colleges must show that they educate students "for citizenship and network leadership" as a condition of receiving public budget.

Rapidly after Friedman's name, the Rockefeller Brothers Fund convened leaders from many fields to make public policy suggestions. Nelson Rockefeller (ultimately New York's governor and Gerald Ford's vice president) chaired the general task, with Henry Kissinger (who later served as secretary of the nation) as its team of workers director. The Rockefeller report, because it was regarded, requested, how "may additionally we great put together our younger people to hold their individuality, initiative, creativity in a surprisingly organized, intricately meshed society? Our conception of excellence should embody many varieties of achievement. There is excellence in the abstract intellectual hobby, in art, in track, in managerial activities, in craftsmanship, in human family members, in technical work."

The Rockefeller document identified that checking out would gain significance for sorting destiny scientists and leaders. however, the panel warned, "selections primarily based on check ratings should be made with the awareness of the characteristics of an individual which are an important component of great performance, aspiration or reason, courage, power or determination."

For the ultimate 20 years, complaints have argued that states must finance "adequate" training, and national courts have had to define what this means. True to American traditions, the courts have proposed definitions that extend ways beyond adequacy as measured via check rankings alone

The earliest choice in this line of cases became issued in 1976 via the New Jersey ultimate court, which found a constitutional requirement for the nation to offer a "thorough and efficient education" that enables graduates to come to be "citizens and competition within the exertions marketplace." The court later elaborated:

Thorough and efficient methods greater than teaching capabilities had to compete in the hard work marketplace. It approaches being able to fulfill one's position as a citizen, a function that encompasses ways more than simply registering to vote. It means the capacity to participate completely in society, within the existence of one's community, the ability to comprehend music, art, and literature, and the ability to proportion all of that with pals.

Those are desires sought by rich districts, the court docket said, and have to be pursued in low-income urban areas as well.

Three years later, in 1979, the West Virginia perfect courtroom issued a decision that has become a model for different states. It defined a "thorough and efficient" education as one that develops "the minds, our bodies, and social morality of its costs to put together them for useful and satisfying occupations, exercise, and citizenship." Then, following closely Thomas Jefferson's language of nearly 200 years earlier than, the court docket required its legislature to fund a faculty machine that would increase "in every baby" the capacities of (1) literacy; (2) potential to add, subtract, multiply and divide numbers; (3) understanding of government to the volume that the kid can be ready as a citizen to make informed selections amongst men and women and troubles that affect his or her governance; (4) self-expertise and expertise of his or her total environment to permit the child to intelligently pick lifestyles to work to realize his or her alternatives; (five) work-training and advanced educational training as the kid may additionally intelligently pick; (6) leisure interests; (7) pastimes in all innovative arts, together with tune, theater, literature, and the visual arts; (eight) social ethics, both behavioral and summary, to facilitate compatibility with others on this society.

Chapter Four

The Characteristics of Effective Educational Goals

The achievement of an agency, society, or group relies upon the effectiveness of management employed. Revolutionary adjustments experienced nowadays in most workplaces have caused the want for competent and effective leaders of character. While many elements lead to the achievement of an organization, the major characteristic that distinguishes a successful employer from one that is unsuccessful is the presence of powerful management. In institutions of study, there may be a demand for a specific form of leadership. College leaders should be in a function to respond productively to the challenging opportunities created in schooling. They form the pillar of the schools that maintain the teachers, students, and employees collectively. Effective principals unfold cohesion and unity in their establishments which might be the general surroundings of teachers. It's far stated that a few leaders have failed to show vital leadership qualities that a good leader ought to possess. They've engaged in sports for their selfish gain. This has created anxiety, animosity, and division in the agency. Chronic strikes and demonstrations in colleges and universities are the results of terrible leadership. Consequently, they had been deprived of peace and balance that is essential for suitable overall performance. However, continuous research and technology have intensified the want for excellent dating among the school administrators and the lecturers. The reputation of academic institutions needs to be constructed by advocating for power management.

College leaders have to be able to lead a way of life that may be emulated by absolutely everyone. It's essential to understand that each person cannot be a leader at an equal time.

Therefore, if an opportunity provides itself for a person who is meant to show the attributes of a powerful chief an excellent faculty chief is anticipated to act decisively to recognize and uphold the confidence and trust in supplying excellent training. Training has been going via drastic adjustments that simplest require powerful management for the implementation of those modifications. An effective major must be available for the advent and sustainability of competitive faculties. He or she has to focus on empowering others to make full-size choices by using giving steerage on strategic planning. in the recent past, training requirements in public establishments have declined because of inappropriate kinds of management. As a result, private buyers have received a full-size proportion of the marketplace due to their effective guidelines which might be in the vicinity. However, the general public schools, schools, and universities can still enhance their academic leadership if they revise the present management styles and integrate them with the new styles.

In line with many researchers, leaders in public institutions ought to be flexible sufficient and embody collaborative sorts of leadership for development to be realized. They argue that attending to others first and being attentive to them is the pleasant model of effective leadership through school principals. The major should be able to contain all stakeholders in enforcing coverage. Powerful leaders are those who are dedicated to serving people by taking note of them, convincing if feasible, and equipped to create awareness of a brand new concept. Qualitative studies suggest that this shape of leadership is more efficient and relevant in faculties in comparison to other kinds of leadership together with transactional, transformational, and ethical management. Serving others includes humility in any respect expenses so one can gain the targeted aim and goal. In a commercial enterprise state of affairs, serving others as for management strengthens the bond between the organization and employees.

Task satisfaction is improved because the employees are given an experience of belonging in the commercial enterprise main to business success. Mind-set is a completely important factor that each chief should be aware of. A fine mindset in the direction of a leader is a nice detail that should be sensitized. Moreover, pupils agree whilst many characteristics of successful leaders can't constantly be delineated but by way of observing that hit management is predicated upon a set of center practices which, while implemented in aggregate, result in advanced getting to know effects for college kids. Even though labeled in slightly extraordinary methods, these fundamental domain names of practice encompass efforts to (1) outline and enhance organizational motive, imaginative and prescient, and course, (2) broaden human beings and encourage their character and collective sense of efficacy for the work, and (3) redesign and improve organizational systems, systems, and contexts. As a consequence, effective leaders work to develop a shared vision of the future, while growing a high level of consensus for the existing goals.

So, one can sensitize the need for effective leadership in getting to know institutions one will be good at reading prior research on the same topic. They will be able to define some of the studies papers that have been completed on powerful management for the aid of the conclusions they have drawn. Specifically, they should be able to deal with the need for powerful management in unique schools and school districts. To look at features of an effective leader, look at will make use of the cutting-edge scenario in a college wherein many instructors are complaining of terrible leadership by using their principals. It is important to use a design of sequential explanation and factor to the important thing, factors, and roles a foremost must play so that it will enhance concord and balance in faculties. School-based total management will be significantly tested for you to display that colleges are factories where destiny leaders are manufactured. Teachers and principals are position models to the students. In case they fail to demonstrate correct and powerful management then we anticipate having a society that has missed the mark. Professional development and ethics have been put into consideration because bureaucracy the essential component in illustrating effective management fashion. The examination will cope with the problem that arises in a scenario wherein the lecturers appear to do an awful lot of the work as a way as teachers are concerned. Moreover, it allows the foremost to understand a way to hold the spirit of cooperation in the instructional agency. It goals at assisting the principals to balance among powerful leadership and managerial duties for the college to realize its venture assertion.

Teachers cite a major's aid and effectiveness as a leading thing that contributes to their selection to stay in teaching. To perceive and apprehend a powerful leader might supply a route to instructors which end up in a common purpose, fulfillment of all college students. Teachers are leaving schooling because there's a loss of powerful management. Colleges aren't as successful within the absence of an effective chief.

A range of recent studies has unveiled various principles on the traits of an effective chief. Those researchers of their qualitative research concluded that extra studies ought to be performed to help us apprehend the want for effective leadership trends. as an example, for the community to be worried about the control of a faculty as a way to improve the educational requirements of a selected college they need to be able to realize the benefits and the meaning of effective management. Some administrative theories also endorse that powerful management should be used for an efficient operation of college activities. They need to help students to become aware of and emphasize the basic characteristics of an effective chief. To make people recognize the characteristics they must realize whilst choosing leaders, following a frontrunner, and understand features of effective leaders. Thirdly, to help human beings to realize now not all characteristics in a pacesetter can be emulated. Subsequently, they can help faculty leaders mainly principals in the near take a look at their effectiveness as a frontrunner. Also, they should intend to highlight the benefits related to having an effective chief in an employer.

In addition, they can focus their intention on informing people on how they can end up powerful leaders via serving others within the future. Then advocate how to start to remodel a school into a successful and powerful business enterprise managed with the aid of a proactive and powerful chief.

The most important have to now not be recognized for establishing stringent policies and rules to be observed but additionally be the first individual to examine them. Every teacher is usually a leader in his or her ability. However, the primary is the top who need to ensure that this leader work collectively in a settlement. Delegation of labor is one of the approaches a powerful leader should discover ways to lead. Additionally, empowering the humans around you has been confirmed to yield a great deal higher dividends inside the boom of a powerful leader. This can enable instructors to reply to the powerful management of carriers in preference to being forced to undertake an obligation. Powerful leadership is driven toward bringing trade-in mastering corridors for the betterment of lives.

This look at to an incredible extent can be approximately self-assessment and the way someone values others. It explores the diploma in which the school leaders, principals believe ineffective leadership for the benefit of the future generations. It forms a platform of education noble and aim-orientated leaders who will stand for the rights of their subjects.

This observation for the motive of this book has been anticipated that it will provide essential facts and it will be a very good useful resource for those intending to end up effective of their leadership. Principals, instructors, and students will locate it as a powerful material which can shape them for management in exclusive regions of life .furthermore, the destiny of appropriate control of tutorial agencies are within the arms of these may be geared up to utilize the records furnished in this exam for you to change their conduct and people who encounter them.

 Satisfactory training is predicated on the established order of effective leadership. This takes a look at could be very vital in supporting us to recognize the effects of management on the student gaining knowledge of and the need for embracing diversity in the leadership of faculties for excellence. It highlights the schemes and methods utilized by specific principals to ensure that the college turns into a hit. The principals are knowledgeable on how they must promote both inner and outside relationships that are simplest viable with the effective leadership style. This takes a look at is also vital because it offers long-term solutions to demanding situations confronted in studying institutions. It offers highbrow stimulation and the correct version of destiny expectancies. It advocates for the spirit of humility which is one of the traits of an effective chief to permit the principals to peer the essence of serving others.

They have a look at will screen that these days many humans have informed approximately the traits of an effective leader. Moreover, the take a look at likely will permit us to understand that our character can also negatively or positively impact the behavior of others. At the end of every day, leadership insists on, relationship, responsibility, and reliability to obtain a certain goal.

-What are the characteristics of an effective chief?

-What are the perceptions and attitudes of the lecturers regarding leadership in their most important?

- How can a faculty utilize the function of powerful leadership to plot a plan to deal with campus weather?

Effective management isn't based on the human beings an essential are confronted with at some stage in day after day operations of a college. There may be no difference in the self-perception of a frontrunner as perceived by a few teachers because leadership is not innate but obtained via schooling. No leader can trade an enterprise without acquiring the ability to be a transformational chief

The position of instructional leadership has propelled itself into an evolving practice and profession because of the 1930s as a supervisor to the 1960s, as a behavioral chief, and now into transitional and transformational leaders. The function of the essential has evolved; however, over the last century, there has now not been tons research approximately the evolutionary abilities of the people that take in this function year after twelve months. Leadership is the lifting of one's vision to higher points of interest, the elevating of one's overall performance to a better fashionable, and the constructing of one's character past its everyday barriers. Within the now not thus far past leadership has developed into a plethora of meanings such as powerful organizational leaders' percentage numerous not unusual traits. With the absence of these characteristics, initiatives and change can fail. Leaders ought to take extraordinary approaches to help preserve their employer from failing. Leadership within the schooling zone is fantastically recognized because it performs an important role in the willpower of the students' outcome. It is ranked second, after classroom teaching on the subject of its impact on the getting to know the manner of college students. Leadership has a massive effect also, on the general college in addition to in assembly the desires of students. through the years, the roles performed by using leaders within the education quarter have emerged as extra traumatic and complicated, requiring a huge range of management attributes as skills, for effective execution of leadership roles. Unluckily, no matter the converting roles of leaders inside the education sector only confined research and substances were devoted to the examination on the way to expand required leadership qualities and talents. Also, in instructional entities, leaders are anticipated to carry out managerial roles, an issue embedded in the organizational structure of most academic facilities these days. In maximum schooling facilities, principals and superintendents are the important thing administrators hence making it tough to segregate between control and leadership, as they coexist. Also, school heads are, as an example, mandated with the function of organizing the imaginative and prescient and aim in their institutions as well as formulating techniques to achieve the imaginative and prescient. This research paper will adopt important literature evaluation regarding traits of effective management in education.

Traits of effective management in training

Even though now not tons of research has been dedicated to leadership in schooling, numerous researchers have undertaken one-of-a-kind studies in an enterprise to establish the traits most not unusual ineffective leadership. Instructional management and hard Work outline instructional management and difficult work educational leadership models emerged in the 1970s and 1980s from early research on effective faculties. These students emphasized the position of the principal as the number one agent of school development, extra, especially inside noticeably challenged city schools. One of the key characteristics of powerful management in education nowadays is the potential to provide academic management. Conversely, with agreement instructional leadership has been "conceptualized as a mutual influence system, rather than as a one-way technique in which leaders affect others". This type of view underscores the necessary effects of tutorial leadership, on the equal time acknowledging "its evolving nature in the context of instructor professionalism". Instructional leadership refers to the commitment of principals and superintendents in their energies and time as well as competencies towards the improvement of teaching and gaining knowledge of nice within their educational centers. Education leaders who have been capable of offer instructional leadership had deep expertise in learning and coaching, together with more modern methods that emphasized more on understanding creation by way of students and hassle solving techniques.

In an evaluation observe, the principals of noticeably excessive-reaching colleges, as measured with the aid of consistent educational success in a ramification of curricular areas, differed from their counterparts in continuously low-reaching colleges "in phrases of the type and effectiveness of instructional management they supplied". In a take a look at twenty-three California elementary schools, fifteen of which have been high performing, and seventeen California high colleges, seven of which have been excessive performing, Heck determined that three academic leadership behaviors have been considered in predicting the levels of student achievement of those schools, including "the number of time principals spends directly looking at study room practices, promoting discussions approximately educational problems, and emphasizing check results inside those discussions". Such leaders were also determined to be strongly committed to high success for all their students; in particular, those deemed as not strong performers, or students who experience difficulties in gaining knowledge. Those research findings are supported via every other examination performed through the America department of schooling which located out that instructional management contributed in large part to the direction of the learning institutions' achievement and stepped forward pupil engagement inside the mastering procedure. Even though crucial leadership first-class, the best 25% of the participants' principals was professional as far as educational management was concerned. This lends itself to the evolving nature of the essential profession. Alongside an evolving career, information has supplied itself in education as a tutorial Positioning system (IPS) for educational leaders. A few have followed facts fashions to resource them within the use of statistics. One especially will be the data-driven academic system (DDIS), which offers a sequential manual to using records to help an instructional chief. Halverson, Griggs, Prichett, and Thomas created this version and organized it in a paper on the Annual Assembly of the National Council of Professors of tutorial management in July 2005 in Washington, D.C. Many principals once more aren't astute in the usage of data to make choices. They are properly-versed in management and enterprise. The six steps that HGPT, advice are:

- Personal Values and Self-recognition

Private values are a number of the management characteristics that build effective college leadership. Values are built beyond regular time from the time one is an infant, and it is nurtured over time and fashioned by way of non-public stories. Values are made from standards, qualities, and ideas that a person deems vital in successful leadership, mainly during decision making. A number of the values that are vital in developing amazing management encompass agree with, loyalty, and a sense of obligation, recognition, selfless service, integrity, honor, and private braveness. A faculty chief needs to be dependable to his or her calling, and the faculty's vision and project. Wavering sends indicators of doubt to the students and the instructor.

Consider is any other value that builds the right leadership in schooling. Without consider, it's miles difficult to motivate and encourage instructors and students. Tutors and students must be capable of agree with their chief. A faculty major has to also show recognize to all the stakeholders (spotting his role within the powerful running of the school and the effect he or she has on the general outcome of the faculty) for him to solicit their recognition. Integrity is likewise every other very strong value that helps in building powerful leadership in training. Integrity entails doing what's proper morally, ethically, and legally. Without integrity, it's tough to motivate, encourage and lead human beings. Courage is also crucial in management. Without personal braveness, communicating with different people and soliciting their confidence in a person is tough.

Educational leadership is constructed upon a framework of non-stop feedback, which aims at encouraging both college students and tutors. Successful principals had been much more likely to have interaction with the whole college through the use of non-stop messages about the work exceptional predicted by instructors, as well as the students. This ends in the creation of an environment wherein success is primarily based on learning profits using college students from their instructors. Any other side that observed crucial in the development of educational management was that it went beyond actually conveying expectancies by way of educational leaders. It changed into discovered that educational leaders did not merely problem orders and commands, but they spend a considerable amount of time in actual studying environments or classrooms, no longer just looking at the behaviors of students, but additionally taking lively participation inside the mastering manner. But, it's far crucial to be aware that instructional management does now not quantity or cause undermining of traditional roles performed through different instructors. Rather, instructional leaders offer steerage and guide to other tutors or instructors. In keeping with Blumberg & Greenfield (1986), educational leaders can compare commands and offer open and effective messages or feedbacks geared toward encouraging instructors to enhance their teaching processes, so one can inspire better student studying. Additionally, academic leaders make sure that the entire college community is engaged in talks about the manner of enhancing learning for students. Instructional leaders also pass beyond the traditional definition of their jobs' expectancies, and they try to limit the bureaucratic burdens, consequently bearing in mind extra participation from students and tutors.

Management capabilities (making plans)

Academic management requires a pacesetter if you want to recognize the needed stability in going for walks in a learning organization. Management skills are hence critical management characteristics that assist in making sure powerful leadership in education. (Leithwood& Riehl, 2004) wrote scholars reintroduced the fourth domain, handling companies, as an important thing of successful faculty management. Though managing an educational facility is a demanding assignment, a frontrunner ought to be in a role to balance among the wishes of the parents, the politicians, the scholars, and teachers, in addition to the entire community. not like in the past when instructional leadership's achievement changed into measured or assessed on the capability of a leader to manage a college's finances, college centers, and buildings, nowadays effective instructional leaders and executives need to take into consideration the desires of different stakeholders, such as the network, and to effectively talk the imaginative and prescient of the faculty.

In keeping with a look at performed by using Steltz (2010) at the effect of control abilities on powerful leadership in training, it becomes found out that management abilities played a key function within the normal success of gaining knowledge of establishments. Even though some powerful instructional leaders had been observed no longer to have educational management abilities, leaders who had excellent managerial talents were discovered to perform properly, as they have been capable of nurture and create a high-quality gaining knowledge of and teaching surroundings, irrespective of the external pressures. The look at also found out that academic leadership abilities were no longer enough to permit academic leaders to be powerful. a few contributors who have been rated high on academic leadership qualities however had low managerial competencies have been discovered now not to be powerful in handling their educational establishments.

SEDL (2012) argues that effective leadership in training goes past robust educational leadership. Given the amount of demand leveled on principals and superintendents, exemplary academic leaders have to also be wonderful managers. To achieve achievement, now and then faculty directors or schooling leaders need to be in a role to barter thru conflicting needs emanating from federal, state, or neighborhood bureaucracies, constituent agencies, politicians, and mother and father. Without powerful control talents, that is almost impossible. Chrispeels (1990), however, notes that at the same time as maximum schooling leaders experience control practices, as most of them are educated on this place, compared to practice, there's a dire want to shift from traditional administration practices, as management demanded these days by using instructional facilities or establishments is exceptional. Education leaders must be able to alternate their conventional consciousness on homes, bonds, books, budgets, and buses to management based totally on community building, collaboration, and communication.

• Community building and Collaboration

Community building, collaboration, and communication are other characteristics that make contributions to effective management in education. Over the years, training leadership has evolved, and today, this shape of management has taken a new measurement that emphasizes the want to collaborate and communicate with all stakeholders, each inside and outside the premises of getting to know establishments. Crowson & Morris (1990) argue that the conventional "top-down model", which turned into characterized by using a hierarchical approach to decision making, is now not applicable in today's education management. Traditionally, school principals and superintendents used to make choices for others (lower in the hierarchy) to execute. Consistent with studies performed through researchers including Kirby, Paradise & King (1992), within the discipline of schooling leadership, located that effective management is constructed on the constructing blocks of participation of parents, members of community, and students in addition to instructors. An effective chief inside the education area is someone capable to influence the people surrounding her or him, with inspirational and significant goals, which lead to the accomplishment of a faculty's imaginative and prescient and mission. An effective training chief is endowed with a powerful approach of connecting with his or her environment, together with all the stakeholders in a schooling organization, and also builds constituencies that strongly endorse for implementation of alternate as well as institutional obstacles breakdown, observed in conventional getting to know and teaching methods. Communication is critical to allow for the continuing connecting of a frontrunner and all stakeholders.

Regular conversation US branch of schooling (1999), however, argue that, in the improvement of powerful leadership in education, allowing conversation and collaboration of stakeholders have to now not translate to consensus in all selections made within a faculty. Although dialogue and lively participation is essential in building effective leadership in education, principals and superintendents have to maintain a few shapes of control and authority. This lets in for the development of appreciation from all of the stakeholders, as well as duty. SEDL (2012) argues that powerful education leaders are those who can create room for speak, without resulting in a laissez-faire form of management style. although speak is recommended, a leader must preserve his authority, especially in faculties facing giant demanding situations as well as in institutions characterized by using an apathetic climate. However, it's far essential to note that the extent of autonomy and authority retained through a most important is dependent on the unique characteristics of a school. At the same time as an authoritative leadership style may be effective in some schools, it may not work nicely in others. Know-how the precise traits of the faculty environment and the stakeholders is hence vital, closer to constructing powerful management in the training area.

• Capability to inspire ardor in All Stakeholders

The ability to efficaciously work with the board of a college is every other feature of effective leadership in training. Steltz (2010) argues that effective school leaders are capable of constructing an effective -manner communique with their board participants, and they're additionally capable of understanding the point of view of the board, work with the board and additionally pursue a unified aim or imaginative and prescient for his or her faculty. But, Chrispeels (1990) notes that constructing a rapport with the board should not quantity to 'bootlicking' activities through the principals. Effective faculty leaders are faculty leaders who're capable of pursuing the imagination and prescient in their schools, without always locating ways to satisfy the needs and demands of the board contributors. The powerful college leaders can join the portions to put in force ideas and exchange with a purpose to advantage college students and no longer a board member's schedule. Capability to implement new ideas and Reforms capacity to set up a "constituency for schooling reform in the larger network" is some other characteristic of powerful management in schooling recognized with the aid of. The schooling constituency must be made up of people who hold various perspectives relating to public education. This calls for school principals and superintendents to have media and public relation abilities, and additionally a political savvy, to permit them to train, and enlighten most of the people on what needs to be undertaken, in addition to, convince them that the goals undertaken with the aid of the leaders are fundamental, not handiest to their children's studying process, but additionally for their destiny lives. Kirby, Paradise & King (1992), argue that a number of the colleges nowadays are experiencing problems due to the fact their surrounding neighborhoods or groups require rebuilding. Powerful schooling leaders are leaders who're able to collaborate with organizations and community companies, with a purpose to establish structures that address households and kids' social carrier necessities or needs. Further, effective leaders can surely define a shared vision to attach the network and college.

- Capability to give you clean vision and dreams

The ability to articulate a feasible vision and aim for an

academic gadget and the capability to come up with a feasible plan to reap one of this purpose or a vision is a feature of effective management identified through Steltz (2010). One of the fundamental facets of management is the capacity to provide you with a viable intention, which stimulates motivation amongst fans, and to come up with a manner of reaching dreams. Effective faculty leaders are capable of set a purpose for their schools, normally aimed at improving the learning revel in of the students and the entire community. At instances, this could include an exchange initiative that requires purchase-in from the network.

• Capability to transport exchange initiatives

Trade is inevitable, even in mastering institutions. according to a look at performed through Fullan (1991), it changed into discovered out that one of the key characteristics of effective schooling leaders became their potential to institute high-quality alternate inside their faculties. The Training region is characterized with the aid of dynamism, especially because of the discovery of technology and the net, which has seen e-studying offerings emerge. Powerful leaders are capable of understanding the need for non-stop modifications of their learning establishments and providing you with the method of reaching or implementing such modifications.

Ability to provide you with New thoughts and put in force Them SEDL (2012) argues that modifications spur powerful leaders to take dangers, which consist of challenging the stakeholder's ideals and attitudes closer to exclusive troubles and changing their historically conceived intellectual fashions of how school training should be, and the way matters must work in schools. A few times, faculty leaders are required to take dramatic but symbolic moves or gestures in an endeavor to stimulate thinking patterns' exchange in people concerning their work.

Boundaries to powerful management in schooling

Powerful leadership in education is critical because it determines the general mastering manner and performance of the students, in addition to the willingness and motivation of instructors. It also allows for the improvement of the college surroundings and the network. However, building effective leadership in schooling is one of the hardest endeavors for principals as well as superintendents. There are numerous obstacles, which avoid the improvement of effective management in training as discussed underneath.

- Lack of aid

Lack of management help in schools from one-of-a-kind stakeholders is one of the key obstacles towards the development of effective educational leadership. In maximum instances, school principals and superintendents enjoy passive or expressed resentment from their fellow teachers and co-workers. Such resentment makes management development hard for school principals, main to problems in implementing adjustments in college's control and studying practices. Additionally, management roles, in most cases, come at the side of constraints in interpersonal relationships, particularly whilst instructors resent the appointment of their leaders. With such a terrible mindset and shortage of guides, growing powerful management will become intricate for principals and superintendents. The unwillingness of instructors to soak up management roles in schooling is another thing that has contributed to the lack of effective leadership in the training quarter. Given the demanding situations associated with education management, maximum instructors are unwilling to take in the mantle of leadership. Without aid from all stakeholders, powerful management development in education is impossible.

- Loss of clear Definition of leadership Roles

One of the major obstacles toward powerful leadership improvement in education is the lack of really defined roles of principals and superintendents. Over the years, management in education has been not noted, not only by using school planners however also by researchers and other good-sized entities. In contrast to in current enterprise environments, training leadership isn't defined, a factor that has left many faculty leaders ignorant of the responsibilities they're required to adopt. The combination of administration, control, and leadership roles in schooling management is every other component that has extended the vagueness of schooling leadership these days. Many school leaders also perform the function of faculty control and administration, and this has created confusion, particularly due to the fact there may be no clear-cut view on what management tasks college principals are expected to perform. This has seen maximum college leaders concentrate greater on management and administration obligations, at the same time as neglecting management roles. Additionally, in maximum schools, there may be no clear definition of the roles of school leaders and that of the board participants.

Lack of training and access to leadership statistics

Management training is vital in the direction of the improvement of effective leadership. But, due to the limited assets and studies committed to management in schooling, most faculty leaders do no longer have to get the right of entry to leadership training, a thing that has contributed to negative management being skilled these days in lots of faculties. Also, faculty leaders have restricted get admission to information touching on leadership consequently enhancing leadership talents is difficult. There is also restrained money and time allotted to high school leaders' schooling in most faculties, and school leaders who desire to adopt non-public studies on leadership discover it difficult because of the number of responsibilities they may be mandated to perform at extraordinarily constrained timelines. Lack of schooling centers for school leaders is a considerable barrier to the improvement of effective management. Even though some leaders are born, maximum leaders are made through a method of continuous getting to know, mentorship and education. But, without getting admission to education centers and management records, growing powerful management in schooling is hard.

Loss of Mentorship

Mentorship is one of the critical factors in the powerful improvement of powerful leadership qualities. Alas, maximum schools today have no mentorship packages to nurture younger leaders in training. In line with a look at performed by using American affiliation of faculty directors, it turned into determined out that maximum training leaders unintentionally fail to nurture leadership features for future leaders. Training leaders locate themselves with a lot of work, leaving restrained room for management improvement and mentorship. Given the reality that most education leaders also adopt control, classroom responsibilities, and management roles, the responsibilities bestowed on them, in maximum cases, make them forget about their management roles, hence; mentorship is critical trouble in education management. Additionally, in contrast to in business settings, leadership mentorship is extraordinarily intricate given that instructors are often transferred from one college to every other, in some instances, within unusually brief durations. Loss of mentorship is one of the key boundaries to effective management in schooling.

The crucial characteristics of powerful coaching education

Teachers input the teaching career to impart their expertise and make a distinction in younger folks' lifestyles. Teachers want students to succeed. The way this knowledge is imparted to a pupil could be dramatically one-of-a-kind from one trainer to any other. Being an effective trainer isn't carried out immediately or "in a single day", however without a doubt using persistent development and reassessing techniques to acquire successful consequences.

Inside the classroom, teachers want to apply many practices to permit college students to examine correctly and reap most abilities. Some of those important characteristics of powerful teaching may be mentioned in this essay. The importance of imparting an advantageous studying environment, creation of dynamic and effective instructions, flexible transport via the usage of several techniques, greatly will increase the capability for college kids to reap their most gaining knowledge. A powerful trainer will attempt for the "Kaizen" and to achieve success in improving scholar mastering consequences.

Sizable proof

For college kids to achieve their most gaining knowledge of capability, instructors should put in force and deliver powerful training. these classes not most effective need to link to the relevant Australian Curriculum Assessment and Reporting Authority (ACARA) strand, but should also be delivered efficiently. Students will learn if the plan is motivating and thrilling, and instructors should healthy coaching techniques to the gaining knowledge of plan objectives. A powerful trainer is a person who displays on their information of the way pleasant to increase a lesson plan this is enticing and thrilling and will deliver the correct expertise within the fine viable manner to the scholar. An effective lesson plan may reflect several coaching characteristics transport of coaching and getting to know strategies, behavior management, and the classroom environment.

Teaching strategies such as Constructivism, direct education, effective wondering are used to make sure the ACARA science strand ACSSU080, is introduced most simply. To be a powerful instructor, a teacher should set up strategies for college students to experience the feel of belonging inside the schoolroom. Presenting a wonderful and inclusive gaining knowledge of the environment allows the student to experience safe and cozy. Students with this sense of belonging are more likely to reply with suitable behaviors and play an energetic element in magnificence participation in preference to against the instructor. A high-quality courting should be fashioned between teacher and scholar, and to set up this courting respect from the scholar need to be gained. To advantage this respect, however, the teacher has to first show admiration, students should sense normal and their contributions valued. The trainer must display a wonderful and genuine subject in the students' hobbies and show superb affirmations and recognition of a college students' contribution, not dismissal - even though the answer to a question is incorrect. A true greeting by way of a trainer after an absence is one example of a way to inspire college students.

Compassion, empathy, and staying power also are attributes for a hit student/trainer relationship. All students attain at specific fees and a teacher ought to be affected person and continual for these college students to be triumphant. Teachers need to be assured of their very own know-how and enthusiasm while offering their lessons. Teachers, who supply their material in this way, are more likely to achieve motivating their college students. Within the technology; Modelling light video, college students had been usually proven to admire using the instructor. In response to student's answers, the trainer gave superb feedback in return showing she valued their input, i.e.: "That's a desirable explanation." in the course of the video lesson, the scholars had been positive in participating within the modeling and school room sports and had been actively concerned in all components of the lesson. In Appendix One hands-on shared experience, whilst transferring from institution to institution as special. The instructor may show reward and advantageous reinforcement with verbal remarks along with "the first-rate team works everybody.

You're working so well as a group."
Some of the study room environment elements have an impact on the successful learning of college students and are crucial for powerful teaching. consideration of: desk and furniture placements; accessibility of high visitors areas; floor space; reducing noise; room temperature; and seating arrangements have to receive excessive precedence and need to be reviewed depending on the teaching venture to hand. The study room environment needs to facilitate the coaching as opposed to impede it. Organization work sports may require desks to be joined collectively or driven to an aspect to maximize pupil participation and organization involvement. This will need to be considered in Appendix One for the duration of the shared experience hobby.

A high-quality mastering surroundings results in wonderful classroom behaviors. A teacher needs to show proactive study room management. How a pupil behaves and acts, is decided through the influences on his/her life, particularly: circle of relatives (care, stresses, parental attitudes to training), peer (social prejudices and authority), private (personality, mastering styles, social) and college (communications, management), all of which have a dramatic effect on a scholar's behaviors. Instructors need to be thoughtful of those effects and the consequences they have within the study room and reduce factors that may also boom the angst that a pupil may additionally sense. College students will feel at ease if they realize the lecture room is continuously a superb and safe environment.

To provide this consistency, the trainer should establish lecture room workouts, rules, and powerful verbal exchange, addressing behavior expectations for effective school room surroundings and a final touch of lecture room sports. A teacher showing this consistency in communication and commands will sell pupil responsibility. These routines and policies may be made exclusively by way of the instructor, or in collaboration with students and consequently giving ownership to the scholars. A routine can be formulated for group work to show respect to fellow college students e.g.: listening quietly to pupil remarks; hands-up for questions; or for the completion of work e.g.: completed workbooks to be placed on teachers' desk. A classroom routine is evident in Appendix One interest closure section, in which college students are anticipated to area finished journal entries on the teacher's table.

Effective teaching also requires the trainer to be bendy inside the shipping of teaching practices or instructional modes, and by using doing so is much more likely to obtain the fulfillment of an effective trainer. Flexibility within the expectancies for students to reach their full potential via nice encouragement and changed coaching strategies, know-how that what is anticipated for one child might be one of a kind to that of every other.

Lively studying with constructivism permits the scholar to assemble relationships and their very own which means thru trouble primarily based on getting to know sports. Students are endorsed thru speak with the trainer and fellow students, and relate new records to that of which they have already got the know-how. Constructivism is the focus on maximizing the information of the pupil and progression via scaffolding and help.

Constructivism educational mode also makes use of collaborative and cooperative gaining knowledge of tactics. Each process is about setting up agencies and operating efficiently in one's companies. Collaborative gaining knowledge allows the student to work independently or within the group whilst important and therefore has much less institution touch than cooperative getting to know. Sports that might be cooperative-based are entirely organization-oriented. Organization work has some risks requiring instructors to devise these elements to contribute to successful results for the businesses. Problems may additionally consist of things which include rivalry among group participants, capacity of man or woman students, interpersonal capabilities, and group size and teacher control talents.

As in keeping with Appendix One, a positive method is displayed within the mirrored image phase. Hassle-based mastering is displayed when students are given time to speak about the questions as a collaborative and demonstrate this corporation's expertise to the magnificence. The seating association also assists inside the shared revel in interest, by taking into account organization dialogue and reflecting on the task requirements.

Another teaching approach is dialogue. During the discussion, effective wandering must be purposeful and inspire the scholars to acquire a better stage of expertise. Dialogue is both trainer and student-directed and understanding when to apply the only fashion of wondering is vital. Education by using the instructor is important. The use of Bloom's Taxonomy comprising of the 6 areas: expertise, Comprehension, utility, evaluation, Synthesis, and assessment, is widely used in curriculum planning, as is the simplified What, While, How, Who, and why? Using each better and decrease degree wondering has to be covered in lesson making plans. Probing higher-level questions are open-ended and require dialogue and the exchange of ideas, in preference to easy lower stage closed questioning. But, the intention of both ought to ultimately be to increase student thinking. Another tool for teachers to sell scholar thinking is the de Bono thinking hats. Comprising of 6 colored hats, the concept in the back of them is to encourage extraordinary student wondering - Blue - manner, White– information, inexperienced–Creativity, Yellow - benefits, and Black – Cautions.

Any other teacher-targeted mode of delivery is direct instruction or explicit teaching. Most efficaciously used for fundamental talents together with analyzing and mathematics, it helps students examine in a little by little procedure. Researchers have compiled a few key elements for powerful teacher-directed education: robust course and manipulation; emphasis is on academic studying; fine man or woman expectations and educational development; scholar cooperation and duty; non-bad - the guarantee of beginners' confidence and experience belonging and protection; and the trainer need to also establish and implement a structure (class regulations). The trainer has to make sure the lesson covers the extent of all scholar capabilities and understanding.

There are numerous different traits equally critical to be an effective teacher. each function meshes with the opposite, and if one factor of the shipping is not organization appropriate, college students will no longer obtain their maximum gaining knowledge of potential and consequently, effective coaching will not result. Powerful coaching requires flexibility and persistent re-evaluation of lesson shipping methods. A lesson plan advanced on one strand for one group of college students will no longer necessarily be as effective brought to any other group of college students. Teachers talented in those characteristics will be powerful educators and could have elevated achievement inside the shipping of effective student learning

Educational leaders play a pivotal function in affecting the climate, attitude, and reputation of their schools. They may be the cornerstone on which mastering communities' characteristics and development. With a hit school leadership, colleges grow to be effective incubators of learning, locations in which college students aren't best-educated however challenged, nurtured, and encouraged. Then again, terrible or absent college management can undermine the dreams of an educational system. Whilst colleges lack a robust foundation and direction, getting to know is compromised, and students go through. in step with a Wallace, basis look at, "management is 2d best to school room training as a power on pupil gaining knowledge of."

The Makings of a successful faculty chief

But what makes a successful faculty chief? How do you emerge as truly powerful as a fundamental or in a leadership position? While there's nobody technique to a hit college leadership, there are certain strategies, abilities, developments, and ideals that many of the handiest school leaders share. The subsequent developments are common among the most a success school leaders.

1. They apprehend the importance of building community

Powerful school leaders construct and maintain reciprocal own family and community partnerships and leverage the one's partnerships to domesticate inclusive, caring, and culturally responsive school communities. To construct those community networks it is important that college leaders are seen of their faculties and network, expand belief and create a feeling of transparency and shared purpose with dad and mom, personnel, community participants, and students.

 In faculties with high ranges of trust:

• Teachers are prompted and willing to strive for new strategies due to the fact they accept as true with leaders to help them.

• College students are stimulated and linked to the faculty because they agree with their instructors.

• families are supportive due to the fact the main and teachers have built trusting relationships with them."

2. They Empower teachers and cultivate management abilities

Remarkable college leaders know that they're no longer jogging a one-guy show; that they cannot do all of it on their own. They recognize that they must surround themselves with notable teachers and co-workers and, no longer handiest that, they must completely guide teachers and personnel with the aid of encouraging them to usually analyze, develop and, possibly most critical, end up leaders themselves.

It is no secret that when people are fulfilled and given the possibility for career increase, in addition to autonomy and manipulation over their careers, they may be greater productive, more engaged, and more effective overall. In a recent Gallup ballot, it was discovered that thirty-three percentage of U.S. instructors are engaged in their work, even as 51 percent aren't engaged and sixteen percent are actively disengaged. These facts are startling to mention the least. via supplying expert development opportunities and guide services to teachers, in addition to developing an environment in which instructors are capable of the test, innovate and lead, principals can make certain healthful surroundings for educators with a purpose to have wonderful repercussions for students. another Gallup examine determined that "surprisingly talented principals on Gallup's main insight assessment have been 2.6 times much more likely to have above common worker engagement at the colleges they lead three years later." Gallup has studied the issue closely, even issuing a file titled "Six things the maximum Engaged colleges do differently."

In his eBook, "What tremendous Principals Do differently," education author and researcher Todd Whitaker wrote: "terrific principal's consciousness on enhancing the best of the lecturers within their buildings. By way of carefully hiring the first-class instructors, using assisting their efforts and their ambitions, via keeping all group of workers contributors to exceed expectations, and by way of running to cautiously aid the individual development of each professional, principals impact student fulfillment."

3. They make use of records and sources

Successful faculty leaders use facts, consisting of standardized and school-based exams, to power continuous improvement via site-based total decision-making for the explicit cause of selling equitable and culturally responsive possibilities for all college students. The opportunities that records gift are many and the simplest leaders are capable of leverage that information to make strategic decisions to benefit their college students.

In step with educational technology, corporation illuminates schooling, "building a basis for statistics-driven decision making" is the primary of "Six Steps for School Leaders to use information effectively."

A document from the Wallace basis asserts that: "in terms of information, powerful principals try and draw the most from records and evidence, having 'discovered to invite useful questions' of the records, to show it in ways that tell 'compelling stories and to use it to promote 'collaborative inquiry amongst teachers.' They view facts as a method now not best to pinpoint troubles however to apprehend their nature and reasons."

4. They have a vision and a plan

The very great leaders are also visionaries. They have an intention that they can unite a group round and a plan to help them get there. No longer just that, but they're capable of truly articulate their school vision and goals. Vision is possibly one of the most critical traits a frontrunner could have as it provides momentum and route, now not only for the group chief but for every crew member. Of path, for leaders to be successful in pursuing their imaginative and prescient and enacting their plan, they must pair their vision with unrelenting ardor.

Imaginative and prescient and ardor from an effective chief must generate inspiration, motivation, and excitement that permeate the course of the faculty.

According to an "a hit school management" record posted by UK-based training improvement accept as true, "effective head instructors offer a clear vision and experience of the route for the faculty. They prioritize. The recognition the eye of personnel on what's important and do now not allow them to get diverted and sidetracked with initiatives with a purpose to have little impact at the work of the scholars."

5. They devise Collaborative, Inclusive mastering Environments

Inclusive studying affords all college students with getting admission to bendy getting to know picks and powerful paths for accomplishing instructional goals in areas where they revel in an experience of belonging. The first-class educators understand this and prioritize inclusivity, developing secure mastering environments that nurture every scholar. Leaders that prioritize inclusive learning additionally normally agree that every person can make contributions to the more learning network and consequently they encourage collaboration between colleges in addition to students.

"Perhaps the most vital role in a success inclusive faculties is the position of the primary," wrote the Inclusive schools network. "The school primary's active participation is the unmarried maximum critical predictor of achievement in imposing trade, improving offerings, or putting a new path. The college important is principal to facilitating systemic change and leading college to adopt new attitudes and new practices."

6. They are captivated with Their Work

Passion is an important element for nearly everyone who wants to achieve success and be satisfied in their activity. But passion is mainly critical for college leaders, who usually have a tremendous impact on their faculty's weather and culture.

Passionate humans have contagious electricity which could substantially have an effect on instructor pleasure and drive as well as student overall performance. "All the knowledge within the world can't make an excellent leader: It's the take care of the work and the folks who collaborate with you that makes the difference," wrote Forbes. "This is in large part because human beings need to observe a passionate leader. Someone who cares about now not simplest the reason for which he or she is running, but additionally the opposite people who are concerned within the attempt. Passion for the initiatives, for the business enterprise, and the human beings involved are key to successful leadership."

7. They encourage danger-Taking

What maximum educators already know is that failure may be the greatest teacher. simply as teachers have to encourage threat-taking among their students that allows you to spur increase, definitely powerful leaders inspire danger-taking among their subordinates and associates via developing supportive surroundings that rewards now not just a hit thoughts or initiatives but effort as properly, regardless of the final results.

"Failure is needed for getting to know, but our relentless pursuit of results also can discourage employees from taking possibilities. To remedy this struggle, leaders need to create a lifestyle that helps risk-taking," wrote the Harvard enterprise review. "One way of doing that is to apply managed experiments — think A/B trying out — that permit for small failures and require speedy feedback and correction. This offers a platform for building collective intelligence so that employees research from each other's mistakes, too."

8. They Lead by way of instance

We've all heard the announcing, "Do as I say, not as I do." Of direction, the irony is that moves are an awful lot greater telling than words. Leaders who lead using example role themselves as exceptional role fashions for no longer only the scholars of their college or district but for colleagues and dad and mom as properly. a frontrunner that leads through example nearly constantly gets admire and admiration, without which he or she will be able to find little luck in management. As truth seeker and doctor Albert Schweitzer once stated, "Instance isn't the main issue in influencing others; it is the only element."

9. They Persevere – Staying with a college for a minimum of five Years

Change, while right, can also be disruptive whilst it happens too frequently. Inside the case of college management, it's been documented that common turnover consequences in a bad school climate, which in turn has a terrible effect on pupil overall performance.

"Dedicated and effective principals who continue to be in their faculties are associated with stepped forward college-wide scholar fulfillment. As a corollary, primary turnover is related to decrease gains in pupil fulfillment," mentioned the gaining knowledge of the policy Institute. "Important turnover has an extra great terrible impact in high-poverty; low-accomplishing schools the very faculties in which college students maximum depend on their education for future fulfillment. The bad effect of foremost turnover suggests that principals need time to make significant improvements in their schools. One examine discovered that it takes, on average, five years of a brand new important leading a college for the college's overall performance to rebound to the pre-turnover degree."

The first-class leaders, consequently, are inclined to dedicate themselves to a college and persevere no matter the limitations or challenges. Despite everything, understanding a imaginative and prescient doesn't occur in a single day; real transformation takes time. a pacesetter's commitment shows now not only ardor however dedication, which can have a surprisingly advantageous impact on faculty way of life.

10. They are Lifelong newcomers

Possibly the most critical of all qualities that a school leader can own is the unquenchable thirst for knowledge. As John F. Kennedy stated, "management and gaining knowledge of are fundamental to every other." The exceptional leaders, irrespective of what enterprise they work in, recognize they'll by no means are aware of it all. They are humble in their expertise but assured of their abilities. They're forever and ever curious folks who never prevent questioning, and getting to know.

The Harvard business evaluation placed it flawlessly once they said: "It takes a real experience of private commitment, particularly when you've arrived at a position of electricity and duty, to push yourself to develop and task conventional awareness. This is why two of the maximum critical questions leaders face are as easy as they are profound: Are you learning, as a business enterprise and as a person, as speedy as the sector is converting? Are you as determined to live involved as to be interesting? Keep in mind, it's what you examine after you are aware of it all that counts."

The document additionally quotes the cited author and Professor John Gardner, who determined, "The excellent leaders I've gotten to recognize aren't just the boldest thinkers; they may be the maximum insatiable beginners."

Leadership and learning are vital to everyone

It is hard to consider an industry where regular mastering is greater relevant than education. To be a successful and powerful leader is not any clean feat. But, effective school leaders are desperately wished in thousands of colleges and academic institutions throughout the US and around the world.

Traits of powerful coaching

Seven principles for appropriate exercise in Undergraduate training" first seemed within the American Association for higher education (AAHE) Bulletin in 1987. Arthur Chickering and Zelda Gamson describe a set of pedagogical requirements derived from decades of educational studies and designed to enhance the satisfaction of teaching and learning in colleges and universities. Those principles have had a great effect on university teaching influencing studies, school improvement, and student learning the world over. They may be referenced, quoted, and remain a cornerstone of coaching and learning practices to this day. Chickering and Gamson nation that correct exercise in undergraduate coaching: 1. Encourages contacts among students and faculty. Common scholar-school contact inside and out of instructions is the maximum vital component in scholar motivation and involvement. Faculty challenge enables college students to get through hard instances and hold on to running. Understanding some faculty participants properly enhances students' highbrow dedication and encourages them to reflect on consideration on their very own values and plans. A few examples: First yr seminars on important topics, students taught by way of senior college members, establish an early connection among college students and college.

2. Develops reciprocity and cooperation among students learning is improved while it's miles greater like a group effort than a solo race. Desirable mastering, like properly work, is collaborative and social, now not aggressive and isolated. Running with others regularly will increase involvement in learning. Sharing one's thoughts and responding to others' reactions sharpens thinking and deepens know-how. Some examples: Even in large lecture classes, college students can analyze from each other. Studying organizations are not an unusual exercise. Students are assigned to a group of five to seven other college students, who meet often at some point of class in the term to remedy troubles set with the aid of the trainer. Many establishments use peer tutors for students who want special assist.

3. Makes use of energetic mastering strategies studying isn't always a spectator game. College students do not

research a lot just by sitting in classes taking note of instructors, memorizing pre-packaged assignments, and spitting out solutions. They need to speak about what they may be studying, write about it, relate it to past reports, and apply it to their everyday lives. They should make what they study part of themselves. A few examples: active mastering is endorsed in classes that use based physical games, hard discussions, group projects, and peer reviews. Lively studying can also occur outside the lecture room. There are hundreds of internships, unbiased take a look at, and cooperative job applications throughout the country in all kinds of colleges and universities, in all kinds of fields, for all forms of students. Students also can assist layout and train guides or parts of courses.

4. Gives set off remarks understanding what you understand and do not know focuses on getting to know. College students need suitable comments on overall performance to gain from guides. While getting began, college students want to assist in assessing present understanding and competence. In training, college students need frequent opportunities to perform and acquire suggestions for development. At various factors at some stage in college, and in the end, students need possibilities to reflect on what they have got learned, what they nonetheless need to understand, and the way to check themselves. VIU teaching and gaining knowledge of handbook some examples: No remarks can arise without evaluation. However, evaluation without timely comments contributes little to mastering. Institutions check entering students as they enter to manual them in planning their studies. In addition to the feedback, students get hold of from path teachers, college students in lots of schools and

universities obtain counseling periodically on their development and destiny plans.

5. Emphasizes time on task Time plus electricity equals mastering. There may be no replacement for time on task. Mastering to use one's time properly is essential for students and specialists alike. College students need to assist in learning effective time management. Allocating practical quantities of time means effective learning for college kids and effective coaching for college. How an organization defines time expectancies for college students, college, directors, and different professional groups of workers can establish the basis of high performance for all. A few examples: Mastery mastering, agreement gaining knowledge of, and computer-assisted coaching require that students spend good enough amounts of time on gaining knowledge of. Extended durations of practice for learning also give college students greater time on projects. Providing college students with possibilities to integrate their studies into the relaxation in their lives enables them to use time well.

6. Communicates high expectations assume extra and you'll get extra. Excessive expectations are critical for everybody for the poorly organized, for those unwilling to exert themselves, and for the bright and nicely-prompted. Looking ahead to college students to perform well will become a self-pleasurable prophecy whilst teachers and establishments hold high expectancies for themselves and make greater efforts. a few examples: in many schools and universities, students with terrible past facts or test rankings do superb work. Sometimes they outperform students with proper training. Most critical are the daily, week-in, and week-out expectancies students and college

keep for themselves and each different in all their training. 7. Respects various talents and approaches to mastering. There are many roads to studying. People deliver specific talents and kinds of getting to know to university. Exceptional students inside the seminar room may be all thumbs in the lab or art studio. Students rich in hands-on enjoyment may not do so nicely with ideas. Students need the opportunity to expose their abilities and learn in approaches that work for them. Then they may be pushed to learn in new methods that don't come so without difficulty.

Some examples: Individualized diploma programs recognize exceptional interests. Personalized structures of preparation and mastery getting to know permit students work at their pace and contract mastering assist college students to outline their own goals, determine their studying sports, and define the standards and techniques of evaluation.

Seven concepts for appropriate exercise in undergraduate schooling

 Seven principles of effective coaching is a complex, multifaceted hobby, regularly requiring us as teachers to juggle a couple of obligations and goals concurrently and flexibly. The following small but effective set of standards could make teaching each more effective and greater efficient, by helping us create the conditions that support student studying and reduce the want for revising materials, content, and policies. 1. Whilst enforcing those standards calls for a commitment in time and effort, it often saves time and strength afterward. Teaching includes acquiring a relevant understanding of students and the usage of that knowledge to inform our course layout and school room coaching. Whilst we train, we do now not simply train the content material, we teach college students the content. A variety of scholarly characteristics can affect mastering. as an instance, students' cultural and generational backgrounds have an impact on how they see the world; disciplinary backgrounds lead students to method troubles in exceptional approaches, and students' prior information (each correct and misguided factor) shapes new mastering.

2. Although we cannot adequately measure all of these traits, accumulating the most relevant facts as early as possible in path planning and continuing to accomplish that at some point of the VIU teaching and studying handbook semester can (a) tell path layout (e.g., choices approximately targets, pacing, examples, format), (b) assist explain student difficulties (e.g., identification of not unusual misconceptions), and (c) guide educational variations (e.g., the popularity of the want for extra practice). Effective coaching includes aligning the three foremost additives of practice: getting to know targets, assessments, and educational sports. 3. Taking the time to do that prematurely saves time in the long run and leads to a higher path. teaching is more powerful and student studying is greater when (a) we, as instructors, articulate a clear set of learning targets (i.e., the information and capabilities that we count on students to demonstrate using the end of a route); (b) the academic activities (e.g., case studies, labs, discussions, readings) guide those learning goals through offering purpose-oriented practice; and (c) the assessments (e.g., assessments, papers, problem units, performances) offer possibilities for college kids to

illustrate and exercise the know-how and capabilities articulated in the goals, and for teachers to offer centered feedback which could guide further mastering. Effective teaching includes articulating express expectations regarding getting to know consequences and rules. There's an excellent variant in what's expected of students across classrooms and even inside a given field. For instance, what constitutes proof may additionally differ substantially across publications; what is permissible collaboration in a single direction might be considered cheating in some other. As a result, college students' expectations won't healthy ours. As a result, being clear approximately our expectancies and speaking them explicitly facilitates students to examine greater and perform higher. 4. Articulating our mastering effects (i.e., the knowledge and abilities that we assume students to illustrate by the end of a route) gives college students a clean target to intention for and enables them to display their development along the way. In addition, being explicit about course guidelines (e.g., on elegance participation, computer use, and late assignment) inside the syllabus and in magnificence permits us to solve differences early and tends to lessen conflicts and tensions which could get up. Altogether, being specific leads to an extra productive gaining knowledge of the environment for all college students.

5. Effective coaching includes prioritizing the information and competencies we choose to awareness of. Coverage is the enemy: Don't attempt to do too much in a single route. Too many topics work in opposition to scholar learning, so it's far necessary for us to make selections – now and again hard ones – about what we will and could now not consist of in a path. This involves (a) recognizing the

parameters of the course (e.g., magnificence length, college students' backgrounds, and studies, path position inside the curriculum collection, a wide variety of course units), (b) placing our priorities for a student getting to know, and (c) determining a hard and fast of objectives that can be moderately executed. Powerful teaching includes recognizing and overcoming our expert blind spots. We are not our college students! As experts, we tend to access and practice information automatically and unconsciously (e.g., make connections, draw on applicable bodies of information, and pick out appropriate techniques) and so we frequently pass or integrate important steps whilst we train. Students, then again, don't yet have sufficient history and enjoy making these leaps and may come to be burdened, draw wrong conclusions, or fail to broaden important abilities. They want instructors to break tasks into element steps, explain connections explicitly, and version procedures in detail. Though it is difficult for experts to do that, we need to pick out and explicitly talk to students about the information and capabilities we take with no consideration, so that scholars can see professional questioning in movement and exercise applying it themselves. 6. Effective coaching entails adopting suitable teaching roles to support our studying dreams. Even though college students are at the end responsible for their very own getting to know, the roles we anticipate as instructors are essential in guiding students' wondering and behavior. We can take on a selection of roles in our teaching (e.g., synthesizer, moderator, challenger, and commentator). These VIU coaching and mastering manual roles need to be chosen to provide the studying objectives and in aid of the academic activities. For example, if the objective is for college students to be able to research arguments from a case or written textual content, the maximum efficient teacher role is probably to the border, guide, and mild a dialogue. If the goal is to help students learn to defend their positions or creative picks as they present their work, our function might be to undertaking them to provide an explanation for their selections and take into account opportunity views. Such roles can be constant or variable across the semester depending on the studying goals. 7. Powerful teaching entails steadily refining our courses primarily based on mirrored image and comments. Coaching calls for adapting. We want to usually replicate our coaching and be ready to make changes when appropriate (e.g., something is not operating, we want to attempt something new, the scholar population has modified, or there are emerging problems in our fields). Knowing what and the way to change requires us to have a look at relevant facts on our very own coaching effectiveness. much of these facts already exists (e.g., student work, previous semesters' path opinions, dynamics of class participation), or we may additionally need to search for extra remarks with assistance from the college teaching center (e.g., deciphering early direction reviews, engaging in attention groups, designing pre- and submit-exams). Primarily based on such facts, we might adjust the mastering objectives, content material, shape, or layout of a course, or in any other case modify our teaching.

Small, purposeful adjustments pushed by comments and our priorities are maximum possible to be workable and powerful. "The mediocre trainer tells. The good teacher explains. The advanced instructor demonstrates. Doing the proper matters together with your coaching is of direction critical however so is avoiding the wrong things. Richard M. Felder, North Carolina Kingdom College, and Rebecca Brent, training Designs, Inc., have given you a list of the ten worst errors instructors make. They may be summarized right here in increasing order of "badness". Mistake #10: when you ask a question in class, straight away name for volunteers. whilst you do that most college students will keep away from eye touch, and both you get a reaction from one of the two or three who usually volunteer or you solution your very own question Mistake #9: call on college students bloodless. In case you regularly name on students without giving them time to suppose ("bloodless-calling"), the ones who're intimidated through it might not be following your lecture as an awful lot as praying which you do not land on them. Even worse, as soon as you call on someone, the others breathe a sigh of comfort and forestall questioning. Mistake #8: turn classes into PowerPoint shows. Droning through lecture notes put into PowerPoint slides is commonly a waste of time for everybody. Mistake #7: Fail to offer range in guidance. Effective training mixes matters up: board work, multimedia, storytelling, discussion, sports, individual assignments, and institution work (being careful to avoid Mistake #6). The extra range you build in, the greater powerful the magnificence is possibly to be. Mistake #6: Have college students work in agencies without a personal duty. The manner to make group work feature is through using cooperative gaining knowledge of, an exhaustively researched academic method that correctly promotes improvement of both cognitive and interpersonal skills. Mistake #5: Fail to establish relevance. To provide better motivation, begin the course using describing how the content material relates to critical technological and social problems and learning guide whatever you recognize of the scholars' experience, pursuits, and career goals, and do the identical thing whilst you introduce each new subject matter. Mistake #4: give exams that are too long. If you want to evaluate your college students' ability to achieve success professionals, take a look at their mastery of the expertise and abilities you're coaching, now not their problem-fixing speed. Mistake #3: Get stuck in a rut. Things are constantly going on that provide incentives and opportunities for enhancing courses.

This isn't always to say that you need to make foremost revisions in your route on every occasion you deliver it you probably do not have time to do that, and there is no purpose to. Rather, simply preserve your eyes open for viable improvements you would possibly make inside the time to be had to you. Mistake #2. Educate without clean getting to know goals/consequences. A secret to meaning guides coherent and assessments fair are to jot down gaining knowledge of objectives-express statements of what students ought to be able to do if they have learned what the teacher wishes them to analyze-and to use the goals as the premise for designing classes, assignments, and checks. Mistake #1. Disrespect college students. if you give students a sense that you don't respect them, the class will probably be a terrible revel in for all of us regardless of what else you do, while in case you certainly bring recognize and worrying, it'll cowl a mess of pedagogical sins you may devote.

What can we imply through "taking getting to know critically?" five exciting questions mirror what is worried in taking up that assignment. I shall ask and answer these briefly to start this newsletter. I shall then problematic on the one's solutions. First, what does it suggest to take whatever severely? I answer that after we take something quite seriously, we profess it. Second, what will we imply by way of studying? I argue that getting to know is some distance greater than bringing knowledge from out of doors the person to the interior. Indeed, studying is essentially an interplay of two tough tactics--getting expertise that is inner to move out, and getting understanding that is out of doors to transport in. third, what does studying appear to be while it's not going well? I ask this query due to the fact I have spent a good deal of my profession in medical schooling, said one educator, so I'm worried now not most effective with health, but with pathology as properly, he said. He suggests that the essential pathologies of learning involve malfunctions of memory, know-how, and alertness and can be referred to as amnesia, fantasia, and inertia. Fourth, what do you need to create to be able to take learning so seriously that you take lively obligation for know-how and treating its pathologies as well as improving its successes? I claim that you have to create a scholarship of teaching to pursue one's desires.

Online mastering

Examples for online Respectful truthful, know-how, bendy, being concerned, patient, beneficial, compassionate, open-minded, honest, diplomatic, worried, reasonable, regular, type, empathetic, humble, honest, sensible Compassionate with regards to students' occasions; open to "stupid" question; willing to explain many times and in one of a kind ways if necessary; uses not unusual courtesy; tactful with criticism; suggests situation for college kids' educational success; inclined to admit very own errors fair, knowledge, bendy, being concerned, affected person, useful, compassionate, open-minded, diplomatic, involved, reasonable, consistent, kind, empathetic, truthful, practical organized to reply extra questions than F2F; gives expressive comments; shows challenge for college students; ought to be able to agree with teacher's answers; fair and reasonable with expectancies, create actual world duties Responsive available, useful, perceptive, accommodating well timed, thorough optimistic comments; set office hours; responds to e mail ASAP; involves college students more in the course of class time; has consciousness of college students' needs; reads college students' body language; accepts that scholars learn at distinctive paces to be had, beneficial, accommodating Responds to posts and questions in a well-timed fashion; asks college students for rationalization to check students' information; builds on what college students already recognize; offers students options to accommodate special getting to know patterns; monitors and participates in dialogue forums knowledgeable flexible, ready, eclectic, credible, modern-day, realistic, reflective, certified should be credible; conveys content material that may be understood; stocks real lifestyles enjoy; varies coaching techniques; relates content to actual-life bendy, in a position, eclectic, credible, contemporary, realistic, reflective, qualified should be capable; conveys content material in a way that can be understood; stocks private anecdotes; uses an expansion of sources to percentage content; should be up-to-date on studies and exercise of their field Approachable friendly, personable, helpful, available, satisfied, effective Smiles; makes a comfy ecosystem; continues suitable office hours and responds to email in an inexpensive time pleasant, personable, helpful, reachable, glad, positive understands that now not the whole lot may be communicated using a written method; makes use of recordings to deliver data; responds directly to questions; makes students feel like trainer desires to be there; uses friendly tone in posts.

Examples for Face-to-Face online

Examples for on line Communicative clear, understandable, thorough, optimistic, attentive Speaks without a doubt; has astute listening talents; makes use of an expansion of coaching strategies; is approachable; is aware college students questions and gets to the factor; is prepared; maximizes use of class time; offers activate nice feedback clean, understandable, thorough, optimistic, attentive clear, "listens" and receives points across thru electronic (written) communication; uses a diffusion of coaching strategies, quick response time; genuinely communicates expectations; non-public remarks helps connect scholar to instructor; offers optimistic remarks organized green, centered, prepared organized lectures, clear visual aids; stays on subject matter; offers sufficient feedback in a reasonable time green, centered, prepared online content material; clean expectancies at the start of the direction; affords timelines; responds to emails and discussion posts right away attractive Enthusiastic, thrilling, passionate, motivating, innovative, high-quality, charismatic, stimulating, interactive, energetic, assertive

Interacts with students, has a ardour for course content material; smiles; varies tone of voice; actively includes students in a lecture; makes use of innovative methods Enthusiastic, interesting, passionate, motivating, creative, nice, charismatic, stimulating, interactive, lively, assertive Posts thrilling information associated with the direction from information; relates cloth to actual life and so forth.; gives innovative discussion subjects professional devoted, punctual, reliable, efficacious, hygienic, assured dresses accurately; is punctual, trustworthy, honest; has properly-deliberate lectures; be faithful to the syllabus; self-assurance allows college students broaden self-esteem committed, punctual, dependable, assured Is willing to research powerful coaching techniques for distance studying; makes certain all interactions are nice interactions humorous friendly, available, superb outlook on coaching, type, glad allows students feel greater comfy; creates a positive learning environment; humor prevents college students from falling asleep in magnificence pleasant, to be had, nice outlook on teaching, type, glad provides a non-public touch to the course; makes the material come

Observable traits of powerful teaching

What makes a powerful instructor? Or more specifically, what observable characteristics would possibly you notice and listen to? The University of Minnesota supplied a few observable characteristics of effective coaching which, while focused on instructor moves rather than the student getting to know, had a few useful pointers—no longer a lot away to train usually, however precise moves that you may use the following day.

In "How an awesome trainer becomes incredible," we

theorized that exact instructors recognize which exams are for 'display' and which is for 'move', this is, which look accurate from 10 feet and which give visibility for each pupil and instructor in which the gaining knowledge of needs to head subsequent, and they version curiosity, collaborate with different notable instructors, and "degree information in numerous approaches."

Twenty Observable characteristics of powerful teaching

1. Starts elegance directly and in a properly organized way.
2. Treats students with respect and being concerned.
3. Presents the importance/significance of information to be found out.
4. Presents clear explanations. Holds attention and respect of students; practices powerful classroom management.
5. Uses active, a hands-on student studying.
6. Varies his/her academic techniques.
7. Presents clean, specific expectations for assignments.
8. Affords common and immediate comments to college students on their overall performance.
9. Praises scholar solutions and makes use of probing questions to clarify/complicated answers.
10. Gives many concrete, actual-lives, and sensible examples.
11. draws inferences from examples/fashions and uses analogies.
12. Creates a category surrounding that's comfortable for college students allows students to talk freely.

13.   Teaches at a correctly fast tempo, stopping to test scholar expertise and engagement.

14.   Communicates at the level of all college students in magnificence.

15.   Has a humorousness!

16.   Uses nonverbal behavior, along with gestures, taking walks around, and eye contact to boost his/her comments.

17.   Offers him/herself in class as 'actual humans.'

18.   Focuses on the magnificence objective and does now not let magnificence get sidetracked.

19.   Makes use of comments from students (and others) to assess and improve teaching.

20.   Displays on own coaching to improve it.

Chapter Five

Effective Goals for Online and Blended Learning

The common learner age in a has a look at ranged from thirteen to forty-four. Intervention/application/exercise: The meta-analysis turned into carried out on fifty results determined in forty-five studies contrasting a completely or partially online situation with a completely face-to-face academic circumstance. Period of practice numerous throughout the research and handed one month in the majority of them. Studies design: The meta-evaluation corpus consisted of (1) experimental research the use of random venture and (2) quasi-experiments with statistical management for preexisting organization variations. An impact size turned into calculated or anticipated for each assessment, and common impact sizes had been computed for absolutely online getting to know and for combined learning. A coding scheme turned into applied to categories each examine in terms of a set of conditions, practices, and methodological variables. Findings/outcomes: The meta-evaluation found that, on average, college students in online getting to know conditions done modestly better than the ones receiving face-to-face preparation. The gain over face-to-face lessons turned into full-size in those studies contrasting blended getting to know with conventional face-to-face instruction but now not in the ones research contrasting in basic terms online with face-to-face situations. Conclusions/guidelines:

research on the usage of combined learning additionally tended to contain extra getting to know the time, academic resources, and direction factors that inspire interactions amongst learners. This confounding leaves open the possibility that one or all of these different practice variables contributed to the particularly wonderful consequences for mixed studying. Similarly, studies and improvement on exceptional mixed gaining knowledge of fashions are warranted. Experimental research checking out design standards for blending online and face-to-face preparation for exceptional kinds of newcomers is needed. Online, studying is one of the fastest developing traits in instructional uses of generation. By using the 2006–2007 instructional twelve months, 61% of us higher education establishments presented online guides. In fall 2008, over four.6 million students over one zone of all U.S. better schooling students had been taking as a minimum one on line path. within the company international, according to a document via the Yankee Society for schooling and development, about 33% of education turned into introduced electronically in 2007, almost triple the charge in 2000 (Paradise, 2008). Even though okay–twelve faculty structures lagged behind different sectors in moving into online studying, this sector's adoption of e-studying is now proceeding unexpectedly. As of late 2009, forty-five of the 50 states and Washington DC had as a minimum one shape of online application, which includes a nation digital college presenting publications to complement conventional offerings in brick-and-mortar colleges, a country-led online initiative, or a full-time online school. The most important country virtual school, the Florida virtual school, had extra than a hundred and fifty thousand path enrollments in 2008–2009. Several states, including Michigan, Florida, Alabama, and Idaho, have made a hit final touch of a web direction a requirement for incomes a high school diploma. District surveys commissioned by using the Sloan Consortium produced estimates that seven-hundred thousand ok–twelve public faculty college students took online guides in 2005–2006, and greater than a million college students did so in 2007–2008: a 43% increase in only two years. Christensen, Horn, and Johnson (2008) expected that through 2019, one-half of all U.S. excessive college enrollments can be online. Online, studying has grown to be popular due to its potential for offering extra bendy get entry to content and instruction at any time, from any location. often, the incentive for online gaining knowledge of applications entails (1) growing the availability of mastering stories for rookies who cannot or pick out no longer to wait for conventional face-to-face offerings, (2) assembling and disseminating academic content material greater price-efficiently, and/or (3) imparting get admission to qualified teachers to freshmen in locations in which such instructors aren't available.

Online mastering advocates argue in addition that additional reasons for embracing this medium of training consist of cutting-edge technology's aid of a degree of interactivity, social networking, collaboration, and reflection that can beautify mastering relative to ordinary study room situations. Online mastering overlaps with the wider category of distance learning, which encompasses advanced technology together with correspondence guides, instructional TV, and videoconferencing. Earlier research of distance studying said universal effect sizes close to zero, indicating that studying with that technology, taken as an entire, become no longer substantially one-of-a-kind from normal lecture rooms gaining knowledge of in terms of effectiveness. Coverage makers reasoned that if the online practice isn't any worse than traditional preparation in phrases of student outcomes, then online education projects will be justified based on value performance or the want to provide get entry to learners in settings wherein face-to-face coaching is not possible. studies locating no distinction ineffectiveness does not justify shifting guidance online in cases in which college students have to get entry to classroom guidance and price financial savings aren't anticipated. But, contributors of the distance schooling community view the advent of online, web-primarily based learning as significantly unique from prior styles of distance schooling, such as correspondence guides and one-way video. Online mastering has been described as a "fifth-generation" model of distance education "designed to capitalize at the functions of the internet and the net". on line and combined gaining knowledge of previous generations of distance training is a function of resource allocation parameters based on the conventional cottage enterprise version, while the fifth technology primarily based on automatic response structures has the capacity no longer only to improve economies of scale however additionally to improve the pedagogical first-rate and responsiveness of carrier to college students. The question of the relative efficacy of online and face-to-face instruction needs to be revisited in light of the arrival of 5th-technology distance mastering and today's online mastering programs, that could take gain of an extensive range of internet sources, inclusive of internet-primarily based programs (e.g., audio/video streaming, gaining knowledge of control structures, 3-D simulations, and visualizations, multiuser games) and new collaboration and communication technologies (e.g., internet telephony, chat, wikis, blogs, display screen sharing, shared graphical whiteboards). Learning this is supported by means that internet-primarily based equipment and assets are a far cry from the televised proclaims and videoconferencing that characterized earlier generations of distance schooling. on-line learning proponents recommend that these more modern technologies support learning that is not just as appropriate as, however better than, traditional classroom preparation. Teaching era researchers to look at the net no longer simply as a shipping medium but also as a capability means to beautify the excellent of getting to know stories and results. One common conjecture is that studying a complicated body of expertise efficaciously requires a community of beginners and that online technology may be used to extend and guide such groups, selling "participatory" fashions of schooling. Studies in this area tend to be descriptive of man or woman studying systems, but, with exceedingly few rigorous empirical studies evaluating gaining knowledge of consequences for online and traditional processes. Another essential trend in current years is the emergence of "blended" or "hybrid" techniques that integrate online activities and face-to-face guidance. As early as 2002, the president of Pennsylvania Country College stated that "hybrid coaching is the unmarried finest unrecognized trend in better education nowadays". Further, in 2003, the yank Society for education and development identified blended mastering as a few of the top ten tendencies to emerge inside the knowledge delivery industry. Gaining knowledge of predicted that the blended approach is in all likelihood to come to be the predominant model of coaching and end up a long way extra commonplace than both traditional, simply face-to-face lecture room preparation or coaching carried out online. The phrases combined getting to know and hybrid getting to know are used interchangeably and without a broadly familiar particular definition. Bonk and Graham (2005) defined combined mastering structures as an aggregate of face-to-face training and pc-mediated guidance. The 2003 Sloan Survey of online teaching supplied a particularly greater element, defining mixed studying as a "direction that may be a combination of the online and face-to-face course. A huge proportion of the content material is delivered online, usually makes use of online discussions, and typically has some face-to-face conferences". mixed studying is defined as "any time a student learns as a minimum in part in a supervised brick-and-mortar location away from home and at the least in component thru on-line shipping with some element of student manipulate over time, place, route and/or tempo". Blended strategies do not put off the want for a face-to-face instructor and usually do no longer yield cost savings as in simple terms online offerings do. To justify the additional time and charges required for developing and implementing combined studying, policymakers want proof that mixed studying is not simply as powerful as, but genuinely more effective than, traditional face-to-face coaching.

In addition, for each combined and simply online mastering, policymakers and practitioners need research-based statistics about the conditions below which online learning is powerful and the practices related to more powerful online mastering. the existing article reports a meta-analytic examine that investigated the effectiveness of online getting to know in standard, and each merely online and blended versions of online studying, in particular, for an expansion of learners and with a selection of different contexts and practices.

Online and blended studying isn't surely described inside the literature. For this meta-analysis, we adopted the Sloan Consortium's definition of online gaining knowledge of as gaining knowledge of that takes vicinity entirely or in good-sized portion over the internet. We operationalized the concept of "huge component" as 25% or more of the education on the content material assessed through an examination's getting to know final results degree. This criterion changed into used to avoid consisting of research of incidental uses of the internet, which includes downloading references and delivering assignments. online and blended mastering which all or notably all of the coaching at the content assessed in the final results degree become carried out over the internet were categorized as "merely online," whereas those in which 25% or more, however now not all, of the guidance on the content material to be assessed came about online have been classified as "blended." Although our studies questions consciousness on the effectiveness of purely online and blended gaining knowledge, we recognize that distinct forms of factors can affect the scale and course of differences in pupil learning results whilst comparing online and face-to-face conditions. Online mastering opportunities fluctuate also in phrases of the putting where they're accessed (schoolroom, home, informal), the character of the content material (both the difficulty vicinity and the sort of study, which includes the fact, concept, technique, or strategy), and the era involved (e.g., audio/video streaming, internet telephony, podcasting, chat, simulations, videoconferencing, shared graphical whiteboard, display sharing).

An evaluation of the moderator variables protected in previous meta-analyses. Researchers informed the improvement of a conceptual framework for the contemporary meta-analysis. That framework includes no longer best online getting to know practices, as discussed, however additionally the conditions under which the observation was performed (e.g., the kind of college students and content concerned) and features of the take a look at technique (e.g., experimental design, pattern size). Forms of variables that could impact effect sizes as the ones referring to the online practice practices, situations beneath which the examination becomes conducted, and components of the take a look at method. within every one of these classes, we specific a hard and fast of unique capabilities that have been hypothesized or observed to influence gaining knowledge of consequences in previous meta-analyses of distance mastering. some of these variables have been coded, and in cases in which a good enough range of research with the vital data have been to be had, a variable became examined as a capability moderator of the online getting to know impact length. As mentioned, from a practical angle, one of the most essential differences among one-of-a-kind online gaining knowledge of activities is whether they may be combined or carried out in basic terms online. Merely online guidance serves as an alternative for face-to-face training (e.g., a digital course), with attendant implications for college staffing and value savings. Only online education may be an attractive opportunity for cost reasons if it is equal to traditional face-to-face instruction in terms of scholarly effects. Mixed gaining knowledge of, then again, is expected to be an enhancement.

Many might don't forget combined getting to know applications that produce learning outcomes that are merely equivalent to (now not higher than) the ones due to face-to-face training without the enhancement a waste of money and time due to the fact the addition does not enhance student consequences. A second salient feature of online mastering practices is the sort of pedagogical approach used. One of kind online pedagogical procedures promotes exceptional getting-to-know reports with the aid of varying the source of the gaining knowledge of content and the nature of the learner's activity. In traditional didactic or expository processes, content is instructor- or laptop-directed and commonly offered inside the form of text, lecture, or teacher-directed discussion. Expository methods are frequently contrasted with active mastering, in which the student engages in sports and usually proceeds at his or her very own pace. Some other category of pedagogical technique stresses collaborative or interactive learning activity, wherein the character of the gaining knowledge of content is emergent as freshmen engage with one another and with an instructor or different expertise sources. Technology can help any of these three sorts of pedagogical methods. In online learning, researchers have described a pedagogical shift in online learning environments from the transmission of know-how to support for energetic and interactive mastering as newer technology has extended online gaining knowledge of opportunities. Researchers are the usage of terms consisting of distributed gaining knowledge of or mastering groups to consult orchestrated mixtures of face-to-face and virtual interactions amongst a cohort of rookies led with the aid of one or extra instructors, facilitators, or coaches over an extended length (from weeks to years). subsequently, a 3rd characteristic usually used within the beyond to categorize online getting to know activities is the quantity to which the pastime is synchronous, with practice happening in actual time, whether in a physical or a virtual area, or asynchronous, with a time lag between the presentation of educational stimuli and student responses, permitting conversation and collaboration over some time from anywhere and every time. An earlier meta-evaluation of distance mastering packages pronounced that asynchronous distance schooling (which blanketed traditional correspondence guides and online guides) had a small but extensive benefit over face-to stand education in terms of student learning, whereas synchronous distance training (on the whole teleconferencing and satellite-based transport of instructions) had a small however significant bad impact. Cutting-edge styles of online studying guide extra interactivity in both synchronous and asynchronous modes, and both conversation strategies have their adherents. Asynchronous pastime offers extra spontaneity, making beginners' experience "in synch" with others, consequently theoretically promoting collaboration however, college students might also feel moved quickly to reply or hampered by using technology breakdowns. In contrast, asynchronous pastime offers greater flexibility to newcomers as it lets them respond at their convenience.

Similarly, a few argue that the time lag offered in an asynchronous activity permits for greater thoughtful and reflective learner participation, enabling "richer discussions related to more contributors".

Some have reasoned further that the asynchronous model has extra potential to supply a learner-centered environment by using encouraging interpersonal, -manner communications between the teacher and a person pupil, in addition to among college students. The meta-evaluation pronounced right here tested the have an effect on of those and other studying practices in addition to a diffusion of conditions and methodological capabilities on the web gaining knowledge of effect length by way of conducting a sequence of moderator analyses.

Associated meta-analyses

Gene Glass and his colleague pioneered the development of meta-analysis techniques for the systematic quantitative synthesis of results from a chain of studies in the Meta-evaluation has been used in a selection of fields to inform policy or the design of latest studies primarily based at the excellent to be had proof. Meta-evaluation makes it feasible to synthesize statistics from multiple research with unique pattern sizes by way of extracting an impact size from and computing a summary effect for, all studies. Researchers have articulated the following benefits of meta-analysis: (1) it calls for an explicit and systematic method for reviewing present research, therefore permitting the reader to assess the meta-analysts assumptions, methods, evidence, and conclusions; (2) it affords a greater differentiated and complicated summary of current studies than qualitative summaries or "vote-counting" on statistical importance by way of taking into consideration the strength of evidence from every empirical observe; (3) it produces synthesized effect estimates with considerably greater statistical electricity than individual studies and lets in an exam of differential outcomes related to distinctive examine functions; and (four) it gives a prepared way of managing information from a big frame of studies.

Online and blended studying numerous meta-analyses associated with distance education have been posted. Generally, those meta-analyses covered the research of older generations of technologies such as audio, video, or satellite TV for pc transmission. One of the maximum complete meta-analyses on distance education was carried out by Bernard and his colleagues. This study examined six hundred and ninety-nine independent impact sizes from two hundred and thirty-two studies posted from 1985 to 2001, evaluating distance schooling with classroom guidance for an expansion of freshmen, from young youngsters to adults, on measures of fulfillment, attitudes, and direction crowning glory. The meta-evaluation discovered a usual effect length close to zero for student achievement ($g+ = 0.01$). As cited, asynchronous distance training had a small but significant nice impact ($g+ = 0.05$) on scholar fulfillment, while synchronous distance education had a small but large terrible impact ($g+ = -0.10$). Bernard et al. discovered also that a wide percentage of the range in effect sizes for student success and mindset results turned into accounted for with the aid of the research' studies technique. Any other meta-evaluation of distance training with the aid of Zhao and his colleagues (2005) examined ninety-eight impact sizes from fifty-one research published from 1996 to 2002. Like Bernard et al.'s observe, this meta-evaluation centered on distance schooling courses added through a couple of generations of generation for a wide kind of novices and found a general effect length near 0 (d = +0.10). Subsequent moderator analyses located that studies of mixed strategies wherein 60%–80% of learning became mediated via technology found substantially extra positive outcomes relative to stand-to-stand guidance than natural distance learning studies did. The difference between blended getting to know and study room education become a whole lot large than that among distance education that became almost absolutely mediated by generation and study room preparation. Like the Bernard et al. meta-analysis, using Zhao et al. blanketed a wide variety of results (e.g., fulfillment, ideals and attitudes, satisfaction, student dropout price). Zhao et al. averaged the extraordinary styles of results used in a look to compute an average effect size for the meta-evaluation. This exercise is elaborate because elements, in particular, route features and implementation practices that beautify one type of student outcome (e.g., student retention) can be pretty extraordinary from people who beautify any other sort of final results (e.g., pupil success) and may even work to the detriment of that different final results. Whilst mixing studies with exceptional styles of outcomes, such alternate-offs might also difficult to understand the relationships between practices and studying. A few meta-analytic studies have centered on the efficacy of the new technology of distance training publications provided over the internet for particular learner populations. Sitzmann et al. (2006), for example, examined 96 research posted from 1996 to 2005 that compared net-based training with face-to-face schooling for job-associated expertise or capabilities. The authors determined that during standard, internet-based education became slightly greater powerful than face-to-face schooling for obtaining declarative information ("understanding that"), however now not for procedural knowledge ("knowing how"). Complicating the interpretation of this locating became the reality that Sitzmann et al. located a fantastic effect of internet-primarily based schooling on declarative information in quasi-experimental studies (d = +0.18), however, a bad impact favoring face-to-face schooling in experimental studies with the random project (d = -0.26). This sample of findings underscores the need to take note of factors of the layout of the studies covered in a meta-analysis. any other meta-evaluation of online learning using Cavanaugh, Gillan, Kromerey, Hess, and Blomeyer (2004) focused on internet-based total distance schooling applications for okay-twelve students. The researchers mixed one hundred and sixteen results from fourteen studies published between 1999 and 2004 to compute an average weighted impact, which was no longer statistically unique from zero (g = -0.03). Next research of moderator variables discovered no sizable elements affecting pupil success. This meta-analysis used multiple consequences from the equal examination, ignoring the reality that the special outcomes from the same student would not be unbiased of each difference. Moreover, the method utilized by Cavanaugh et al. assigns greater weight to studies with extra consequences than to studies with fewer results. In precise, even though some meta-analytic research has investigated the results of distance education for a huge range of novices not one of the large-scale meta-analyses making use of methodological great standards in the choice of research remote gaining knowledge of results with internet-based mastering environments from other sorts of results and older distance education technologies. Studying contains advances in internet-primarily based studying gear and their expanded reputation throughout unique learning contexts warrants a rigorous meta-analysis of students' gaining knowledge of results with online studying. Past meta-analyses usually blanketed research with vulnerable research designs (i.e., quasi-experimental research without statistical control for preexisting variations), thereby summarizing findings that might be themselves problem to threats to internal validity. The finding in several meta-analyses that the scale of a take a look at effect is associated inversely to research design exceptional implies the want for computing a usual online mastering impact with information drawn completely from studies with acceptably rigorous research designs;

Mixed and online gaining knowledge of

Online guides are those in which a minimum of eighty percent of course content material is added online. Mixed (now and then referred to as hybrid) education has among thirty and eighty percent of the direction content added online with a few face-to-face interplays. Combined and online publications no longer handiest change how content material is added, additionally they redefine conventional academic roles and offer distinctive opportunities for mastering.): This teaching guide offers studies on the studying possibilities presented thru online and combined getting to know, as well as powerful practices for facilitating online courses.

What does the research say about mixed and online getting to know?

Online mastering is one of the quickest growing traits in educational uses of the era. A recent survey of extra than 2,800 schools and universities suggested the following:

In 2010, the U.S. department of training released a meta-analysis and overview of empirical studies focused on online getting to know k-12 faculties and better training from 1996-2008. Their findings discovered that "college students in online situations carried out modestly higher, on common than those learning the equal fabric via traditional face-to-face instruction". Further, they reported that combined preparation combining online and face-to-face factors had a bigger gain than in basic terms on-line preparation.

Although these consequences recommend that mixed mastering environments can offer a getting to know benefit whilst compared to merely face-to-face training, the researchers emphasized the findings "do not reveal that online studying is superior as a medium. It became the aggregate of factors within the remedy conditions (which was possible to have protected extra learning time and materials as well as extra opportunities for collaboration) that produced the located gaining knowledge of blessings". In different phrases, the trainer must create an interactive, supportive, and collaborative gaining knowledge of environment for college students to attain the potential blessings afforded using online gaining knowledge of. Precise tips for facilitating a powerful blended or online elegance may be discovered within the accurate practices segment of this teaching guide.

What are the factors that could make combined and online learning successful?

As mentioned above, the studies indicate that once facilitated correctly, online schooling can't most effectively suit, however additionally surpass conventional face-to-face mastering. Here are some of the capacity blessings of online education:

• Learner-centered training: A powerful online teacher is a person "who's open to giving up manipulate of the getting to know procedure" by making students energetic contributors of their gaining knowledge of the method. A learner-centered method acknowledges what students bring to the web classroom—their history, wishes, and interests—and what they get rid of as applicable and significant effects. With the trainer serving as a facilitator, college students are given greater management and obligation around how they learn, together with the opportunity to teach one another via collaboration and personal interactions.

• Collaborative & Interactive mastering: research has discovered that online practice is greater effective when students collaborate in place of working independently. There is a diffusion of methods for students to collaborate online, consisting of synchronous and asynchronous discussions and small group assignments. Similarly, the relative anonymity of online discussions allows the creation of a "stage gambling field" for quieter students or the ones from typically marginalized companies. Whilst posed questions earlier, students have the opportunity to compose considerate responses and feature their voices heard, in addition, to reply to one another in a way no longer typically afforded through face-to-face preparation.

• Metacognitive recognition: in view that online beginners have extra autonomy and duty for carrying out the gaining knowledge of method, it's critical that students apprehend which behaviors assist them to study and practice those techniques proactively. This consciousness and knowledge of one's studying procedure includes accelerated metacognition—a key exercise for scholar success

• Expanded Flexibility: online gaining knowledge of offers more flexibility due to the fact college students can manipulate while and wherein they research. Through self-monitoring their time and pacing, students can spend greater time on unexpected or tough content material.

• Immediately feedback: online novices normally have greater get right of entry to teachers through email and can have questions responded to using their peers in a well-timed fashion on discussion forums. In addition, online checks and quizzes can be constructed with automatic grading functionality that offers well-timed comments. Instant and continual comments all through the studying method are beneficial for gaining expertise of tough standards, as well as triggering retrieval mechanisms and correcting misconceptions.

• Multimodal content material: The net gives an abundance of interactive and multimodal materials that may be used to boom engagement and attraction to numerous newbies. Click on here to find out about unique methods to deliver multimodal content material online, together with thru videos, podcasts, screencasts, video conferencing, and presentation software.

Designing your online route

•	recognize Your Learner: A recent survey of one,500 people nationwide, who have been recently enrolled, presently enrolled, or planning to sign up for an internet direction determined that a wide style of college students were attracted to online learning. But, they also identified the subsequent key topics in online students' responses:

•	Most online students have several obligations in lifestyles so that they are trying to find comfort and versatility while furthering their training. hundreds of thousands of post-secondary students have grown to become to online education as it allows them to suit schooling around their work and own family duties and to have a look at any time and anywhere.

•	On-line students price the independence, self-course, and manage online education gives them. Among several factors that pressure them to online programs, students most usually point to "the capability to examine when and in which I need" and "the potential to take a look at my tempo".

As you lay out your course, it's crucial to expand as complete a photo as feasible of the unique students who will be enrolling within the class. Gaining an experience of their earlier knowledge and technology competency will help you to understand what helps they'll want and tailor your training as a result. a few methods to gain these insights include asking students to complete a web survey, idea inventory, or pre-evaluation. in addition, college students can mirror their previous understanding and reports via an internet discussion or blog publish.

• Expand getting to know desires: As with face-to-face instruction, it's imperative first of all the lead to mind by way of developing learning desires first. Ask yourself, what are the important thing concepts and/or talents college students want to master by way of the give up of the direction? the solution to this question will help in developing path content, sports, and assessments that align along with your mastering desires, as well as choosing the appropriate technology.

• Have clear expectancies: gift clear hints for participation inside the elegance, as well as precise data for students about path expectations and approaches. Similarly, use rubrics to talk mastering goals and grading criteria for every studying interest inside the path (e.g., exceptional online discussions) and comprise them into scholar tests. Lauren Palladino's online module for a graduate astronomy class is a splendid instance of the way to gift clear expectations early on.

Organizing direction content material

• Offer an obvious direction thru the cloth and make certain guideposts are clear to the pupil. The organization is vital because online rookies need to healthy the route into their crowded schedules. He emphasizes the importance of posting route assignments and due dates early and having clear instructions. Shea and co-workers also defined the significance of absolute labeling and organizing route-level and phase-stage materials as a good way to create a path the one's college students can follow.

• Organize the content material in logical units, or

modules, wherein each module is organized around a first-rate subject matter and includes relevant objectives, material, and related sports. Inside the advent to the module, consist of records approximately how long the pupil has to count on to spend operating on the module. This allows holding college students to shift along at a comparable pace. The route demo from Boston college right here illustrates this modular business enterprise. Within every module, gift content material in effortlessly digestible chunks.

• Whilst imparting textual content, format the content for the internet using breaking it into short paragraphs and the usage of headings, bullets, pics, and different formatting gadgets that make webpages less difficult to read and realize. The "7+/-2" instructional layout rule of thumb, based totally on the work of psychologist George Miller, indicates the inclusion of five to nine pieces of information in a section. This self-paced asynchronous direction from UC-Irvine demonstrates numerous of those ideas.

• While offering audio or video, encompass a short description and information approximately the length. Maintain the segments quickly, from twelve to fifteen minutes, to help maximize listeners' retention. Strategically chunking content material facilitates students to soak up the records, avoiding records overload and exhaustion.

• Assist your college students' digest the chunks of

material via imparting short don't forget or application questions after each one. Research has verified the crucial role of retrieval practices for conceptual getting to know. Facilitating online mastering

• Promote metacognitive attention. on account that online novices have greater autonomy and obligation, it's far vital which can be supported in planning, tracking, and assessing their information and performance. As referred to earlier, presenting clear expectations and a clear direction through the material can help college students reveal their pace. In "selling student Metacognition," Tanner (2012) gives a handful of adaptable unique sports for selling metacognition, along with pre and submit-assessments, reflective journals, and questions for college students to ask themselves as they plan, screen, and examine their thinking.

• Hold a Social Presence: live the present and be attentive to scholar desires and concerns. The instructor needs to have interaction in a balanced level of participation and verbal exchange; both publicly and privately, so students realize he or she is engaged and available. This includes modeling correct participation by often contributing to discussions via responding to students' posts and asking similar questions. The teacher is instrumental in growing heat and an alluring environment that promotes a web experience of the network.

• Sell Collaboration: Collaborative studying processes assist college students to reap deeper ranges of expertise generation thru the creation of shared desires, shared exploration, and a shared process of that means making. Further, collaborative activity can assist to reduce the sensations of isolation which can occur whilst college students are operating at a distance". Collaborative getting to know maybe promoted via an expansion of activities, consisting of small group assignments, case research, simulations, and group discussions.

•   Promote active studying: gaining knowledge of isn't a spectator recreation need to talk about what they may be studying, write reflectively about it, relate it to beyond reviews, and apply it to their everyday lives. They have to make what they study a part of themselves". Retaining in mind the characteristics of online rookies, it's also critical to make obligations authentic for college students. These are, complicated tasks related to actual-lifestyles reviews that also can be applied to destiny activities. Here are some specific thoughts on online activities.

•   Comprise a couple of Media: A key mistake teachers make is, in reality, converting print substances for internet surroundings. as an alternative, leverage the possibilities of the net by using considering diverse content sources and media codecs to encourage getting to know and appeal to one-of-a-kind getting to know patterns. CIRTL indicates that when choosing media for a direction, think about the way it accomplishes mastering desires and the way the medium will affect the learner (e.g., generation desires, download time, disabilities). Similarly, Kapus (2010) recommends that when incorporating streaming media in a course it also publishes entire transcripts and inspires students to both watch the content material and examine the transcript.

• Provide ok Technical assist: It has to no longer be assumed that all college students have reveled in online mastering or using the essential technology. Offer ample technical guide for inexperienced persons by inclusive of hyperlinks to resources, making yourself to be had to college students, and promoting collaborative peer hassle fixing on the discussion board.

What you want to build a powerful combined getting to know study room

As online learning takes over education, a brand new approach to K12 studying is emerging in school rooms the world over. Mixed learning integrates face-to-face instruction with virtual training to provide upward push to an effective gaining knowledge of revel in. It requires a good-sized departure from the two character techniques and constitutes an essential re-orientation of coaching practices.

Mixed getting to know gives enormous blessings to college students – they stand to enjoy the established practices of the classroom while studying at their own pace, owing to the adaptive and personalized nature of online gaining knowledge. Educators must then focus on growing combined mastering guides that can effectively merge these two strategies to create informative and interactive gaining knowledge of environments. Building an effective blended getting to know study room calls for cautious planning and practice. The following great practices are beneficial in creating an "a hit" combined study room surroundings.

1. A complete gaining knowledge of management system

A complete studying management gadget (LMS) is a

prerequisite for developing an immersive gaining knowledge of surroundings. It must function as a principal repository of statistics –direction fabric, assignments, net sources, and so on. Open for getting right of entry to and use to all students. It also acts as an easy device to assess student development via assignments, and so forth. a very good LMS offers flexibility, ease of use, and unhindered accessibility. It must additionally make it clean for both students and educators to get admission to, streamline, and track route-related information.

2. A nicely-defined course define

At the very outset, teachers ought to prepare a specific route to define to guide newbies – they ought to lay out path content material and shape and the equipment to be employed for coaching. The course define must include route sources, objectives, challenge information, checks, and their grading percentage. Teachers should also genuinely outline the elements of the fabric that might be covered online and those that might shape a part of study room conferences. They ought to also actually kingdom hardware and software program requirements. A properly defined course outline helps students keep track of their learning, a need in a path that promotes unbiased gaining knowledge of. The trainer can use the outline to preserve the song of route development and pace. An appropriate evaluation strategy will assist instructors to identify improvement regions and work on them to acquire advanced mastering results. Educators should additionally plan suitable assessment strategies to create a holistic blended learning software. Figuring out the top-rated approach to test studying outcomes and tracking path development is essential – they have the choice of accomplishing online quizzes, in-magnificence objective or subjective assignments, school room discussions, etc.

3. Clean learning objectives

Instructors ought to become aware of and outline clean studying targets to assist students to understand what they can assume from a route. An effective combined learning classroom mandates a specific knowledge of direction dreams earlier than educators begin developing content. The goals function as a roadmap, assisting every person to understand wherein studying is headed and the topics that want to be blanketed to correctly achieve route objectives. There should be good enough readability in setting up how to 'mixture' online with the hooked-up methods of teaching. To decide course objectives, teachers ought to discover the competencies that the newcomers need to increase during the course; the statistics to be included; and the sorts of schooling gear and sports that form part of the path.

4. Constant Aesthetics

Believe in a learning management device with constantly shifting factors and changing layouts. No longer the best might this bring about a first-rate deal of bewilderment, it would additionally obstruct easy learning. The primary structure and layout of the LMS need to be constant with good enough visible and image elements to useful resource understanding. There should be uniformity in terms of the format of videos, assignments, games, and many others, assisting rookies to navigate via the direction material without getting careworn. This goes on to reinforce the overall readability and scholar engagement.

5. Correct communication

Effective communication among the teacher and college

students needs to be mounted to obtain advanced studying results in a blended studying program. There need to be a good enough alternate of queries and feedback with ordinary study room discussions. Teachers can offer their touch statistics and encourage students to talk in case of queries and worries to set up a positive rapport. Towards the end of a route, they can also engage inexperienced persons in life or online surveys, evaluations, and reviews at the high quality of the course and its delivery.

Imparting normal and constructive remarks is a vital element of effective communique. Using starting up lines of verbal exchange, instructors can imply the availability of a perennial support machine.

6. A properly-educated instructor

A combined mastering course necessitates the right trainer education to facilitate foremost getting to know. They have to recognize pupil needs and accordingly layout courses. Effective blended-learning professional education ought to consist of educational procedures which can be primarily based on knowledge scholar views. By encouraging teachers to revel in combined studying as newcomers, they receive the primary-hand revel in that's required to create applicable and interactive content for college kids. On account that blended school rooms can be tough to devise and control, teachers must additionally gain knowledge of management strategies tailored for such school rooms. They should be nicely-versed with the technology required to execute blended mastering, and as a consequence need schooling on the software programs and hardware management as properly. There may be no denying the reality that online mastering is right here to stay. The importance of blended classrooms in this context becomes clean. In a hyper-related international, both physical and digital gaining knowledge of areas remember. Educators ought to catch up with this trend and assist college students to succeed through an effective blended gaining knowledge of technique.

What are the blessings of combined learning?

Blended getting to know, which combines conventional face-to-face schooling with the generation, has grown to be more and more popular in academic institutions over the years. This fashion of learning affords a way for faculty to have interaction with students thru visuals and online interaction. Seventy-seven% of academic leaders declare that online education is both equal and superior to stand-to-face schooling and may be finished for a fragment of the price.

So, how can mixed get to know benefit faculty and college students alike?

Advantages to college

Trade can be tough, particularly for college who have taught the usage of conventional strategies for years. However, as blended getting to know will become greater commonplace in academic institutions, the blessings are becoming more apparent - making the adoption charge well.

1. Song and improve engagement

Mixed learning allows making a clear roadmap for college kids, which includes what is anticipated of every pupil and the necessities to attain the very last intention or grade are. With blended studying, teachers can visualize and track every student's development. This system can make it easier to identify symptoms of a student suffering or instructional strengths and act upon them for that reason. For example, educators can examine metrics to see what applications and modules students are engaging with. With expertise in which each scholar's passion lies, it will become less difficult to cater to and regulate every student's getting to know behaviors. If college students are falling at the back, it turns easier for a trainer to become aware of the problem, and step in earlier. Take the Commonwealth Connections Academy for example. Using pulling reports from their online studying platform teachers could analyze take a look at scores, route activities, and portfolio assignments. If a scholar is falling behind in a particular place, they're cautioned to attend a drop-in center that offers college students more face-to-face time with their trainer. Instructors and college students agree that the middle is a useful manner to zero in on a pupil's learning limitations and offer custom training for development. Every so often the solutions are as easy as presenting higher organizational abilities.

2. Beautify communique

Younger people nowadays are developing up with extra generation than ever. We've already seen shifts in verbal exchange patterns, beginning with millennials. Watching a generation who became saturated in the digital international can display how communique is evolving. An observation from LivePerson discovered that within the US and the UK, about 75% of internet customers surveyed said in place of communicating individual, they have been more likely to speak digitally through:

•   Electronic mail

- Text message
- Social media

The findings may be a trademark that blended gaining knowledge of, which has an emphasis on technology, reaches students better than traditional methods. By way of catering to a scholar's favored method of verbal exchange, online forums can join academics with college students extra efficaciously.

3. Allows edtech

Via combining new era like AR and VR with conventional education techniques, students are getting a more inclusive studying revel in. A look at by EdTech review shows that AR and VR technology has mass appeal, too. Purchasers price AR merchandise 33% higher than non-AR offerings. Google Expeditions and Titans of space are tremendous examples of AR and VR in the study room. Both offer digital field trips like tours of the solar gadget to enhance science classes. These adventures are each attractive and valuable methods to educate. The growth of tech methods that coaching online is becoming more effective and less difficult.

4. Personalization

Within the U.S. the student-to-trainer ratio has risen to nearly 30 students in keeping with trainers. With class sizes this huge, it can be difficult to personalize lessons or understand the character wishes of each scholar. Mixed getting to know offers the opportunity to change this. Scholar-centric, mixed studying makes it less complicated to individualize gaining knowledge of modules based on competency. College students inside one lecture room can move at special paces, and teachers can see more without difficulty, which college students either specific more hobby in a specific location or show the need for extra interest in a particular concern.

5. Reduces cost

Mixed learning saves educators money in several ways. for example:

1.   Repurposing content reduction and money spent for direction preparation.

2.   Virtual tutoring can help to get rid of employee and venue charges.

A paper through the Fordham Institute located that the national average for according-to-scholar charges for classic mastering in ok-12 became approximately $10,000. Virtual colleges' prices have been $5, $500 to $7, $100 in step with pupil, whilst blended learning charges began at $7, $600. Fees may want to upward thrust to around $10, $200 in line with scholar relying on how a lot of face-to-face training is emphasized within the plan. With the aid of implementing mixed gaining knowledge of strategically, an organization could reduce fees by way of almost 50%.

Benefits to students:

School members aren't the simplest ones to advantage from combined learning. Perhaps more importantly, students are given an extra comprehensive educational revel that may improve retention and engagement.

1. Peer guide

In Aspden and Helm's examine 'Making the connection in blended studying surroundings', they determined that online verbal exchange, thru a combined gaining knowledge of surroundings, advanced social components of students. Particularly, they said that mixed getting to know allowed college students to make and preserve connections with different students, and their mastering group, even when off-campus. With the aid of presenting online discussions in real-time, or in an asynchronous version like dialogue forums or chat rooms, open talk is continually handy. The consistency of communication enables a 24/7, community-style assist system this means that continuous peer support.

2. Easy get entry to and flexibility

By having sources online, students can access fabric with no constraints consisting of agenda conflicts. Online materials may be found on smartphones, pills, and computer systems that are the generation we're already the usage, daily. In truth, GlobalWebIndex discovered that on a normal day, internet users a while eighteen to thirty-four spend three hours, thirty-eight minutes surfing the web via their smartphones on their own. Moreover, many college students inside the USA fail to finish faculty. As many as 7% of high faculty college students drop out before commencement. Worse nonetheless, almost 1/2 of the students who start college don't finish within six years. One end is that most people of college students who start college and don't end are element-time enrollments that may advise that scholars are juggling have a look at with work and private commitments. Due to the fact mixed learning platforms are available at any time, it's miles handy for those who are trying to finish training whilst taking on other obligations like running or parenting.

3. More suitable retention

Blended getting to know may have the capability to educate students with greater success than traditional face-to-face schooling. The English department at Manhattan

College (LIU) Brooklyn is currently trying out blended getting to know as a manner to enhance retention for their students. To start, LIU offered iPads for all its incoming college students. The wish is that by using incorporating technological components into their lessons, it will help alternate the manner college students reflect on consideration on their writing. The data LIU has collected, though more often than not qualitative, is beginning to paint the photograph that mixed studying has a nice impact on retention. Other studies imply that studying online can grow retention costs from 25-60% as compared to the handiest 8-10% for face-to-face gaining knowledge.

4. Increased satisfaction and effectiveness

College students these days opt to have a spread of methods to research. As digital natives, many younger college students are familiar with an internet environment and in reality, prefer it. The varied formats of training also serve a purpose outside of scholar enjoyment and pride; it also may be a more effective manner for college students to learn, too. Mixed learning encourages self-gaining knowledge, where students are compelled to search for facts online independently, instead of just sitting in a lecture room setting and relying on a lecturer. Inside the e-book mixed learning: Uncovering its transformative capability in higher schooling, the authors argue that mixed getting to know is effective due to the fact in contrast to the traditional lecture-based teaching model, combined studying opens school room time to consciousness on more energetic and meaningful activities that can cause advanced effectiveness.

5. Boosts gentle competencies

Soft competencies or skills which might be required inside the place of business for expert success are certainly fostered in a web learning area. Especially, capabilities like referring to properly to others, time management, important wondering, and crew cooperation are nurtured in a mixed model. A study published with the aid of Elsevier examined a set of calculus college students to look at how a blended mastering version impacted gentle talents. The belief in their observation became that the ability to communicate via electronic mail or online improved participation. And that due to the fact students were actively discussing and vocalizing their information of standards, blended gaining knowledge of helped build self-assurance and fulfillment. It became concluded that verbal exchange abilities changed favorably with a combined getting to know the direction. It is clear that mixed gaining knowledge of offers new ways for educators to engage and connect with college students. With falling enrollments and the project of the digital panorama putting pressure on structures, faculty, and syllabus, introducing blended gaining knowledge ought to assist tap into a new cohort of students and create a brand new sales circulate.

Chapter Six

Goal-Setting through the Lens of Motivational Theory

Do you often locate your self-suffering to alternate your conduct, irrespective of how willing you are to set objectives? If your desires rarely reach fruition, you are not on my own. For lots, there is the 'you who you would like to be, after which (more consistently) the 'you' which you are. Those variations of yourself aren't constantly aligned. If they had been, we might all be superheroes. Disillusionment may additionally comply with the wide variety of factors you "ought to" have accomplished if only you were chronic for your endeavors. Research in psychology is here to orientate ourselves in a complex world, and even assist us to live our lives in greater pleasant and effective approaches. Locke's purpose-setting theory of motivation, which has been examined and supported through hundreds of research related to thousands of contributors, constantly provides positive changes within the lives of individuals internationally. What's the intention-putting idea?

A take a look at Edwin Locke's idea

Does this quote sound acquaint? it is essential to the trendy aim-setting principle, even though it is over 2,500 years old. While it is obvious that the dreams can't be reached, don't alter the goals, alter the motion steps. In case you are new to this quote, it can be time to write it down and memorize it.

Most desires are possible to acquire, but human beings are unsuccessful at intention-putting once they omit to remember the maximum critical substances to any given intention. Perhaps you decided on a glass of wine on New Year's Eve, or while you have been sitting at the subway getting back from work, determined to maximize your agency's outputs. You had been taken by the belief, then, which you could teach for more than one months before jogging that summer season marathon; that your crew-building sporting events would enhance the bonds among your employees and in turn, undoubtedly impact their performance at work; that you could write 500 phrases an afternoon and complete your first novel. You have got already been uncovered to infinite inspirational quotes. As one instance, J. okay. Rowling has an amazing inspirational quote. In any case, she drafted Harry Potter at the return of a napkin in a restaurant in Edinburgh. She believes that:

"The whole lot is possible in case you've were given enough nerve."
If this quote evokes you, this is appropriate. It isn't always continually enough, however, to study a quote like this and exchange your intention-pushed moves. Regardless of someone as inspiring as in 90% of the instances, analyzing a motivational quote and promising yourself to work harder, alternate this or that dependency, or enhance a thing of your life ensures failure. Why is this? If putting goals and succeeding is part of what makes 'human,' then how do we deal with this fail-susceptible tendency?
It subjects, to gain your dreams, as running towards meaningful dreams presents us with a feel of the path, motive, and meaning in lifestyles. The extra dreams we set

within healthful barriers and the much more likely we're to build self-self-assurance, autonomy, and happiness. It's time to explore the science behind intention-putting. Allows flip that 90% failure fee on its head.

Aim-putting studies: Findings and records

Many research on goal-placing display that the addiction of creating goals is strong, cross-culturally; but, the rate of accomplishing the ones goals through small, viable adjustments is weak. The subsequent findings summarize the closing 90 years of goal-putting:

• Cecil Alec Mace carried out the first observe on aim-placing in 1935.

• Individuals who write their goals are much more likely to achieve their purpose than folks who don't through 50%.

• Motivation professionals agree that goals have to be written down, and carried with oneself, if possible.

• 92% of New Year resolutions fail by using the fifteenth of January.

• Carefully mentioned desires, which may be measured and set within precise timeframes, are more powerful.

• Explaining your dreams to someone you are near, or making the dedication public, significantly will increase your possibilities of attaining your purpose.

• Via contrast, dreams which can be kept to oneself are more likely to be blended up with the 1,500 minds that the common person stories by way of the minute.

• Often, achieving a purpose means sacrificing something or putting aside certain behavior, or beliefs about yourself—it can even result in an emotional or bodily toll.

• Harvard studies document that 83% of the population of America do now not have dreams.

• Aim-placing normally yields an achievement rate of ninety%.

• Dreams have an energizing function. The higher the goal, the more effort invested.

Theoretical Definition(s) of aim-putting

To offer context, right here are some definitions of aim-setting defined with the aid of experts inside the subject: Extensively defined, aim-setting is the process of setting up clean and usable goals, or targets, for gaining knowledge of. Goal-putting concept is summarized concerning the effectiveness of specific, difficult goals; the relationship of dreams to affect; the mediators of goal outcomes; the relation of goals to self-efficacy; the moderators of aim effects; and the generality of goal results throughout human beings, obligations, nations, periods, experimental designs, goal resources (i.e., self-set, set jointly with others, or assigned), and dependent variables. Edwin Locke's purpose-putting principle argues that for intention-setting to achieve success with preferred outcomes, they ought to comprise the subsequent unique points:

• Readability: goals want to be precise;

• Difficult: dreams must be tough yet practicable;

• Goals must be normal;

• Remarks need to be supplied on aim attainment;

• Desires are greater powerful when they are used to assess the performance;

• Closing dates improve the effectiveness of dreams;

• A studying purpose orientation ends in better

performance than an overall performance aim orientation;

• Organization intention-putting is as critical as character aim-placing.

The following video offers a concise explanation that summarizes the actions and steps to attain unique desires. It's less than 3 minutes and informative.

To make the memorization of those factors simpler, the acronym clever may additionally assist you to remember what the most vital attributes of powerful intention-putting are:

• Precise
• Measurable
• Practicable
• Practical
• Time-based totally

How do those work out in exercise? In brief, the answer pertains to specificity, which we can address next.

Examples of the goal-putting idea of Motivation in exercise

Positioned apart the impossible to resist wanting to make your goal as vague and romantic as possible and stay with the uncooked stuff. What action items do you need to do, to reap this intention?

The anagram "smart" is here to help you with this technique.

Getting clever

The first factor of the anagram says that dreams must be 'particular.' All you want to do is make certain you are clear about what your purpose is concretely going to cope with. For instance, in preference to announcing, "I ought to end up greater social" (if say, you're a lonesome cat girl who gets visits as soon as a month), first define what you mean through being social, what your expectancies are of social lifestyles and the methods in which you feel a greater social presence to your life could decorate it.

Then, caricature out a plan to place into movement straight away, tackling instances of the day by day lifestyles you can work on (inside the administrative center, in already existing relationships, all through everyday encounters) and the more incentives you can take to get out of your way to fulfill new people and experience new stories and activities.

Write down what you are aiming to achieve and what you may try this may additionally positively impact your socializing efforts (e.g. turning into extra hospitable, relaxed, being concerned, kind, compassionate, empathetic). Alternatively, specificity can also talk over with putting unique dates, instances, locations at which you'll commit to spending time dedicating yourself to your aim. Subsequently, we need to keep in mind what measurable goals imply.

'Measurable' is that you must be capable of measure in a single way or another whether you have got finished your purpose or now not, or still in the system of doing so. How your purpose needs to be measured is as much as you. Nonetheless, you ought to have a clear concept and expectation as to how your aim, once finished, might appear to be. If your intention became to become more social, that would imply constructing sturdy friendships with two new people and deciding to attend one social event every week for an entire year.

Preserving tune thru 'dimension' facilitates to provide you

an experience of where you presently discover yourself with regards to your goal and wherein you're heading subsequent. Dreams have to be 'proper' to you. That means that you must not best pick out with them but also, feel like they are in line with your cost device and they gained lead you to transgress your sense of integrity in any way. If the aim is to be greater social, the 'acceptability' element comes into play at the level of what you sense an ok friendship might appear like. Whether or not it's sharing fun activities, emotional and intimate conversations, cooking, or playing sports activities collectively, it's important to be self-conscious, to recognize what you're after, and the way your beliefs and feelings are entangled with the purpose you're about to set for yourself.

Your intention should be sensible. In other phrases, you need to work with what you have got even as pushing yourself slightly past so one can exchange your contemporary reality. Going back to the example of the lonesome catgirl (not anything wrong approximately that), a sensible aim would be to make efforts to expand at least new friendships over the following six months, and no longer, say, to end up a famous member of the network, as accomplishing this may take notably more time. We've simply briefly referred to the time framework, however, it's worth re-emphasizing as a lot as vital. The time frame is all approximately setting a fixed closing date by which you must have completed your intention. Regardless of what you have determined to do, ensure you interconnect your intention along with your calendar, and that you make the necessary modifications in your daily existence so that operating in your goal happens easily and step by step.

Key studies related to the aim-setting idea

Regardless of the responsibilities worried, the goal supply, the setting, or the time frame, it is the tenets of Locke's goal-putting principle that stay solid. Through the years, the clever concept has proved powerful for growing overall performance in a variety of settings. Here are five case research exploring numerous approaches of goal-setting and its results.

Five interesting Case studies on the intention-placing theory

Performance, if set as an intention, does not result in the same outcomes without the specific dreams of gaining information and skillsets. Researchers determined that inside the study room, recurrent persona developments can be found. Students are mainly divided into classes: those often focused on gaining understanding and abilities, and those frequently worried about their grades and performance inside the class. It became discovered that the first cohort performed higher on taught topics than the second one. Aim-setting, however, isn't best approximately the decided item of consciousness. There are, in reality, many determinants that shape the goal-setting and goal-crowning glory system. Any other have a look at highlights how the problem of the given undertaking additionally acts as a factor that hinders or improves overall performance. The best stage of effort passed off while the challenge turned into reasonably challenging, and the lowest level whilst the task was both too clean and too difficult. Moreover, the social measurement which accompanies aim-placing must be taken into consideration too, every time feasible. For example, a primary look at done at

Dominican University, list members recruited from the enterprise sector confirmed that:

• Informants who sent weekly reports to someone they had been near-completed extra than folks that had not written their dreams down. People who had written desires mentioned with unique ways they intended to fulfill the one's dreams had been as successful as those who just know their aim intentions to a pal;

• Informants who informed their pals in their goal had been able to acquire a great deal greater than people who most effective wrote down motion commitments and people who did in no way;

• Usual, folks that wrote down their dreams achieved a good deal greater than individuals who had now not.

In brief, this observation furnished empirical proof to help the declaration that duty, commitment, and writing down dreams have a primary influence on an individual's commitment toward achieving self-imposed desires. Intention-placing allows humans to stay focused and discover meaning in what topics in their lives. In reality, Boa et al. (2018) declare that desires additionally offer many people a sense of cause, as well as a power to stay as active as possible till their death; this proves in particular proper in the context of illness. The researchers conducted a comparative case look at ten healthcare experts in a hospice, to practice patient-centered aim-placing. The consequences indicated that rather than centering the approach on sufferers, members tended to articulate them on the subject of what they appeared to be essential (problem-solving, alleviating symptoms).

This has a look at by way of Boa et al. (2018) burdened the

importance of making the desires appropriate for the priorities of the individual so that it will maximize their effectivity and beautify humans' excellent lifestyles. Some other study performed via Carr (2018) sought to gauge the consequences of an already current intention-setting strategy in an elementary school serving many college students from a disadvantaged socio-monetary heritage. The conclusions talked about that intention-placing, when implemented continuously, had a tremendous impact on scholar self-efficacy, motivation, and studying scalability. This, car argues, took place whilst the dreams being set were particular, measurable, attainable, reasonable, well-timed, and difficult at the same time. Essentially, the smart anagram prevails in many conditions, backgrounds, and views.

In protection of mastering dreams

For plenty, the notion of performance as an accomplishment intertwines with aim-putting. Just valuing or wanting the "give up-product," and omitting what it takes to get there, is a not unusual mistake made by many. That's why research expresses how dreams about getting to know (instead of performance) have better success fees than dreams being met. The emphasis on learning has a trickle-down effect that sincerely benefits overall performance after all. The 5 research indexed below spotlight the difference between performance and understanding-based dreams:

• Putting a mastering aim in preference to a performance goal for responsibilities (for people with inadequate information) is most effective.
• In addition, people with a hard and fast getting to

know the goal for themselves perform better than individuals who had set a performance-associated goal on an assignment that concerned predicting stock-market fluctuations.

• Informants who had been assigned a tough studying intention reached extra market share on an interactive, pc-primarily based simulation of us cellular telephone enterprise than members who had been assigned an excessive-overall performance goal instead.

• Assigning a studying purpose stepped forward the self-regulatory affective and cognitive mechanisms, in evaluation with an intention emphasizing high-performance.

• Those who had a learning purpose have been less susceptible to anxiety. in addition, they accomplished better even after bad comments, in comparison to the ones only assigned a performance purpose.

To put in force studying-driven goals, it is essential to recognize how they fluctuate from overall performance goals. An overall performance purpose might be something like, "I need to come to be fluent in XY language," while gaining knowledge of aim would be:
"Using subsequent December, I want to learn the way to talk conversational XY language. So, I can be taking numerous classes every week, download the Duolingo app, and work at least an hour each day on memorizing a few phrases in my chosen language. I will additionally try and get in touch and meet folks who communicate this language to enhance my exposure to it."

Self-Efficacy and aim-setting

Self-efficacy is an idea coined and developed by way of Albert Bandura. It's far a cornerstone concept inside the discipline of tremendous psychology. It's tough to do justice to the titanic significance of these studies for our theories, our practice, and indeed for human welfare. This emphasizes how the assembling has had an effective effect on numerous areas ranging from phobias and depression to vocation preference and managerial organization.

Akhtar (2008) defines self-efficacy as:

"The notion we have in our very own competencies, in particular, our capacity to meet the demanding situations in advance folks and whole a task efficiently." The concept that "what we assume" affects "what we do" isn't new. The sector of high-quality psychology has explored the effect of our beliefs and worldviews on our fitness and the way we live our lives.

As Mahatma Gandhi famously said:

"A man is however a made of his mind. What he thinks, he will become." It is essential to distinguish a person's functionality from how they perceive their functionality. Regularly, there's also a discrepancy between the man or woman's preference and the capacity, which leads us to self-efficacy. Self-efficacy is a shape of self-assurance which embraces an 'I can cope with this attitude. It has an empowering effect on the moves of the person in query. Motivation, however, refers to a person's willingness to meet a given venture or intention.

Locke's purpose-placing idea objectives to encompass both, through formulating goals which no longer simplest are in keeping with someone's abilities but additionally gives the important resources so that the individual is stimulated by the aim even as stimulating his or her sense of self-efficacy. Even as it isn't precisely viable to instill a feeling of self-efficacy in someone who disbelieves their capability to perform well and push themselves beyond what they assume they can achieve, setting goals within a high-quality framework can make a giant difference.

The intention-setting Framework

What is the fine technique to undertake while implementing dreams? We have seen, little by little, how they should be dependent. But not the general framework in which they need to ground themselves for maximized effectiveness. Relying on how they are framed, desires could have precise consequences on a given person's studying manner and overall performance. They can be framed negatively, by emphasizing how a person should prevent losses and failure at all prices.

A negative goal-setting technique may want to look like this:

- My intention for subsequent yr is to stop myself from gaining any weight at all.

- All personnel ought to purpose to not lose greater than fifty out of the enterprise's two hundred and fifty modern-day clients.

- College students whose grades fall beneath the average will be penalized and given greater homework for the second semester.

This technique tends to be ineffective and degrading. Research indicates that punitive strategies often bring about anxiety, lower endurance, and overall performance, especially in contrast with goals that can be set with a high-quality outlook.

Frese et al. (1991) have advanced the concept of "mistakes

management," which intends to reframe mistakes during the technique as opportunities for the man or woman to research from. Framing mistakes and poor remarks with statements that include "errors are a herbal part of the gaining knowledge of system!" and "The greater errors you make, the more you learn!" and are beneficial. In short, discouraging worry-based environments encourage human beings to try once more, in place of giving up on their desires. This 'forgiving' factor also enables people to assume, and not understand, failure as part of the increased technique. Intention-setting isn't a directly forward course to achievement, and it's miles crucial to sense as you can actually "fail" and still a goal for their intention, maybe with introduced specificity.

As such, if framed undoubtedly, the appearance of the previously cited desire greater like this:

• This year, I can try to adopt a food plan so that it will allow me to lose weight. I aim to attain 80kg, and given that I currently weigh 85kg, my goal is to lose 5kg overall. the first eating regimen I try won't be the proper one, and I may additionally need to strive numerous before I find one which works, this is, one which permits me to lose weight and with a specific regime that I will stick to at the identical time. I'm able to reveal my development because the months skip and sign up for a gymnasium membership.

• The organization strongly values courting with its clients. We presently have two hundred and fifty and our intention for the imminent year is to preserve this range constantly. Your role, therefore, can be to make sure that customers are glad about our offerings through diversifying what we provide and the manner wherein we relate to them. The most effective manner to achieve this is with one-of-a-kind methods and strategies that we can reveal and investigate the results of.

• College students whose respective grade has expanded by way of factors may be rewarded with much less homework within the 2d semester. If the grade does no longer grow two factors, the individual efforts of every can be considered in the final selection of who has to be rewarded in the classroom. Such an approach provides clean guidelines and expectancies of a given purpose and also triggers advantageous emotions. Places of work, schools, and environments with positive purpose-putting get to revel in the power, creativity, and motivation of inspiring spaces. Human beings like an assignment, especially when it appears tough however possible.

How is aim-putting related to Behavioral change?

To date, we've got visible what goals do, but we've unnoticed to mention what takes place to people once they do no longer set dreams in their lives. Indecision, lack of focus, boredom, and no longer having something unique to strive for, can result in a sense that one is dwelling a dulled, much less significant model in their life. Signs and symptoms of despair, amongst different intellectual fitness struggles, regularly seem in those perceived unchanging spaces. That is because specially-written goals can offer people an experience of existential structure, purpose, and that means. As Locke argues, goals are "immediately regulators of behaviors and that they provide the self with an imaginative and prescient for the future and a clear direction to try toward a specific objective.

Greater so, goal-directed movement coupled with

reasoning capabilities is an essential element of what makes us human. Even the "non-human" global flourishes with purpose-setting parallels. This is not to mention that plants write down their goals in pencil. But allows have Locke explain how:

"The lowest level of goal-directed movement is physiologically controlled (plants). The next degree, the gift inside the decrease animals, entails conscious self-regulation thru sensory-perceptual mechanisms inclusive of pleasure and ache. People possess a better form of cognizance; the potential to reason. They have the power to conceptualize dreams and set long-variety purposes".

The human capability to mirror is a curse and a blessing.

It liberates us from the constraint of absolutely the determinism of factors however it additionally means that we are liable for the choices we make and whether or not they will make a contribution to our welfare. For instance, those who start an exercise and feeling the numerous fitness blessings frequently emerge as seeing fee in making additional way of life changes, along with a healthier recurring and weight-reduction plan. For this reason, if a purpose is perceived by the person as something that could contribute to their experience of well-being or that of the institution they're a part of, then it can additionally serve as a source of suggestion and esteem. This regularly ends in a ricochet effect on different behaviors linked to performance and efficacy.

Can aim-placing assist selection-Making?

Goal-placing and decision-making are the two voluntary

acts that can extensively transform a person's life. You possibly have heard the adage, "you can't keep a person who doesn't need to be saved." About helping others, it is not viable to accomplish that except they want the assist, and also feel sufficient motivation to take the perfect steps forward—no matter how tiring this will show. Setting dreams empower decision-making, and the alternative is authentic as well. It permits people to filter out what's huge, worth pursuing, and what isn't always.

Goal-putting vs. Expectancy theory

The expectancy idea was turned into evolved by Victor Vroom (1964) and looks at the mental approaches which underlie motivation and desire-making. Vroom outlines three fundamental factors which shape how humans determine to move about their lives and the steps needed to acquire a given result: expectancy, instrumentality, and valence. He argues that 'motivational force' may be calculated using multiplying expectancy with instrumentality and valence.

The actual components seem like this: Motivational force = Expectancy x Instrumentality x Valence. Installed a literary manner, Vroom's factor is that motivation emerges from someone's notion that an invested effort will allow them to obtain a certain favored performance, and that the way this overall performance is played out, will lead to the achievement of a selected goal. On the flip, the extent to which the man or woman perceived this very last purpose as desirable (valence) can even shape the degree of motivation for the man or woman to pursue a given aim.

In different phrases, self-assurance, evaluation of what is required, and the value perceived at the precise final results equal the strength a character might also experience toward a particular aim.

The expectancy concept provides an interesting measurement to Locke's goal-setting concept. Locke provides insight into which goals are applied in powerful approaches. Vroom, on the other hand, sheds light on how shallowness, character notion, and the value system of individuals come into play. The theories coined using Locke and Vroom do intersect in how they emphasize the importance of putting goals that might be tailor-made to subjective wishes and capacities.

To spark the vital 'motivational force' for any given task, there has to be momentum. With this momentum comes success, especially when failure is recommended as part of the learning process.

First-rate journal Articles for similarly reading

One of the super factors of purpose-setting is that it's far relevant in maximum domains of lifestyles. For more detail regarding the exclusive studies noted, you may discover the original assets inside the bibliography. It's far viable to locate information associated with aim-placing in nearly every situation. As an example, if you have specific goals to become a posted creator, there are masses of step-through-step publications supplied on the internet. There is additionally a wealth of literature documenting the advantages of goal-placing inside the context of workplaces, in particular for the reason that idea began as a try to enhance employee motivation in the workplace. In your comfort, we compiled a listing of currently posted magazine articles regarding aim-putting, carried out to a range of contexts. If you don't have get admission to instructional fabric and would like to consult on any of the subsequent articles, don't hesitate to drop us a message. Goal-putting inside the expert world

• Exercising Self-Efficacy as a Mediator among intention-placing and bodily hobby: developing the place of job as a setting for promoting bodily activity through Iwasaki et al. (2017)

• Fulfillment aim Orientation and its Implications for a place of business intention-putting packages, Supervisory/Subordinate Relationships and training with the aid of Rysavy (Dissertation, 2015)

• Experiential sporting activities on goal-placing, leadership/Followership, and administrative center Readiness.

Purpose-setting with college students/children:

• What are the impact of peer-monitored fitness gram checking out and private aim-setting on performance ratings with Hispanic middle faculty students?

• Effect of student smart intention-setting in a Low-appearing middle school.

• Does Participation in prepared sports activities have an impact on faculty performance, intellectual health, and/or lengthy-time period aim-putting in youngsters?

Intention-setting in Healthcare/ with patients

• Intention-putting in neurorehabilitation: improvement of an affected person-targeted tool with theoretical underpinnings.

• Rehabilitation intention-putting: theory, exercise, and proof.

• Comparing the shape of the patient assessment of persistent infection Care (PACIC) Survey from the patient's attitude.

A Nuanced attitude

Staying informed with how to improve oneself and others is important; however, an excessive amount of absorption with the subject might also overlook the very price of life. It's not sufficient to be busy, so are the ants. The query is, what are we busy about?

Henry David Thoreau

Thoreau's brilliant phrases invite us to mirror the broader photo. Do our goals push us to pursue in-reality topics? if so, then keep. If not, possibly it's time to pause. Even though aim-placing can indeed improve someone's experience of motive, self-belief, and autonomy, the habit of placing desires can lead us off course from our core values.

The modern trend, regrettably, is following this "busy route" wherein burnout is ingrained with modern company tradition (Petersen, 2019). It is, in particular, affecting the millennial generation. As Petersen's (ibid) article shows, it can be hard enough to carry out the most primary duties, such as answering emails, doing household chores, registering to vote, calling human beings on their birthdays, and many others.

Burnout, Petersen argues, is a part of the over-involvement of infant-boomer dad and mom in their kids' lives, in addition to the moving of modern-day exertions members of the family and social media technology. In lots of methods, this has blurred the line that used to exist among professional and private lifestyles that is largely nonexistent now.

Many people feel pressure to usually logo or marketplace who they're or what they do to be able to sense connected and compete for social repute, even when now not inside the expert global. For lots, this shows as the internalization of a feeling that one has to be working 'all the time.' This pushes people to compare their lives or 'effect' with others and make goals out of social assessment and insecurity, as opposed to goals focused on a proper preference to alternate something. A culture of self-care has arisen, as a possible response to burnout and overwhelming instances.

Self-care, however, is not a whole solution given that "The trouble with holistic, all-consuming burnout is that there's no technique to it. You couldn't optimize it to make it give up quicker. You may see it coming like a chilly and start taking the burnout-prevention version of Airborne. The first-rate way to deal with its far to first acknowledge it for what it's miles — no longer a passing ailment, but a chronic sickness — and to apprehend its roots and its parameters."

Peterson also recalls the words of the social psychologist Devon price, who, writing on the topic of homelessness, argued that: "Laziness, as a minimum in the way maximum folks usually conceive of it, genuinely does now not exist. If a person's conduct does no longer make experience to you, it's far due to the fact you're lacking a part of their context. It's that simple."

Hence, this comes as a cautionary message against excessive purpose-setting and the madness of steady self-improvement and improvement. Present-day society encourages us to sense that we are by no means "desirable sufficient." How do we stability the self-compassion that we are enough, with the preference to be better and set dreams? Possibly one solution is to avoid desires that do not align along with your core values, in addition to desires that do more damage than correct.

On the equal observe, researchers warned approximately what happens whilst 'desires go wild:' whilst dreams are too slender, too difficult, too severe, and enacted inside an unrealistic time-frame, they could result in disastrous outcomes. Those effects variety from unethical conduct to mental pitfalls connected with experiencing failure. For instance, if an organization's boss aims to increase income by way of over-operating and underpaying a group of workers, this is not a sustainable or moral intention for everyone concerned.

The authors, basing on control studies, additionally screen how intention-setting can also come at the fee of getting to know. Once more, how can we avoid feeding a competitive tradition, and as an alternative, promote cultures of growth and intrinsic motivation? To keep away from this, Steve Kerr from widespread electric powered advises managers to chorus from setting goals that are in all likelihood to grow their personnel' strain stages or comprise punishing failure; instead, Kerr wants to equip the body of workers with the vital gear to satisfy the difficult desires.

This approach, Ordonez et al. argue, will encourage managers to keep in mind whether the aim-putting way of life blessings the organization's outputs and the properly-being in their personnel.

Locke & Latham (2002) additionally warned approximately the capability pitfalls of mixing goals with monetary rewards in the place of business; this usually brings employers to set as a substitute clean dreams as opposed to more challenging ones rather. Before rushing to set non-public or enterprise desires, it is vital to take into account your motivation.

Four PowerPoint about purpose-setting idea (PPTs)

Hopefully, your thoughts are now humming approximately the methods you may percentage the cost of this content with others. Possibly this article should encourage your place of work, your classroom, or truly, your lazy and incredibly unmotivated pal. Reading lengthy articles on the net isn't always available to everybody for the reason that now not everybody has the time or hobby to make investments in the effort.

Our function at PositivePsychology.com is to translate and synthesize educational thoughts and studies into easily reachable writing. Our readers play a crucial position in phrases of speaking these assets and ideas to the wider public. PowerPoint may be mainly impactful tools that could transmit vital facts concisely. They're consequently the best manner of getting the message throughout to a wider audience.

Chapter Seven

Assessment, Goal-Setting, and Academic Motivation

Whilst nearly all students apprehend that getting to know is important, some are honestly now not inspired using lecturers or love of getting to know by myself. However maybe if that studying had been reframed as a way to obtain a certain intention, these students could be higher capable of seeing its fee. All of us have buddies who're in particular goal-orientated, whether they're "type A" individuals who love crossing things off their to-do lists or huge-picture those who dream about plans and work difficult to fulfill them.

For a few people, honestly having a certain give-up point to aim for is motivation enough. It makes experience, then, that a few students could be inspired through putting dreams—whether quick-time period, concrete desires, consisting of passing a check or reaching a sure grade, or lengthy-term, summary goals, consisting of stepping into university or pursuing a positive profession. This sort of intention-orientated motivation must not be stressed with the more extrinsic idea of profitable students for reaching positive benchmarks, with a right away venture and next reward every few weeks. Even as some of the principles are the same, that is a broader idea of goals that frames learning and achievement as a gateway to something else. So what forms of goals are commonplace in schooling? Dreams overlap; being a terrific student and entering into university each involves doing properly on checks, which may additionally be visible as a goal in itself. Dreams additionally alternate through the years and can be as unique as reading a book or as large as turning into a better pupil. Similarly, every scholar, regularly with guidance from the family, sets individual desires based on his or her particular scenario. To make the scope of this paper extra attainable, it focuses on the whole on forms of goals that might be ubiquitous in training and function "gateways" of a type: doing well on tests and attending postsecondary schooling. Tests in their diverse forms, consisting of standardized checks, diagnostic checks, teacher-designed classroom exams, and different types, are encountered by each scholar. And the intention of attending postsecondary education is commonly upheld as the "mild at the top of the tunnel" of ok-12 education.

This book examines various applications that use test performance or postsecondary attendance as motivational desires and the effects of these goals on students. How do guidelines surrounding assessments and university readiness affect engagement? How does the destiny possibility of higher training affect motivation? Before thinking about one's questions, it's miles beneficial to check the concept and studies behind the usage of goal-setting as a motivator. Then we can turn our interest extra particularly to assessments and postsecondary schooling as motivational dreams.

Purpose-setting through the Lens of Motivational idea

The scale of motivation and the theories or mindsets summarized can shed mild on the position of intention-putting in scholar motivation. Goal-putting and the 4 dimensions of motivation; each of the four major dimensions of motivation, competence, control/autonomy, price/interest, and relatedness can play a vital position in goal-placing. To feel able, students want to look at their goals as sensible and doable, which can also require altering the goals or altering college students' perceptions of their abilities. To experience control, college students need to be capable of seeing a clear direction to achieving the aim, through a manner they can control rather than through luck or hazard. Manage is also maximized when college students set goals themselves, or at the least agree with and internalize goals set for them through someone else. Student aid for the aim can even foster interest and fee. finally, relatedness may be stricken by what students understand is predicted of them with the aid of society, how they will be judged through human beings of social importance, or what dreams different participants in their very own social group or every other suited social institution are pursuing. Motivational theories of the several theoretical perspectives most usually utilized in motivation studies, achievement purpose theory is, as the name indicates, most directly relevant to purpose-putting. "Success goal idea posits that scholars' educational motivation may be understood as tries to achieve desires," writes Seifert (2004). Intention theorists normally damage down schooling dreams into two organizations: "mastery" (or "getting to know") dreams and "performance" desires. Mastery dreams involve demonstrating accelerated expertise, skills, and content material expertise. Overall performance goals, on the other hand, involve achieving a pre-described overall performance degree or outperforming others. Researchers have continually found that scholars who have a mastery-purpose mindset exhibit deeper cognitive strategies, strategize more effectively, and are extra adaptable to demanding situations. Performance-orientated college students display greater destructive reactions to failure, see much less of a link among effort and final results, and cognizance greater on their performance relative to the overall performance of others. For that reason, mastery dreams are extra powerful and appropriate from a mental perspective. The same scholar may have specific mindsets and desires in different contexts, however; he or she may have a mastery orientation in one state of affairs and a performance. Therefore, college students' mindsets can be modified; setting powerful desires may be one way to perform this. What does research endorse approximately goal setting? Findings from research approximately how desires are set and what varieties of goals are effective motivators have implications for packages that use desires as motivators. Who sets the aim? An aim is a specific concept that one forms consciously, as opposed to motives or desires, which extra frequently arise on a subconscious level.

This makes goal-placing an interesting hybrid of the inner/external motivator dichotomy mentioned inside the first two papers of this series. It may almost be stated that an intention is an extrinsic manifestation of intrinsic motivation. Curiously, students missing intrinsic educational motivation may be incapable of setting their desires however if they're helped to set dreams, they may be able to set up motivation and improve their fulfillment. any other way to consider this is as a spectrum of externalization alongside which desires ought to fall as both in part externalized, if set through oneself, or completely externalized if set arbitrarily via a person else.

This is remarkable because of the high correlation between intrinsic motivation and fulfillment, and the poor results sometimes correlated with extrinsic motivation. Indeed, Rigby refers to this in his categorization of "interjected law," which's described as being inspired by internal stress pushed using external needs in other phrases, pressuring yourself to do something due to the fact you watched you "must" or are anticipated to. Even though students who show this kind of motivation typically work very difficult, it's also correlated with dropping out of faculty, tension, and maladaptive techniques for dealing with. In precise, goals are intentionally mounted, allowing us a first-rate amount of management over what precisely they are. We must be careful about who units desire for college kids if they're advocated by using an outside celebration, then they must at the least be based on students' inner, intrinsic motivation. This is vital due to the fact research has also proven that the actual dreams themselves can affect pupil success degrees. Placing the "proper" goal Researchers at the University of Michigan examined the varieties of future identities (in other words, lengthy-term desires) that students predicted for themselves. They determined that almost 90% of eighth-graders in three Detroit middle colleges, a lot of whom had been low-earnings and minority students expected to wait for college, however approximately half of these equal students did no longer select the classes or exert the instructional attempt that could earn them college admission. Even though the students had set the admirable purpose of attaining higher training, it did no longer have an impact on their educational behavior. What should explain this gap between goal and action? The researchers hired identity-primarily based motivation idea, which holds that human beings act in approaches they sense correspond to their hooked-up identification and that those identities are sensitive to contextual cues. They found that elements are wished so as for destiny-related dreams to improve instructional overall performance: the destiny identification college students are striving for has to be education-structured, and the identification ought to be applicable while students are making educational alternatives.

In a single experiment, researchers determined that even as maximum children desired to wait for college, kids who held destiny expert dreams that had been education-dependent spent extra time on their homework and had a better GPA at the give up of the have a look at. To establish causality, the equal researchers completed every other test wherein they showed one organization of children a graph of destiny profits linked to educational degree and any other group a graph of median lifetime profits in comparison with the income of sports and music stars. eight times as many children from the primary group (who have been considering training structured dreams) as from the second (who were thinking about non-education-dependent desires) finished an additional-credit homework challenge that night, and extra reported that they intended to spend time beyond regulation on studying and homework. Consequently, the sort of intention and the context wherein it's set can determine how a good deal impacts educational motivation and attempt. in addition, research by way of Schultheiss has proven that "while specific desires and implicit motives are congruent, then individuals are greater stimulated and perform better". Finally, one of the maximum vital guidelines for setting dreams is that the aim needs to be of appropriate trouble. Atkinson (1964) located that goals which can be too hard are truly demotivating. Human beings exert the maximum effort closer to a venture that is moderately difficult and the least amount of effort towards a goal that is quite easy or pretty tough. This can appear abstract however makes feel within the context of the four motivational dimensions: if the aim is set too excessive, it's going to undermine competence and control, but if the purpose is just too smooth it's going to have no fee. Those findings were reiterated through Locke and Latham (1990), among others. In popular, motivational concepts and studies support aim-setting as a powerful way of growing student motivation, if the dreams are installed properly. Now, allows flipping our attention to how the exercise of intention-placing is being utilized in schools and how that practice is probably advanced to have a greater sizable nice impact on motivation. Assessments, intention putting, and educational Motivation tests are a hotly debated topic due to the fact their outcomes are increasingly more getting used to judging students, instructors, and faculties.

The No baby Left at the back of the Act mandated that states and districts assess scholar success in math and studying every twelve months and set outcomes for colleges that didn't carry enough percent of college students to a designated degree of scalability. A few teachers also are starting to see their pay connected to students' performance on tests. College students themselves are judged based on check ratings; in a few cases, an end-of-direction assessment can be the maximum vital component in a pupil's grade, and in twenty-five States, College students aren't accredited to graduate from high school without passing an exit exam. it's miles consequently in everybody's first-rate interest that five middle on training coverage The George Washington University Graduate school of education and Human improvement 2012 students are encouraged to excel on various kinds of tests, making it a goal around which the work of instructors, administrators, and college students revolves. No longer exceedingly, to a few college students, it appears that evidently, the most effective purpose of learning is to excel on exams. The conventional awareness has been that the way to spur extra effort is through intimidation by way of the danger of dire effects for low take a look at ratings. So, the intention of succeeding on assessments, whether for graduation, responsibility, or grades, is getting used to increase students' instructional motivation. variations in motivation relying on kind of tests as defined in advance, there is a difference between extrinsic and intrinsic motivation and therefore among extrinsic and intrinsic dreams. So which sort are assessments? Few tests are fun to take and intrinsically motivating. a few checks offer concrete extrinsic dreams to college students, via grade promotion, graduation from excessive faculty, or university admission. Other exams offer extrinsic goals to teachers and directors due to the fact they may be used for school responsibility purposes; the stress of these dreams may be handed on to students. One-of-a-kind types of assessments are motivating to one-of-a-kind extents, relying largely on what is at stake—commencement, grade promotion, and class grades matter maximum to students. The effects of checks, and therefore motivation for college students to excel on them, can vary throughout a continuum. Study room assessments designed and administered with the aid of instructors can be even greater motivating to college students than the excessive-stakes standardized exams administered by way of the nation if the lecture room tests have an immediate impact on students' grades. Then again, a few lecture room checks are used for diagnostic purposes and may not affect students' grades in any respect. A few country-mandated standardized checks are used to determine grade promotion and graduation fame and consequently count greatly to students, whilst different external exams like NAEP have honestly no consequences for character college students. So there are excessive-stakes and low-stakes assessments, and external and internal exams, comprising a continuum of motivation. The same scholar might be differently stimulated by each of those styles of assessment. tests which are used to offer college students with facts approximately wherein they stand academically, as opposed to determine rewards or sanctions or make an overall judgment approximately pupil ability, maybe motivating by increasing emotions of competence and manage.

The maximum motivational purpose isn't always too difficult but also no longer too easy, and aligns with college students' private pastimes and desires. If an evaluation meets these criteria for a sure student, then it'll probably be a powerful educational motivator for that student. Much has been written approximately the impact of high-stakes checks on curriculum, instruction, and scholar fulfillment. Although few of these studies have looked especially at the impact of excessive-stakes assessments on student motivation, some findings from research on excessive-stakes assessments apply to our purpose right here. Pupil success on country responsibility exams has progressed in most states since 2002. Those state checks have excessive-stakes for schools, instructors, and directors and comparatively high stakes for students, in particular when the consequences are also factored into selections about commencement, promoting, or direction grades. even as the research suggests that test scores have stepped forward for the reason that adoption of high-stakes checking out, one should be careful about concluding approximately the effectiveness of these testing regulations, and one should be in particular careful about inferring that test rankings have multiplied due to the fact students are extra stimulated. The primacy of check results in-country and federal accountability structures have modified academic practices. While some of these adjustments, which include imparting more practice to low-achieving students, could typically be considered fantastic, many others have distorted education in methods that would undermine motivation. for example, in response to stress to elevate test rankings, many schools, administrators, and teachers are devoting more instructional time to subjects and content which are probable to be tested and much less time to crucial but untested know-how and abilities. This will result in a discount or elimination of content that is thrilling and precious to students and a decrease in motivation. some other final results of excessive-stakes checking out is an excessive emphasis on check guidance practices that are designed to elevate test rankings without always selling broader expertise of the topics being tested. For examples, instructors might also respond to check based accountability via the usage of study room physical games based on a particular take a look at the layout, drilling students with exercise examples just like those used on important exams, or converting the sequence of topics to accommodate the trying out agenda. Whether or not these practices are properly relied upon on the best of the check. If the take a look at is a complicated, overall performance-primarily based evaluation, then making ready for it can lead to a more emphasis on trouble-fixing within the study room, which may be useful and motivating, however, if the take a look at is the more common kind of multiple-preference check, then extensive practice on this checking out format may be counterproductive from a learning and motivational perspective. Studies at the results of high-stakes testing on college students' motivation are particularly combined.

 On one hand, high-stakes checking out can breed anxiety and different emotions that can undermine pupil motivation. A survey of two hundred and thirty-six teachers in sixteen colleges and five districts of North Carolina, performed after the nation carried out a high-stakes accountability software, 28% of teachers answered that their college students were extra prepared for getting to know because of the program. but sixty one% said that their college students felt extra anxiety, 24% indicated middle on schooling coverage. The George Washington University Graduate school of education and Human development 2012 their college students had been much less assured, and nearly 49% said this system "had a terrible impact on students' love of getting to know". Then again, a few college students can be inspired by the high stakes and risk of effects. Researchers on the college of Chicago surveyed 102 low-performing center school college students in Chicago earlier than the management of

Iowa take a look at of basic abilities, which underneath a brand new coverage might be used alongside instructor exams of students and scholar statistics to determine whether or not the scholars should flow on to the next grade. The general public of students seemed to enjoy a growth in motivation under the brand new coverage, reporting elevated interest in their classwork, elevated attempt, and extra time spent out of doors of the school on magnificence work. however, about one 1/3 of the students still reported especially low stages of instructional attempt, especially the students who had been the furthest at the back of their friends in terms of educational skill stage. Likewise, a 2006 CEP look at excessive faculty go out exams determined that some college students replied to these exams by using working more difficult in school, while others had been resentful and dubious approximately their capacity to be successful. Evaluation and the four dimensions of motivation; a look back to the 4 dimensions of motivation; competence, autonomy/manipulate, interest/fee, and relatedness can assist explain why using exams as an aim, specifically excessive-stakes assessments, will have a terrible effect on motivation for a few students. most exams, as they're currently implemented, strongly encourage a performance purpose as opposed to a mastery-purpose mindset, and so it's miles no marvel that a few college students reply with the aid of feeling traumatic or pissed off, fearing failure, and usually becoming unmotivated. If they take a look at measures overall performance level rather than increase, and if college students feel that accomplishing at the prescribed stage is out of doors in their talents, competence could be undermined. research has additionally consistently shown that, whilst presented to genuinely explore new fabric or try to recognize it for the cause of explaining it to a person else, students keep greater hobby and more understanding of the material over the longer term than if they are advised really to memorize it for a take a look at.

Likewise, maximum excessive-stakes checks are administered once in a while, requiring months of practice; if college students don't apprehend what steps they could take to be successful on the examination, or have opportunities to put together for it, they experience hopelessness, and their manipulate and autonomy are undermined. If the consequences tied to the exam aren't crucial to college students, there may be no interest or value. And if positive meaning or effects is tied to low rankings on the examination, college students who fail or fear failure on the exam ought to show off a "profound and long-lasting loss of self-assurance". Even the finding that nations wherein greater students are forced to repeat grades have overall decrease fulfillment on the PISA math and technology checks makes sense if we accept social relatedness as a motivational element. Students who fail to move on to the following grade with their peers can also lose feelings of relatedness and thereby suffer a decline in motivation. Therefore, even as high-stakes tests may also offer motivation for a few high achievers, they appear to have a disproportionately poor effect on students who're already at threat of losing motivation. Differences between students; an extra factor to take into account is which college students are maximumly stricken by having assessments as a purpose. For college students who bypass tests without difficulty or need a stopping point for which to goal, having checks as an aim may be an academic motivator. At the equal time, if excessive achievers assume the examination is just too smooth, it can cause them to experience cynical or green with envy in the direction of the college. However, for students who conflict academically, that equal exam may additionally appear like an insurmountable obstacle. One pupil said about the Washington kingdom examination, "For a while, the WASL made me experience dumb". Nichols and Berliner (2008) note that for students who warfare academically, high-stakes checking out can decrease self-worth and educational motivation; for college kids who see assessments as clean, "a faculty tradition shaped around high-stakes checking out is uninteresting and unconnected". Additionally, the intention of checks will form pupil behavior otherwise. When college students determine to manipulate the potential threat of punishment using studying very difficult and learning plenty, then the behavior management device works as favored, no degree of intimidation will change their view of themselves. No statewide assessment and no hazard of an 'F' on their report card will carry them to trust in themselves as freshmen, they've stopped being concerned". So there can be a few negative motivational results related to assessment desires for some students. it's far hard to use tests as dreams due to the fact, as mentioned earlier, to be powerful a purpose has to be tailored to the man or woman. If the aim is simply too hard or too smooth, it isn't motivating, however, in some types of exams, all students take the equal check, irrespective of their skill stage.

If a purpose is imposed upon a student rather than grounded in something the pupil autonomously cares about, it's going to no longer be motivational. based totally on goal theory, exams may additionally boom motivation if they coincide with desires a scholar already holds, however, whilst all college students are required to take the identical common checks, it is going to be motivational for just a few and can undermine the incentive of others.

Kinds of exams with the capability to encourage

This dialogue of exams and motivation isn't always supposed to signify that checks themselves are inherently terrible. They provide beneficial records to students, instructors, and parents approximately which college students want help and whether or not college students are studying the understanding and abilities they're expected to research. If exams are for use as a motivational purpose, then the key is to remember what kinds of assessments ought to offer that sort of information and at the identical time more intently align with the intention-putting principle to increase college students' educational motivation.

Of path, there may be no perfect assessment, and assessments fluctuate primarily based on their cause, content material, and type, so identical recommendations do not observe to all exams. However motivational theory is supported by way of tests with the subsequent characteristics:

• Exams that reward effort, innovative strategy, and gains in expertise or mastery instead of the attainment of a specific success benchmark are more likely to promote growth and mastery aim thoughts-set. While adults reward students' intelligence after a student plays nicely, they ship a fixed mindset message: you're sensible and that's what I fee in you. Whilst adults praise effort (or techniques), but, they send an increase thoughts-set message: you could build your abilities through effort.

• Checks that include quick-term, without difficulty practicable dreams after which steadily boom in difficulty can build competence and self-assurance, in addition to a feeling of manage within students. Additionally, those varieties of assessment can permit students to look at a clear direction to achievement and understand the hyperlink between effort and fulfillment.

• Checks that permit college students to recognize what they will be tested on beforehand of time can provide them a clear understanding of what's predicted of them. In truth, some scholars endorse permitting college students to be a part of this technique using inquiring for their input on which testing standards and check to apply and what styles of effects must be predicted. Even as this could not be possible for larger-scale exams, regarding college students in a discussion about the evaluation and its reason can be helpful.

• Any other promising approach is to allow students to first grasp ideas in pursuit of a non-formal purpose and then later apply their understanding to a graded assessment, instead of administering a one-time examination, research has again and again determined that children who had been asked to master new cloth with an end intention of a quiz or take a look at ended up preserving less of the fabric than did students who have been given the material and told to grasp it so that they might answer a few widespread questions or give an explanation for it to others. Being allowed to first exhibit their understanding through opportunity way may increase students' self-belief and feelings of competence in training for greater formal tests.

• Although they have got drawbacks, overall performance goals are essential to growing social fulfillment and adaptive coping behaviors; however, if checks are administered often instead of as soon as in step with semester or year, they could offer more overall performance remarks so that scholars can better recognize in which they're acting relative to expectations. Low-stakes assessments that allow college students a threat to fail without dire consequences can be greater supportive of studying than tests with performance desires. "Performance comments are unlikely to undermine studying dreams when it's miles seen as an evaluation of present ability degree. it's miles most effective when problems and mistakes are considered as judgments of extensive, underlying competence or capability . . . that ten centers on training policy The George Washington College Graduate Faculty of training and Human development 2012 people are probably to be deflected from mastering pursuits".

In brief, exams aren't inherently motivating or not motivating; rather, the form of checks and the way they're provided should be cautiously taken into consideration. Postsecondary training, aim to set, and educational Motivation one of the hugest goals in k-12 schooling is to prepare college students to preserve their schooling beyond high school, whether this means attending a four-year college, community university, or technical institution. President Obama (2009) has stated that through the year 2020, he wishes the US to "have the very best proportion of college graduates inside the world," and the Lumina basis is running to make certain that through 2025, 60% of American citizens keep a fantastic postsecondary credential. reaching some form of postsecondary education has essentially grown to be a country-wide goal, set by using society on behalf of all college students so that students end their education prepared to be productive members of society. However, is that this a good manner to motivate college students? The possibility of college as a motivator for college students to answer this query, we want to think about how the 4 dimensions of motivation are probably applied to make post-secondary schooling a powerful motivational purpose:

• Competence: college students want to sense organized to prevail at every step that is required to enter post-secondary training. They need to experience able to preserve precise grades, pass a go out exam if required take and rating nicely on university front checks just like the SAT or ACT, and sense organized to succeed in college. In different words, students want to sense academically and for my part qualified.

• Manage/autonomy: college students want to look for a clean pathway to postsecondary training. This may appear obvious to some, but regrettably, many college students don't develop up in a context wherein these pathways are nicely hooked up. To a well-known degree, many college students, in reality, don't recognize what kind of grades are required or predicted, which excessive faculty courses to take, how extracurricular and leadership reports can make their software extra competitive, or a way to frame their studies in a way that could be beneficial for postsecondary admissions. On a greater primary level, a few college students lack even rudimentary expertise in the way the postsecondary method works, which may be overwhelming. if you are the primary in your family or neighborhood to go to university, scholarships, monetary useful resource bureaucracy, and faculty packages can appear daunting, leading college students to sense that the procedure is past their manipulate. For others, there can be a concept that best "rich children" or "clever kids" visit college, leading them to feel that it's worthless to attempt. Further, a few students assume their households don't have the economic manner to pay for school, and without an understanding of scholarships or useful resources, they bargain the option of post-secondary schooling.

• Hobby/cost: Having a discern or teacher tell them that higher training is critical does no longer make students adopt the goal as their own, and therefore received be motivating; students need to understand the price of post-secondary schooling. For some, it's a hassle to get entry to statistics: students might not understand approximately the lengthy-time period effects (income, exceptional of life, and many others.) related to higher schooling, or won't recognize that a postsecondary degree would possibly now be a demand for the task they need. a few college students might imagine they'll be successful in a process that doesn't require additional schooling and therefore do not formulate an alternate plan.

• Relatedness: Postsecondary education has to be supplied in the right social context, if students see their friends invested in reaching a postsecondary diploma, they're much more likely to be as nice, and vice versa. Similarly, if college students experience that happening to higher education is anticipated of them using society or reputable adults that can act as a motivational cue, instead of students wondering that no person expects them to be the "college type".

For postsecondary schooling to be a purpose that honestly spurs scholar motivation, schools, districts, households, and teachers want to establish regulations and packages that make certain college students feel prepared, realize the steps they need to take, see the value in continuing schooling, and a sense that it's socially advocated. Examples of programs to encourage postsecondary as an intention Now let's take a look at a pattern of the packages and guidelines presented in the region to encourage college students to move on to post-secondary training and the extent to which those programs are engaging in that reason. While most of these packages have not passed through formal studies research, they have produced some records and anecdotal proof to indicate their lengthy-time period impacts. The subsequent instance illustrates what took place whilst an application to start with tried to use college as a goal without providing essential supports to increase motivation.

• Say sure about the training program. In a single interesting example, philanthropist George Weiss has made it a personal mission to provide scholarships to fortunate cohorts of college students. The project first began in Philadelphia's Belmont elementary school in 1987, when Weiss promised the participants of the sixth-grade magnificence that he would pay for their university schooling if they have been admitted. Given that time, he has spent $33 million creating comparable packages thru his Say yes to education application in NY, Connecticut, and Massachusetts. But of those first one hundred and twelve college students from Philadelphia, best 20 finished a bachelor's diploma—and twenty ended up in jail. Sixty-two graduated from high faculty, earned their GED, and thirteen finished exchange faculty. Ten earned associates' ranges. Weiss now feels that he began while the kids were too antique and didn't have enough time to exchange their mindsets or behaviors; his newer programs also provide the trainer and parent training. Of a 1990 elegance of seventy-eight third graders, eighteen entered university, and eight graduated from college four years later. Unluckily, when truly applied, applications to encourage postsecondary attendance have produced mixed consequences.

This may be because so many other factors play into students' motivation and capability to maintain university as a reasonable purpose; any of the 4 dimensions of motivation could be undermined, even supposing college students see a clean way of financing postsecondary training. Ann Coles, former senior vice chairman of the education assets Institute, cited that it miles tough to distinguish whether or not the far-off prospect of an unfastened college schooling is surely motivating or whether the actual motivating elements are "the help offerings, the caring, the mentoring" that accompany the extra complete postsecondary motivational packages. Numerous other packages no longer handiest use college as a motivational goal but additionally provide vital help:

• The Kalamazoo Promise. In Kalamazoo, Michigan, the Kalamazoo Promise program promised students who graduated from a district high college and have been admitted to Community University, alternate faculty, or a public country college that the entire fee of their lessons could be paid for through a group of nameless donors.

Consistent with the sentiment noted using Ann Coles, this application used a complete, community-based totally layout, although the Promise did now not specify what steps the faculty district ought to take. The program turned into to start with meant to spur local financial development however ended up leading to whole-school reform a perfect instance of how a goal can function as a motivator and agent of alternate if enacted well. The key came whilst district management applied a complete bundle of reforms from pre-k via twelfth grade. these protected instituting regular preschool, adding half-hour of daily writing to 3rd grade English coaching, transferring sixth grades to the middle faculty building so students had been exposed to difficulty-unique teachers, and sending all incoming sixth graders an ebook to study every ten days over the summer season holiday. different reforms spurred by way of this system covered growing the range of AP topics offered in high faculty from 8 to twelve, encouraging more college students to take AP classes with the aid of giving extra emphasis to grades from these classes in GPA calculations and making a host of other changes that had been now not especially dramatic or costly. In different words, the Promise led to a reassessment of curriculum, structures, and programs, all based totally on one aim. school climates also modified; in a survey of all three excessive faculties inside the district and interviews with forty-two students, twelve principals, nine counselors, and twenty teachers, researchers found that teachers drove college students tougher academically, which expanded expectations in addition to educational guide. Students noticed "their teachers the use of the incentive of the Promise to encourage modifications in college performance [and] conduct"; students said that they had been "exerting impact on peers to 'stay at the proper song' and college students requested for assist extra often and self-regulated their conduct greater. Of most of the educators surveyed, forty% suggested a normal wonderful trade-in faculty climate, and 20% said a sturdy nice alternate. The network turned into also very enthusiastic: dad and mom said they were greater focused on their children's lecturers and enforced more subjects at home, and community companies started out supplying tutoring and mentoring programs. According to district leaders, the Promise worked due to regular feedback, as faculties talked with mother and father, students, and the network and made modifications to this system. Every person felt as though they'd a stake in its success. This fostered massive amounts of interest, relatedness, and management, and consequently a brilliant diploma of motivation. Because the major at one excessive school stated, "It's not simply the money. It's the academia. It's the social capabilities.

Proof shows that about 84% of eligible college students are the use of the scholarship, and others are attending out-of-kingdom or personal universities. Approximately - thirds of scholarship recipients attended a four-year public Michigan college and extra than 1,500 college students have used the scholarship to this point. Colleges have visible a 71% increase in AP route enrollment and consistent increases in student achievement on country checks. The one's accomplishments blended with big reforms to the entire ok-12 system and changes in faculty climate and network mindset advise this approach is a first-rate way to enforce the aim of postsecondary schooling as a motivator.

• Houston. in the Houston unbiased faculty District, 35% to 50% of college students dropped out before graduation, and many who graduated did now not go on to university. In 2008, the district used a $1.1 million grant from the invoice and Melinda Gates basis, in partnership with Houston community college, to revamp its faculties' college guidance packages. The district ensured that each high faculty had a specialized college counselor (that could assist to foster students' emotions of control over the technique). The superintendent also mandated that each faculty create a "university sure way of life" (which addressed the price and relatedness dimensions of motivation). District leaders encouraged extra college students to take university-stage publications (building competence), and almost all high colleges hooked up "university centers" to assist students to navigate applications and financial useful resource. those modifications not best helped college students practically (filling out applications, applying for economic resource, getting advice from counselors) but also signaled to college students that they're expected to visit college, that it's a realistic goal for all of them, and that there's community help for that purpose.

• Assignment GRAD. In early 2000, below the management of then-Superintendent Beverly hall, the Atlanta Public schools required its faculties to take part in challenge GRAD, which aimed to higher prepare students for university. challenge GRAD worked to improve math and reading competencies (fostering competence); partnered with groups in colleges to offer to tutor (additionally growing competence), and helped provide university counseling and help with admissions and financial useful resource forms (giving students a few control). The challenge additionally ran trips to college campuses (interest/cost), mounted a summertime enrichment program (competence), and presented $4,000 in scholarship money to students who were able to meet numerous requirements (manage).consequences have been promising to this point. At Booker T. Washington high faculty, the 4-12 months commencement fee expanded dramatically from 62% in 2003 to nearly 87% in 2007. The previous government director of assignment GRAD in Atlanta also noted that this system helped to grow parents' expectations of their youngsters and helped higher schooling establishments see the Atlanta public colleges as a supply of high college graduates who can achieve college. In different words, society expects those college students to be triumphant, motivating them through growing relatedness. Assignment GRAD also runs comparable partnerships with colleges in extra than ten locations around the US, supporting heaps of low-earnings students put together for postsecondary training. College students who bypass thru the program whole college at almost twice the charge of college students from similar socioeconomic backgrounds.

College-sure basis in Baltimore. The Baltimore faculty district has attempted to foster a college-going culture that isn't always just about counseling and filling out programs—even though that technical guide is vital for college students to experience in control but is also augmented by way of many levels of history assist. "It's approximately putting the fire of their bellies, the concept of their heads," stated Mavis Jackson, a college counselor in Baltimore. Body of workers and schools at each level are tasked with creating surroundings that demystify the idea of postsecondary education for students who aren't otherwise uncovered to it. this is executed through matters as easy because the fundamental making day by day bulletins, instructors attempting to observe how lessons will follow to university work, the school posting recognition letters in hallways so students see what their friends are accomplishing, or teachers wearing t-shirts or redecorating lecture rooms with trademarks in their alma maters so that scholars have a concrete example and role version of a university graduate. Via moves like these, students start to view postsecondary schooling as something that's expected of them, because of the cease intention in the direction of which the complete college is running. Baltimore faculties decided to position up the money to carry the CollegeBound basis into twenty-eight of its thirty-four everyday public excessive colleges. The muse affords to assist like university festivals, visitation journeys, advising and counseling, charge waivers for programs and front tests, and scholarships and presents.

As Baltimore schools CEO Andres Alonso explained, "we're an urban school machine placing a full-size quantity of sources into preventing violence in faculties, building network helps, building after-school programs, constructing supports to help our youngsters stay in school. Using the definition nearly overwhelms our potential to do certain different things. So the program is filling an essential area of interest in those colleges", and indeed, the program is producing outcomes. The number of college students completing college programs almost doubled between 2002 and 2009. Of the excessive faculty seniors who participated within the application in the 2007-08 faculty twelve months, 79% have been well-known to two- or four-year schools, an increase from 47% in 2005. The variety of students taking the SAT examination within the district increased by using 70% over ten years, compared with an increase of 30% nationally. Of the hundred and eighty college students who went via three years of this system and had been tracked as they went on to university, 90% returned for their sophomore year of university, while the country-wide average was only 70%. Anecdotally, a few students credited the program's relentless barrage of data and assist with assisting them to do not forget university as a goal and making the instructional modifications necessary to be an aggressive applicant. In precise, research has proven that the maximum a hit packages to inspire college-going is carried out in a way that fosters the four essential dimensions of motivation. While packages that virtually endorsed children to wait at university had some confined achievement, applications that targeted enhancing attendance, grades, counseling, and ratings on admissions tests and on maintaining the goal of college foremost in students' minds had more effective outcomes. What can we do better? The latest research shows that there are a few specific areas wherein schools can do a higher activity of assisting students to include postsecondary education as a motivational purpose.

Many college students do now not experience they are academically prepared for university. In the latest surveys, carried out by the College Board and advanced respectively, most effective 1/2 of recent high college graduates stated that they had been properly organized for university and work, and over 60% said that their high college did an underneath truthful process of preparing them for post-secondary training. Preserving their high school educations in such low regard undermines emotions of competence and motivation and makes students experience that postsecondary education isn't always an affordable aim for them.

College counseling is regularly weak, if no longer completely absent, in the schools that need it maximum. In step with the director of public policy and studies for the countrywide association for college Admission Counseling, even in faculties with steerage counselors, college advising often takes a back seat to different duties of counselors and directors, including dropout prevention and sophistication scheduling. That is exacerbated by using the fact that the common high college counselor has a caseload of near three hundred college students. Popular counselors additionally often receive little professional education on how to help college students prepare for postsecondary schooling.

 A few colleges and universities recruit college students who have little or no hazard of being admitted. College students who take the preliminary SAT exam (PSAT) have the choice of providing their cope with to acquire informational mailings from faculties. Regrettably, a few college students get hold of these mailings and think they must practice, spend time and money at the software, and are rejected whilst colleges did now not intend to confess most of them inside the first area. Of direction, students ought to understand which faculties are practical for them to use to, but figuring out that may be a complicated and overwhelming method; for example, the director of college counseling at a San Francisco high school known as mailings from Harvard "misleading." there may be no evidence to suggest that schools are doing this on purpose, but huge software swimming pools improve scores of college selectiveness, and alertness fees convey money into the school. For college students who had their hopes raised after which dashed, this undermines emotions of competency and hobby and humiliates, frustrates, and disappoints, underscoring the want for higher university counseling and advising. As the studies and applications described above advocate, dreams in popular can assist motivate students to work harder if sure conditions are a gift. Findings from studies and practice have also addressed the motivational cost of the two particular dreams analyzed in this paper passing checks and attending post-secondary training. Desires in widespread, regardless of the specific intention, it's far much more likely to be motivating if it has the subsequent characteristics:

• The aim is practical and viable, but difficult. The aim is acceptable and education established.

• The aim is recommended, or as a minimum embraced, by way of the pupil, and the pupil can see a clean course for reaching it. It also allows if the goal is supported by using human beings essential to the pupil.

• Goals may be tailor-made to apprehend that distinctive college students may additionally need one-of-a-kind types of goals, based on their mindsets and motivational patterns.

• Mastery-based dreams, which contain demonstrating multiplied information, abilities, and content material know-how, are leading to performance-primarily based goals, which contain reaching a pre-defined stage of overall performance or outperforming others. Via the identical token, goals can undermine motivation if they may be too difficult, or if college students feel a goal has been imposed on them or that failing to satisfy it'd have dire outcomes. Exams as motivators' intention concept, the four dimensions of motivation, and the research summarized above recommend several classes about assessments as motivators:

• Assessments are not inherently motivating; rather, their motivating power varies relying on the stakes connected to them, how they're offered, and how a man or woman student reacts to them. When tests are used as motivational gear, it's vital to recall which varieties of tests can offer beneficial statistics approximately students' gaining knowledge of and are aligned most carefully with the important thing dimensions of motivation.

• For an evaluation to be motivating, educators want to make clear to college students what they want to learn to do nicely on the evaluation. The motivational principle additionally indicates that checks that praise creativity, effort, growth, and strategizing and that permit college students to use failure as a mastering tool can have a stronger effect on motivation than checks that emphasize competition or overall performance levels. more frequent tests that start with easier goals and steadily boom in trouble can build students' competence and feel of manage, as can possibilities for students to demonstrate their understanding with performance responsibilities or low-stakes checks earlier than taking an assessment that counts. Ultimately, supporting college students to recognize what's expected of them on the evaluation beforehand of time can increase feelings of competency and control.

• Even as high-stakes checks do spur some college students to work harder, they can have a bad effect on the motivation of other college students by using evoking tension, frustration, or fear of failure. A few critics also preserve that the forms of drill and practice regularly used to prepare college students for high-stakes tests can reason college students to become bored and motivated. Postsecondary training The goal of attending university or some other post-secondary institution may be academically motivating for essential and secondary college students if it is presented successfully and if students obtain the academic, social, and other supports they need to feel able and in control. Studies indicate that the usage of postsecondary education as an aim is simplest when it embraces the four dimensions of motivation:

• College students' emotions of competence, self-assurance, and control are extra after they have to get admission to and are academically organized for the type of high school instructions they will need to be equipped for university.

• Presenting college students with statistics, recommendations, and steering approximately university admissions necessities, front checks, packages, and monetary useful resource also can boom their competence and management.

• Relatedness is helped by way of developing a "university-going culture" wherein college students get hold of cues from all members of their network that they're expected to pursue post-secondary training.

• To spur hobby and price, students may additionally need help with know-how the significance of postsecondary schooling in a context that applies to their private life goals. a top-rated motivational surrounding lets in the coordination of dreams within the carrier of long-time period studying and fulfillment and that teaches children how to coordinate these desires on their own.

To encourage and increase studying and newbies, teachers can assist students to set sensible, relevant, and practicable desires which could produce academic fulfillment and promote self-efficacy. As an ancient Chinese proverb states, "No wind is favorable if one does no longer recognize to which port one is cursing," so it's miles with college students who do no longer have a popular through which to gauge their development. By using establishing available dreams and allowing them to measure their progress against a particularly fantastic impact of personal aim placing Smithson 58 goal, students advantage self-assurance and motivation to study offered standards. In the end, students can then perform higher on both brief-term and long-term assessments. This has a look at came due to looking for the exceptional way of coaching for my 0.33-grade students at Cherokee Ridge standard school in Chickamauga, GA, to be successful each at every year standardized trying out and short-term assessments alongside the way. for the second semester, each trainer in my school becomes given a breakdown of the number of accurate responses out of overall solutions that a student needed to gain to pass in every challenge region domain in reading, Language Arts, and Math on the imminent achievement check. On the flip, each character trainer became to set a schoolroom purpose for every challenge region and plan how to assist the students to meet those goals. As I pondered this venture and pondered on beyond check preparations, I developed a trouble assertion which said, "I want to plot a plan to get my students to want to do well no longer most effective on the excessive-stakes check however at the groundwork steps alongside the manner."

Consequently, my research query requested, "How many want to instill intrinsic motivation in all of my students, said the educator. Now so that they make the right gaining knowledge of arrangements vital for educational achievement on the upcoming achievement test?" In previous years, the basis for the standardized check had consisted of challenge-based workbooks and online packages inside the layout of the take a look at. Some students had set desires in a location with these as the premise. He desired to construct at the aim placing idea. But, he knew that lots of my college students did now not have laptop get entry to at home and that pc time with the most effective two computer systems in my schoolroom and one laptop lab to accommodate almost 9 hundred college students could not be enough. He wanted all of my students to be actively concerned about my plan. Then, it passed off that he was already administering several weekly exams geared in the direction of the imminent check. He ought to use those assessment gear as the idea for adopting private goal setting for my complete elegance. Consequently, my plan became sensible action studies in that it emphasized a manner or "how-to" method in making my students extra academically sound and equipped for the upcoming excessive-stakes test. My reason became to instill intrinsic motivation via the intervention of personal intention putting to master principles offered every week that could finally allow the students to bypass the upcoming Georgia CRCT (Criterion-Referenced Competency Test). My research changed into driven through the person dreams outlined in the weekly exams in reading, Language Arts, and Math. The context for the examination turned into my classroom of 1/3 grade college students from Cherokee Ridge simple school in Chickamauga, Georgia. Chickamauga is a small, rural city placed in north Georgia just over the state line from Chattanooga, Tennessee. The school includes pre-kindergarten through fifth grade and is constructed from approximately eight hundred and fifty students. The ethnicity is in the main white Caucasian students. The faculty is an identified college with over 80% of the students on unfastened and/or decreased lunch. The topics for the have a look at were my eighteen ordinary schooling college students, which means that they were in a self-contained classroom and have been no longer pulled out for special offerings in content region topics with individualized coaching.

consequently, there was one unique education advantageous effect of private intention setting Smithson fifty-nine pupil on the lecture room roster who became no longer a part of the observe. The group consisted of ten males and eight girls. By ethnicity, the individuals have been fifteen white Caucasian students, black students, and one Asian scholar. The general public of the group become from low socioeconomic families as evidenced using the unfastened and/or reduced lunch status. College students whose households earn one hundred thirty percentage of the federal poverty degree or less qualify without spending a dime faculty lunches, while students whose households earn among a hundred and thirty and one hundred and eighty-five percent of the poverty level qualify for reduced-rate lunches. The federal poverty degree is $22,050 or much less, meaning that a student in a circle of relatives of four can obtain unfastened lunch if the entire own family earnings are $28, 665 or less and a discounted charge if the earnings are between $28,665 and $40,792.50. Negotiations for the challenge have been restricted because it changed into my very own lecture room of which he used to be reduced in size to teach and to establish high-quality practices in teaching. He did, but, cozy permission from my primary to behavior the take a look at. He adhered to moral standards by keeping all names and rankings personal and nameless. The timeline for the project changed into approximately six weeks. This was the period before the administration of the standardized trying out. The first three weeks turned into without intervention while the second one three weeks covered the personal aim placing. This research was crucial to me as a classroom teacher because it reflected how private intention setting can be related to assessment. His speculation changed into that if the scholars set their personal goals for mastering content material, then their academic overall performance could increase as considered from the baseline evaluation rankings before the intervention to the rankings received after the intervention of personal aim placing. moreover, my research question, "How ought to be instilled intrinsic motivation in his students now so that they make the right getting to know preparations vital for educational fulfillment on the approaching standardized check?" is critical to all educators because motivation is the using pressure in the back of learning. He firmly believes that it is a lifetime skill for fulfillment. Dreams define the "wants" that make people perform and emerge as a success. If educators recognize what will energize and activate the scholars to analyze and master the fabric, then teaching can emerge as extra self-directed and the students will analyze self-efficacy that can close an entire life. This ought to be the goal of all educators, to need college students to come to be successful and accountable for their work, grades, and ordinary educational overall performance.

Hit humans Have desires. As previously stated, "A purpose is a dream with a definite plan." In different phrases, a purpose is a behavior or outcome that someone is consciously seeking to carry out or reap. Goals are in my opinion important, in the attaining of the person to read it, and sincerely defined with a selected plan. If studying had been a race, the purpose will be the finish line. Purpose placing, then, is the system for aiming at that stop result. Bandura (1991) articulates that desires specify the requirements for personal success by prompting self-tracking and self-judgments of overall performance attainments. The greater successful human beings choose themselves to be, suggests that the better the desires they set for themselves and the greater firmly they're devoted to those desires. From the world of enterprise, folks that achieve fulfillment are folks that are engaged in planning, figuring out precise dreams, and designing strategies to work closer to them. Likewise, for college kids to obtain academic fulfillment, educators want to train college students to observe intention-setting standards. Whilst he in comparison the goals of underachievers and achievers, he determined that underachievers had no particular desires or that they had set desires past their attaining whereas achievers set practical, practicable dreams that have been associated with their lecturers. Greater difficult dreams among students caused better success. Dreams grow people's cognitive and affective reactions to performance effects because goals specify the necessities for personal fulfillment. These researchers concluded that once simple students are taught to use goals and to carve up big, remote desires into smaller sub-desires, then they make faster development in mastering abilities or content. In essence, they grow to be more academically successful. When college students have a role in forming the dreams, they take possession and turn out to be responsible closer to the dreams. Students grow to be even extra independent whilst growing private dreams, or ones which are precise most effective to themselves. Once the desires are set, they assist to maintain both the scholars and the trainer focused on what's maximum relevant and what can be strived to gain. Then, whilst goals are actualized, the scholars have an experience of achievement. Providing students with an aim-putting technique or hints can help them more correctly set and reveal the development in achieving certain goals. suggestions consist of mentioning the aim in written form, making the goals as concrete as possible, conceptualizing the accomplishment of the goal, figuring out the stairs to gain the goal, receiving trainer remarks as to how they're progressing, and speaking what worked and what did no longer. Dreams need to be specific and Incremental. It isn't always enough to tell college students to "do your quality" on an assessment or mastering activity. Unique desires are far greater effective as a clear performance fashionable is set. It alleviates plenty of guesswork about wherein to intention. a selected aim is significant to the student and is nicely described. In essence, it's far clear to absolutely everyone. it's also measurable because of this that the scholars recognize if the aim is potential, how far away the finishing touch is, and whilst it has been executed. it may be measured by a rating on a check or a completed project. Schunk (1991) conducted studies of essential students who obtained guidance on math operations and were given practice time in solving problems.

One organization turned into given a specific goal denoting the number of problems to complete while the other organization changed into given a general goal of operating productively. The ones running towards the precise aim promoted higher math success. dreams that use unique requirements such as complete twenty troubles in one hour are much more likely to decorate motivation and getting to know than popular desires along with "do your high-quality." in addition they referred to that in fashionable, hard dreams such as to study a thirty-page bankruptcy in the one-night tremendous impact of private intention setting boosted motivation higher than easier dreams together with to study five pages in a single night time. They attributed this to the scholars' endurance and more attempt to pursue a greater tough aim. Aim setting needs to be in obtainable, incremental steps. Teachers want to assist college students set small, possible dreams that can be carried out quickly as they pass toward a larger purpose. One success can cause some other as the pupil profits a bit more confidence with every met intention. This procedure helps internal motivation. Siegle (2000), as well as Zimmerman et al. (1992), advise from their studies that after students are taught to obtain distant dreams in a procedure of achieving smaller sub-dreams, then they can make quicker development in mastering talents or content. The responsibilities are subdivided into proximal, or close to hand, particular steps with instructor feedback to allow the scholars to understand how they are doing in terms of both the sub-goals and the distant goal. in the course of this time, in addition, they examine the skill of self-regulation and improve their self-efficacy and interest in the venture. Desires Are Strongly Correlated with Motivation and academic performance. Educators around the US warfare with college students who're disinterested and/or unmotivated to learn and partake inside the classroom. One purpose for this will lie in a student's motivation or lack of it. Mastery motivation, a pupil's preference and pride with turning into proficient, is a predictor of educational achievement, specifically with 0.33 graders. They studied groups of first and third graders and connected higher math and analyzing grades in third graders to higher tiers of attaining their favored intention. Further, intrinsic motivation is the motivation that is characterized using personal amusement, hobby, or pride rather than tangible extrinsic rewards. Intrinsic motivation and self-reliant internalization lead to effects that might be useful each to person and society. Personal aim placing is one form of intrinsic motivation. It may facilitate higher ranges of academic participation in college students.

One technique for affecting college students' motivation is through the schoolroom environment, and especially, with intention-oriented school room systems. A few experimental research monitor that coaching low achieving students to set desires for themselves improve their instructional success and their intrinsic interest in issue matter. Whilst students set and obtain their own goals, they're much more likely to acquire an experience of self-efficacy and turn out to be more academically engaged. Personal intention setting had a rippling effect. As the students set affordable goals to gain and attained them, they were capable of setting up higher stages of educational engagement and motivation. There has a look at blanketed three information collection strategies of pupil journals, student questionnaires, and letter-grade averages of students. College students started every day by setting a personal purpose in their preference. Then, they needed to complicate their journals on their choice of the purpose and how they were to accomplish it. On the give up of each day they contemplated and wrote about their overall performance and if they had attained their aim. They had been given three questionnaires periodically throughout the observation to derive how many dreams they'd accomplished and their degree of motivation approximately achieving the goals. Even though the evidence for growing letter-grade averages become inconclusive inside the have a look at, it changed into mentioned that scholars have become extra involved in classroom discussions, handing over homework, being prepared, and taking note of the teacher throughout the length of the take a look at. If students feel that they can effectively accomplish an undertaking and/or the undertaking pastimes them, then they may have interaction in that project. Moreover, college students end up greater invested in responsibilities in which they have selected the desires that they may be operating towards. They experience as though they have done something non-public which offers them extra motivation to acquire their next intention. In different phrases, with the aid of permitting the students to select their desires, it will make sure that the one's goals maintain the price to them and boom their motivation to reap the goals. Educators could agree that dreams are very essential for achievement as evidenced in in-person life in addition to scholarly lifestyles. "Dreams are primary to modern treatments of work motivation and aim commitment and one's determination to attain an aim is a critical construct in know-how the connection between desires and overall performance". Learning is a herbal technique of pursuing my part meaningful desires. Educators additionally agree that goals are important for the academic boom in the schoolroom. However, to date, there may be an absence of studies at the intrinsic motivational elements relating to setting individual personal goals and next educational overall performance on particular exams.

The concept of control by goals has lengthy been used in enterprise in improving exact team of workers overall performance. There was a developing hobby among teaching researchers in exploring the impact of desires in the instructional subject. a great deal of the early work in this place of motivational research has been performed with youngsters as opposed to with college students. Handiest currently have the theories been prolonged to university school rooms. Intention putting can dramatically influence college students? Self-regulated mastering and motivation. In this book, the author discovers if purpose placing can function effective motivational tool in enhancing their self-regulated mastering technique, consequently academic performance for university college students. Intention setting as motivational device Zimmerman and Risemberg diagnosed six additives of instructional self-control: motivation, methods of learning, use of time, physical surroundings, social surroundings, and performance. Via getting to know these self-control competencies, college students can exert manipulate over their learning and thus promote instructional fulfillment. Within the gift look, the focus is on inspecting how students use intention setting as a motivational device in the procedure of self-regulated gaining knowledge of the procedure. If motivation is one vital factor, how can instructors understand that students are encouraged of their mastering? Ames (1992) defines student motivation as purpose-directed behaviors that involve extraordinary approaches of wondering and are elicited underneath numerous inner and outside situations. He augmented that motivational goals provide the mechanism for filtering perceptions and different cognitive manner. Zimmerman & Martinez-Pons (1986) recommend one-of-a-kind approaches for college students to manipulate their motivation: placing aim, growing high-quality ideals about one's ability to carry out academic challenge, and arranging rewards or punishments for success or failure at academic tasks. Students who experience greater confidence in their ability concerning a project are probably to have interaction with their repertoire of techniques and persist in their use than those having no self-belief of their competence. academic studies Quarterly 2004 educational studies show that excessive achievers record the use of goal putting more regularly and greater always than low achievers. furthermore, college students are extra inspired to perform what they have got planned for themselves and they generally tend to work more difficult on self-made desires than externally imposed desires and that participation in goal putting can result in excessive aim commitment, for this reason, beautify performance also advocates that the school must help students in developing desires for themselves and that teachers ought to give a boost to those same goals. Indeed, some researchers advocated that a few college students are motivationally oriented toward getting to know dreams; others are orientated toward overall performance goals.

Differences in such orientation may additionally affect their classroom overall performance. for example, performance-oriented college students tend to be discouraged when faced with limitations, at the same time as studying-oriented students would be encouraged instead of discouraged through boundaries, thus nonetheless preserve attempting and result in better overall performance. Performance-orientated students who understand their capabilities to below are more likely to possess a feeling of helplessness; while studying-oriented students who perceive their capability to below are greater worried about how an awful lot they can research, paying little attention to the overall performance of others. Also, gaining knowledge of-orientated college students are much more likely to use self-regulated gaining knowledge of techniques. Moreover, as students develop in the school years, they generally tend to shift from gaining knowledge of desires to overall performance goals. This is now not unusual inside the nearby setting wherein the schooling device has advocated students and adoption of overall performance as opposed to mastering orientation.

A prime factor in setting up motivation for students is to ensure that they take possession of their studies and goals. Intention putting can allow students to focus extra on their math and reading comprehension because they have the opportunity to self-inspire to fulfill their dreams based on an evaluation of preceding educational performance or previous set dreams. If intention-setting procedures are applied, students can set measurable and meaningful desires and take enormous possession over their mastering. but, many basic students fail to set goals to improve motivation or instructional fulfillment because non-lecturers, along with intention placing, are not addressed inside the schoolroom. Rowe et. al. (2017) states that these non-instructional abilities can help boost and could boost student's academic talents. goals that might be set by using college students permit them to develop in their purpose-setting talents, as they emerge as greater comfortable with aim-placing approaches, to enhance academic scalability because they can make better selections to focus on precise talents to improve their academics. Whilst college students can take greater possession over their gaining knowledge of, through intention-placing, they can attend to their motivation closer to their math and English Language Arts (ELA) work. Students also war to set desires because they may be unaware of what particular standards want to be mastered in each content region to fulfill country-mandated scalability. Standardized testing changed into initiated by the regulation No Child Left in the back of, which changed into intended to assist college students to come to be more successful.

But, college students nevertheless struggle to preserve a nice mindset regarding teachers because the full-size increase isn't always a gift according to the outcomes of standardized trying out. Aim-setting in a Fourth-Grade school room found that for the reason that No child Left behind legislation become implemented, the scholar boom has been minimal because of the new and better educational expectancies. The present-day examination targeted determining if there has been a correlation between purpose putting an educational fulfillment in math and studying comprehension based totally on country standards. The goal of this takes a look at turned into to assess whether or not coaching purpose-placing approaches and having students set weekly desires, had any outcomes on students' math fulfillment, studying comprehension abilities, and motivation to complete academic work. Review of Literature in this literature evaluate, three foremost regions of research have been studied: motivation, achievement in math, and achievement in analyzing comprehension. When college students input the fundamental lecture room, they frequently lack the motivation to finish their math and studying work and to improve their academic fulfillment. There are numerous reasons that students come to the classroom with a negative demeanor toward academics in a college. Standardized tests, and the point of interest completely on tested topics, could cause students to experience much less inspired to teach. College students sense the stress from the legislation No infant Left at the back of, even without knowing the definition of these federal rules. "Districts use check consequences as the basis for accreditation, and nearly every nation has currently "raised the bar" for college kids' success. The pressures related to these movements are big". The strain that is related to the "elevating of the bar" has caused the inducement in students to decrease because college students do now not experience as if they can whole challenging work or display intention-placing in a Fourth-Grade study room five proficiency at the standardized tests used for accreditation. The incentive idea and the aim-placing concept, referred to underneath, help to describe how goals help in motivation to aid in the training of youngsters. Motivation theory Motivation principle is specially related to learning in a lecture room. The incentive concept states that humans can be more inspired if their wishes are met. This theory can be connected to teachers in the schoolroom using investigating how and why college students lack the inducement to complete academic duties. Motivation is defined as beginning and keeping favored conduct for a tremendous outcome.

Motivation and studying can have an effect on each other in a manner that improves student success in the schoolroom. Unlike instructional fulfillment, motivation isn't always directly observed within the lecture room, but, it can be inferred with the aid of verbal exchanges or surveys given to college students. Nearly all the success made via students must be stimulated if you want to create better fulfillment. Motivation can also be connected with self-law. Self-regulation may be described because of the potential to maintain awareness of academic work and to present a consistent attempt to tough work. Self-regulation is a key talent that may help students become a greater success in purpose-setting and turn, increase their motivation to finish academic work, and increasing their academic achievement inside the study room. Goal-putting theory addresses the project of placing dreams to improve overall performance. Locke and Latham (2002) define an aim as "the item or goal of a movement". Putting an effective and rigorous purpose leads goal-setting in a Fourth-Grade classroom 6 to better fulfillment stages for teachers. Rigorous and particular dreams result in a top-notch attempt toward a project, in comparison to simple and indistinct desires. While goals are set, college students direct their attention closer to precise responsibilities and maintain their interest in that project for a longer time frame. This look at determined the stamina, from trying to meet their purpose, helps students whole more complex instructional work and could result in higher academic success because of the extra complicated responsibilities students have completed. Part of the intention-putting idea addresses gaining knowledge of dreams. These studying dreams are intended to awareness of studying unique content and are primarily based on country requirements. however, a pupil may want to, unintentionally create "tunnel vision or a focal point on accomplishing the goals in preference to obtaining the talents required to satisfy the purpose", once they set they're getting to know dreams. To keep away from this, instructors can help college students create their dreams until students feel secure doing it independently. Whilst college students set a selected instructional fulfillment goal, they could become motivated to finish their work and have higher educational success. No toddler Left behind and high-Stakes exams No child Left at the back of changed into implemented in 2002 to pick out the colleges that had been no longer making ok every year progress, based on high-stakes, and standardized tests after each school yr. This legislation has brought on many unintended, harmful results on teachers in addition to college students. It states that scholars want to have better educational achievement in the schoolroom; however, this is best assessed with standardized trying out, and many college students war to meet skillability benchmarks. Due to this law, students sense the increase in stress put upon them via educators. Teachers and management experience the purpose-setting in a Fourth-Grade classroom strain of this legislation extra in a monetary manner.

Each Lee (2010) and McCullough (2003), said that states use these standardized check rankings to offer to fund to faculties. This means if the students do not meet proficiency tiers, then schools do not get investment. This lack of investment, because of low fulfillment on the standardized exams, has teachers trying to find new and higher ways to motivate college students to want to do nicely. Some states use test outcomes as the idea for accreditation, and states have recently accelerated the standards for college kids' fulfillment. Intention-placing talents are meant to help grow the educational success of college students by using motivational techniques to complete their everyday educational work. Motivating college students in a classroom has become increasingly difficult because of the instructional pressure located upon each of the teachers and the students because of the rules No infant Left in the back of and standardized tests. With the implementation of standardized checking out each year, colleges and instructors are constantly looking for new methods wherein they could help students sense much less stressed approximately their lecturers, as well as teaching their college students non-educational competencies, which include aim-placing. outcomes of intention-placing on Motivation putting dreams is a non-instructional skill that teachers have become to a good way to assist college students end up extra stimulated throughout the school day. Whilst teachers help their students set goals, they also assist them with activities such as independent mastering, achieving desires, and resiliency. Self-regulation and aim-setting are carefully aligned with motivation. Students become greater self-regulated due to the fact they take the wished steps to create an intention, plan strategies to satisfy that goal, and correct their very own errors at the same time as trying to meet their intention. Goal-putting in a Fourth-Grade study room stated that "a chief component in setting up motivation for college kids is to make sure that they take possession in their mastering and dreams". When students can take ownership over their getting to know, they can increase their motivation to meet the desires they've set. Students who learn to use the non-instructional ability of purpose placing can build their motivation for the lecturers within the schoolroom that could improve each ability education and non-academic abilities. The goal-putting process ought to assist fundamental age youngsters to emerge as extra aware of their abilities and may motivate them to retain making and accomplishing their dreams. While college students are capable of set their character goals, this helps them come to be more self-aware of the work they are finishing, independently, in preference to that specialize in what other students are completing. College students need to keep in mind what outcome they would love to perform while considering putting their goals. With educational intention-putting as a method, it's far critical to bear in mind what's taken into consideration mastery for you to be successful in a selected project.

Mastery is measured based totally on nation requirements and is assessed the usage of standardized trying out at the end of each college yr. setting dreams has a positive effect on success for students and it helped college students pass more in the direction of mastery. When students create a goal to enhance success, it helps provide the strength to master a concept. While college students set an educational purpose and strive to meet that purpose, academic success can be stepped forward. Purpose-setting coaching "is powerful in improving the academic overall performance of students". College students who always make goals that are based on their lecturers have the opportunity to enhance their academic achievement at any stage in college. Aim-putting in a Fourth-Grade lecture room nine research has proven that when students create goals, it may grow their motivation to study because they may be capable of taking possession of their gaining knowledge. Creating personal goals helps students focus on their wishes and what they want to perform for themselves. While students are furnished time to set individual desires, they validated higher educational achievement and engagement in the classroom. Students who possessed the motivation to learn focused greater on their abilities and were more motivated to complete their academic work. In addition, they observed that students who had an aim-setting attitude had a better self-efficacy after they got here to high school, as opposed to those college students who did not set dreams. Setting desires now not best presents a clean route for what educational work wishes to be mastered, however, it additionally facilitates students' hold centered on the favored outcome. The keys to organizing goals are making them as precise as viable, cause them measurable and attainable, and making them time touchy. Amy Snyder (2016) used graphs and visible aids, even as conferring with college students, to help them see how they've progressed thru aim-placing to enhance their motivation. The use of visible aids, in her, observation, enabled greater motivation for college kids due to the fact they were able to visualize boom and persisted in making significant desires. When instructors confer using visual aids, as Snyder did, and had conversations about their desires, college students felt inspired due to the fact they knew that the teacher might help them overcome limitations that had been encountered. While instructors well-known college students who're meeting their purpose-putting in a Fourth-Grade classroom 10 desires, the scholars are much more likely to increase the amount of time spent doing preferred behaviors because of the hobby of the teacher. Additionally, instructors who check with college students commonly make greater high-quality comments to college students; consequently, increasing students' motivation to continue to grow and increase the quantity of time spent operating on instructional work. wonderful consequences of aim-placing on instructional success As college students improve their potential to set and reap desires, they come to be extra aware of their accomplishments, which inspires them to preserve putting desires and achieving better educational fulfillment. In an examination accomplished with the aid of Morisano et al.

(2010), it changed into concluded that purpose-placing helped college students develop their grade factor common (GPA) from a 2.2 to a 3.0. Those who did not set desires expanded their GPA, from a 2.2 to a 2.4. Ronnie Dotson (2016) discovered the equal trend whilst looking at purpose-setting with college students. In his have a look at, 69% of the scholars made academic growth after goal-putting techniques have been applied, in comparison to 60%of students who had not participated inside the intention-setting processes. In these studies, Morisano et al. (2010) and Dotson (2016) display a correlation between purpose-placing and academic success. Ervin et al. (2010) additionally found that students performed better on the degree of instructional progress evaluation, or MAP checking out, after placing goals for themselves based totally on previous tests. In common, the Montessori students in this observe scored 10 percent higher than college students who were no longer in a Montessori classroom and had been no longer teaching the equal intention-putting method. The preceding research, Ervin, et al. (2010) and Dotson (2016), had been each finished by way of comparing one pupil's achievement to that of any other. Intention-placing is a fine, non- aim-setting in a Fourth-Grade classroom eleven educational ability that may offer the opportunity to boom students' academic success. Effects of intention-setting on Math success Zachary Mayse (2016) based his instructional achievement study for math on a path or group goal. This kind of aim is while every student has the same fulfillment intention. Usual, the mathematics path aim in his take a look at changed into no longer met. However, there was a boom inside the fulfillment made utilizing his subjects. Snyder

(2016) determined that when her topics set math dreams, they grew from a median of 58 percent on their evaluation to an average of 84%. She concluded that fourth graders who were following the goal-setting method had been encouraged to fulfill their dreams and that helped to produce better math fulfillment. So, even as students won't constantly meet their character math goals, development became made, and students stepped forward in their abilities in their math achievement. Consequences of intention putting on ELA fulfillment Susanne Lee (2010) centered on pure goal-setting particularly, with college students' reading competencies. She referred to twelve of the sixteen college students in her study handed their goals primarily based on their MAP assessment. All of the students, in her, examination, made profits from their studies, however, not each pupil met their goals. One pupil from the sample, who handed the self-described intention, grew twenty-four points in studying for the duration of a five-month duration of statistics series. Mayse (2016) discovered an equal increase in his study on intention-putting consequences on instructional fulfillment. In English Language Arts or ELA, his students who set personal goals grew a median of eighty-one factors. Snyder (2016) found that the scholars in her study did not grow as a great deal in ELA as they did in math.

This discrepancy changed due to high baseline intention-putting in Fourth-Grade classroom information leaving little room for big amounts of the boom. She determined that scholars made growth from a 98.8% accuracy to a 99.3% accuracy. Instructors and researchers have tried to determine if aim-setting can grow college students' educational achievement, in addition, to help the scholars in becoming extra self-sustaining of their abilities to set goals. As the studies suggest, goal-putting had an effective impact on college students' motivation and educational success inside the study room. Even if college students did now not meet their purpose(s), educational achievement and character motivation improved and college students have become more confident of their abilities. Teachers are always looking for new and higher ways to help their students senselessly careworn approximately academics and help them be influenced to triumph over barriers. simply aged children ought to use the aim-putting approach to assist improve their motivation closer to school work and academic achievement as they preserve their academic adventure.

Chapter Nine

Supportive Environmental Conditions

Creating a supportive mastering environment

A supportive getting to know the environment is much less approximately the bodily lecture room and assets (although those are vital) than it's far about values and relationships. In truly supportive getting to know surroundings, every student feels valued, protected, and empowered. For this to occur, each pupil needs to recognize that their tale matters. For teachers, this means listening, and taking the time and suitable possibilities to research:

- In which their students have come from
- In which they may be now
- In which they want to move in the future.

Powerful teachers do not educate training; they educate students.

Selections referring to program layout, texts, assets, and contexts are made based on sound understanding approximately the students within the elegance: know-how about their college students' linguistic history, their ethnicity, their expectations of their mother and father and their pursuits, their abilities, their prior studying and so forth. These factors all contribute to the formation of each scholar's identity – who they're and the way they see themselves. Finding out approximately your college students is simply part of the large inquiry cycle that also involves consciously making plans and implementing programs of mastering which might be designed in particular for them. The resources you operate may be selected as part of this equal inquiry.

Here are some steps you may take at the start of new college months to start to create a supportive studying environment:

- Creating a learner profile
- Building relationships with your college students
- Building relationships between college students

Growing a learner profile

Start constructing a learner profile (paper-primarily based or virtual) for every student. In it, you would possibly maintain a tune of:

- English curriculum progress (See, as an example, progression in thoughts)
- Key capabilities progress
- The student's studying desires.

How may want to you and your college students update those throughout the year? How could your students percentage their profiles with their families?

Allowing eLearning: ePortfolios

Learn about e-portfolios. You will be able to create an e-portfolio the usage of your college's getting to know control device or LMS (for example, expertise net, Moodle, Ultranet). Inspire your college students to individualize their portfolios; as an instance, with the aid of linking remarks or work to a music video to track or illustrate a particular gaining knowledge of the episode.

Instructors and college students at Mt Roskill Grammar faculty have been exploring the way to beautify gaining knowledge through the usage of online environments. They may be the usage of gaining knowledge of management gadgets to organize and percentage sources. Teachers have also identified the cost of designing responsibilities and possibilities that inspire reflective thought. Excessive faculty investigated the collaborative development of e-portfolios to interact in a learning partnership with students.

Building relationships along with your students
How might you pass about constructing relationships along with your college students to speak your notion that everyone student has the capacity to be a beginners and achievers?
• Are there ways in which you and your college students ought to introduce yourselves, sharing who you're, wherein you're from, your likes, dislikes, and hopes and goals for the future? Ought to you do that orally thru, for instance, a mihimihi or talanoa?

• What about bringing or developing and sharing visual tales, collages, or artifacts? Ought your students make, for example, thoughts maps, mosaics, tapa, Korowai, layout, or coat of palms?

• Should you ask your college students to percentage their role models, and what kind of person they aspire to be? Who do they look as much as in their network? What are their strengths and needs? What are they obsessed with (it can no longer be English!)? How should you operate this data to make English studying relevant to your college students?

Video gaming as a context, to learn the way one trainer inspired his students to study in English in reality by using a context that encouraged them.

• Can you operate your students' personal reading or viewing to apprehend and verify their feel of identity and belonging?

Building relationships among college students

How should you construct relationships among college students so that they sense security and value?

• Challenge college students with unfamiliar textual content that is open to unique interpretations. Discuss viable meanings, accept all responses, and encourage students. How are you going to well known, admire, and price their voice?

• May want to you operate your faculty's mastering management system to create a discussion forum (as an instance, what function film must we take a look at this year)? How may you have interacted with college students in responding to each different post?

• Do you have strategies a good way to permit students to get to get to understand every other and you?

From such activities, collate data about your college students' writing, speaking, and supplying competencies. Fostering a healthy, secure, and Supportive mastering environment: How HP/HP faculties do it. Many don't care approximately all of the matters that went incorrect to your different faculty. They're records. Now you're right here. You visit work, you display us what you have got, and agree with me, we're going to get you there you'll trap up and walk across that stage. To study, kids and youth want to feel secure and supported. Without those situations, the thoughts revert to a focal point on survival. Educators in excessive-acting, high-poverty schools have long identified the important importance of offering a healthy, safe, and supportive classroom and college environment. At Port Chester middle school and different HP/HP faculties, this means all varieties of safety and security at the same time as at college—food if hungry, smooth garments if needed, clinical attention while necessary, counseling, and different own family services as required, and a maximum of all caring adults who create an ecosystem of sincere aid for the scholars' properly-being and educational success. While students who live in poverty experience a complete guide that works to mitigate the proscribing, on occasion unfavorable poverty-related forces of their lives, the chance for fulfillment is greatly better.

Comprehensive support uses the needs-based method and "something it takes" thoughts-set. Striving to create and keep a wholesome, secure, and supportive learning environment for each toddler, leaders in HP/HP colleges adhere to the key principle of continuous development—acknowledging that the work is by no means absolutely achieved—and ask questions including those to guide their moves: Is our college safe? Can we recognize the effect of poverty on scholars getting to know? Have we fostered a bond among students and schools? Do we have interaction with dad and mom, households, and the network in actual ways?

We offer historical past useful in answering questions. Those identical questions function as leverage points for enhancing the studying surroundings in any high-poverty college. A healthful, secure, and supportive studying environment allows students, adults, and even the faculty as a machine to examine in powerful methods. Such an environment promotes innovation, inquiry, and hazard taking. Furthermore, such an environment reinforces and enhances the management capability in the school due to the fact ready, super, and committed educators need to work below such conditions. Is your school fostering a healthful, safe, and supportive gaining knowledge of surroundings?

Is college safe?

Many are scared at times. In many colleges, the gangs seemingly have control of the vicinity. Teachers are afraid to field children because their motors might get keyed. Neighboring schools need to rent safe parents to escort their teams for athletic events, and the worst becomes when a variety of our kids no longer have a secure vicinity to examine.

A faculty must be secure. growing this condition calls for considerate and constant attention to the safety and safety of the centers; advent of clean rules and methods for student and team of workers behavior; common and powerful verbal exchange with mother and father, households, and the faculty network; and attention to classroom management as well as the needful professional development. Without those conditions in the region, mastering cannot end up a college's recognition.

The information base on HP/HP colleges is steady with the practices of the schools we studied, especially the secondary colleges, in which leaders emphasized safety for students and the body of workers as a prerequisite to gaining knowledge. At Port Chester middle school, the previous principal, Carmen Macchia, defined, "inside the starting, youngsters might presale-layer bladders all-day trip of fear of what may occur to them within the toilets." To assist st, college students emerge as answerable for their actions, the college established structures, together with the common presence of college workforce in lavatories and hallways. via truly placing expectations and modeling suitable conduct and exact citizenship, group of workers advocated college students to assist sell college protection, which authentically contributed to converting students' views from one in every of "ratting out" their friends to one in every civic responsibility to their school.

Each scholar needs and merits to feel respected and free from physical damage, intimidation, harassment, and bullying. To make sure a safe mastering environment, leaders attend to all elements of the day-by-day lifestyles in colleges. They make certain protection at bus stops and on playgrounds, as well as in lunchrooms, bathrooms, hallways, and lecture rooms. Matthew Mayer and Dewey Cornell (2010) talk over teasing, hateful language, and social exclusion as elements of "low-stage incivility that impact a scholar's adjustment and psychological health". Via day-by-day vigilance, regular effects, and continual tracking of progress with frequent mid-course corrections by way of the adults, HP/HP faculty's salary struggle on such low-stage incivility. Nonetheless, leaders of those colleges document that the school did now not come to be truly safe till the scholars got here to agree that detrimental behaviors might no longer be tolerated. Most effective than did they feel relaxed enough to trust every different and to sign up for the adults in together operating in opposition to inappropriate behavior. As of important, an HP/ HP college at the West Coast explained, "as soon as the children allow the other children (particularly new children) know that we don't do that stuff in our school, it all started to trade. They were taking responsibility for his or her faculty and favored the manner that felt."

Faculty way of life alert

At the same time as a staff has to be aware of early caution signs and symptoms of harassment and bullying and act unexpectedly to interfere if warranted, this attention, motion, and timely intervention will best take place when trust has developed and relationships of mutual admire were shaped among college students and adults. Organizing day-by-day touch and demonstrating challenge for every infant presents a comfort area for communication among teachers and scholars. Leaders within the HP/HP colleges they visited and those in another research report that their concerted mission to take away aberrant conduct required each day interest in the early weeks and months. Their tenacity in successfully addressing students' bad behaviors paid off. Subject referrals dropped, average behavior progressed, and relationships of mutual recognize became the norm in the school tradition. They also explain that as guidance has become greater focused and applicable, pupil engagement in learning improved, which in flip had a nice impact on conduct. while children and teenagers willingly engage in efficient getting to know reports in their lecture rooms, which includes solving challenging math trouble or writing a compelling creation to an essay or greedy how a consonant blend works, they start to see value in learning and revel in fulfillment, and their need to act out or disengage diminishes. The negative conduct is changed by a newfound self-belief that fulfillment in a lecture room or course is something they can attain. This phenomenon bills for why, even in a notably dysfunctional school characterized by rampant misbehavior, some instructors are still able to hold respectful, productive school rooms. Those environments emerge as islands of protection for the children fortunate sufficient to be in them. High-performing, high-poverty faculties strive to create a similar environment of protection and safety schoolwide.

Making sure school safety is going hand in hand with the development of top-of-the-line operating situations for teachers and the body of workers. In 2006, Eric Hirsch and Scott Emerick examined working situations for teachers in North Carolina and produced a document entitled instructor operating conditions Are scholar getting to know situations. not relatively, they observed that student studying will increase whilst schools create safe, supportive, and trusting faculty climates. They also discovered that teachers and staff regarded any such climate as immediately related to their running situations; while secure and trusting, they felt compelled to do all they could to decorate students getting to know. Leaders in HP/HP colleges optimize the link between expert getting to know and student mastering. They remember the fact that teachers' working conditions are college students' mastering situations, and as such, making sure protection for all novices (college students and adults) turns into a concern. As soon as the status quo of safe studying surroundings is underway, the hard work of improving practice can appear. As an HP/HP high faculty foremost within the West defined: "as soon as we reestablished law and order, we had been poised to take off. It's our basis we needed to get it constant, and we did."

The district's "benefit point"

Count on safety—assist faculties

Setting up regulations and strategies does now not, in itself, make certain that each faculty in the district might be safe. District leaders now not only keep a valuable gain in this area but additionally have a duty to actively help a college's efforts to make sure safety. Specifically, district leaders can help with assessing a school's protection wishes, help schooling and acquisition of materials and gadgets, and facilitate the improvement of community partnerships, and resource inside the selection and evaluation of precise applications.

Will we understand the influence of Poverty on students getting to know?

This morning I used to be asked to sign up for two officers from our county fitness and welfare department on a go to the house of 3 of our children. What we discovered become a small trailer house wherein our three college students, their infant sister, their adolescent siblings, and 5 adults had been residing—eleven people in a -bedroom trailer. There was little or no meals, a blaring television, a blue haze of cigarette smoke, and a completely unhappy toddler. I wanted to cry. How in the international can we anticipate these three children to return to high school each day prepared to analyze? Yet they do … and we will teach them!

A second query that drives the establishment of secure,

wholesome, and supportive learning surroundings relates to knowledge of the consequences of poverty on scholars gaining knowledge of. Although the concept of a subculture of poverty has been refuted, too many educators retain to agree that individual who live in poverty proportion a not unusual set of ideals, values, attitudes, and behaviors (including a bad work ethic, alcohol or drug abuse, or apathy towards faculty). To counter those myths, leaders in the faculties we studied and in different HP/HP schools use facts and research to guide the high expectancies of students.

School subculture alert

An ethos of expert accountability for gaining knowledge is tangible in all of these faculties, status in stark evaluation to the numerous educators in public colleges who retain responsible college students and households for poor achievement.

How Does Poverty influence Live?

Even though a few students and practitioners contend that educators can higher apprehend the everyday realities of poverty by specializing in "patterns or tendencies" ascribed to people who live in poverty, this stance can be a slippery slope that perpetuates unfavorable stereotypes. No one theoretical framework can completely describe the existence reviews of these living in poverty. People in poverty are as various as humans in every other socioeconomic elegance (Bane & Ellwood, 1994). The gift, like other groups, a wide array of values, beliefs, inclinations, and experiences, backgrounds, and lifestyle changes. This range makes ascribing unique characteristics to those who live in poverty at quality tough and at worst harmful. A higher approach considers the constraints that poverty frequently locations on humans' lives, specifically children's, and how such conditions have an impact on gaining knowledge of and educational achievement. As witnessed in HP/HP faculties, this approach is not about "fixing" college students; alternatively, it's far approximately reworking colleges so that they higher serve students who stay in poverty—college students who are as worthy of superb faculties as are their center-class peers. As we've already cited, residing in poverty does no longer inherently bring about a shared culture. Alternatively, poverty impacts intervening elements that, in flip, have an effect on outcomes for humans. These intervening elements or constraints are extensive ranging and complex, and they could compound each other. They may be skilled directly or indirectly as a person, a circle of relatives, a neighborhood. What will we suggest by intervening factors? They can encompass students' fitness and well-being; literacy and language improvement; get the right of entry to physical and fabric resources; stage of mobility; and degree of continuity among domestic and school in terms of expectancies, values, and ideals.

On an essential level, for instance, with earnings at or beneath the federal poverty stage, it is very tough to provide for one's basic needs. Underneath such circumstances, choices in housing and the pleasant and quantity of meals available in addition to getting entry to fitness care are all significantly circumscribed. Uninhabitable dwelling conditions, perpetual starvation, and sporadic get right of entry to health care can bring about bad physical and emotional fitness, which in turn can inhibit cognitive improvement and one's readiness to analyze.

Having money provides a sense of strength and manipulation over one's life and the way to make alternatives for one's self and circle of relatives. This case contributes to the improvement of private enterprise, that is a perception in one's ability to impact alternate or motion and in a single's potential to behave on behalf of one's self, circle of relatives, or community. By using the definition, those who stay in poverty have restricted economic capital (money). Nevertheless, it isn't always the most effective lack of money that could compromise the capacity to increase personal agency. Three different kinds of capital regularly affect the personal company: human, social, and cultural. limitations in every one of those styles of capital also can adversely affect college students' achievement in school.

Restricted possibility to develop Human Capital. Human capital refers back to the abilities, skills, and expertise that a man or woman brings to the table, including the "capability to cope with abstractions, to recognize and cling to guidelines, and to apply language for reasoning". Terrible groups offer fewer possibilities to develop human capital than do wealthy communities because, as an example, they regularly have insufficient faculties, libraries, and clinical centers to sell healthful improvement.

Constrained possibility to increase Social Capital. Social capital may be a valuable resource to mother and father. It is gained using forming relationships in formal and informal social networks, even though participation in such networks necessitates knowledge of the organization's norms and gaining individuals' consider. Those networks frequently advantage dad and mom with middle and top incomes as they negotiate the bureaucracy of schools and propose for their children. Individuals who stay in poverty, for a selection of reasons, are frequently isolated from such networking. Restricted possibility to increase Cultural Capital. College students living in poverty regularly do not begin college with the equal sort of cultural capital as their extra prosperous friends. Upper-center- and upper-elegance college students have a cultural gain due to the fact they have got frequently been socialized to the cultural blessings of exposure to libraries, museums, books on Western civilization, theater, or journey. Such expertise is rewarded in schools. Studies have proven that parents, no matter earnings level, regularly share similar aspirations for his or her youngsters in terms of cultural capital. Some families actually have more methods (money), enjoyment time, and assets (together with transportation) to obtain their dreams.

How Does Poverty impact gaining knowledge of?

In general, youngsters and children residing in poverty are not nearly as organized to benefit from college as their greater prosperous counterparts. Poverty-related factors that interfere with students' potential to research encompass health and properly-being, limited literacy and language development, get right of entry to material sources, and level of mobility. Health and well-Being. As formerly cited, those factors are interrelated, and one issue can compound another. For example, substandard housing, inadequate medical care, and bad vitamins can have an effect on the fee of childhood disorder, untimely births, and occasional start weights, all of which affect a child's physical and cognitive improvement. Such factors influence students' capacity to gain from schooling. Residing in the day-by-day economic problem also can adversely affect students' intellectual health, self-image, and motivation to do nicely in the faculty.

Language and Literacy development. Children who stay in poverty regularly come to high school behind their more prosperous peers in phrases of literacy and language development. In educating the opposite us, Susan Neuman, (2008) states that greater than fifty years of studies "indicate that youngsters who are poor hear a smaller wide variety of words with greater confined syntactic complexity and less communique-eliciting questions, making it difficult for them to fast collect new phrases and to discriminate among words". A considerable frame of literature also points to differences in getting entry to studying materials using students from low-earnings households in evaluation to their extra affluent friends.

Cloth sources. Poverty often places constraints on the family's capability to provide other material assets for his or her kids as nicely. for instance, they'll have limited access to top-notch daycare, limited get right of entry to earlier than- or after-faculty care and limited bodily area in their homes to create personal or quiet environments conducive to look at. They may no longer very own a pc or have the financial sources vital to finish out-of-class initiatives.

Mobility. Poverty regularly places every other sort of constraint on households—the potential to offer strong housing. Students frequently pass from one area to another because their mother and father are searching for work or are handling other troubles that require them to transport. Frequent moves nearly usually have a poor academic and social impact on college students.

Unusual feel

Dayton's Bluff primary college, wherein forty percent of the pupil body is a cell, takes a competitive method to counter the ill results. The school plans for mobility in preference to reacting to it while it occurs, lessening the unfavorable impact that moving in and out of school creates for such a lot of underachieving children who stay in poverty. Group of workers don't forget pupil mobility as each day, expected incidence, and intervene as they do with some other instant pupil want. A group of workers member stands prepared with intake substances, and the essential reserves each day time for meeting each new scholar and family the day they appear to provide excursions, explain available sources, and introduce new teachers. Ability and location diagnostics start on arrival, however most vital, the brand new scholar and family are met in a pleasant, welcoming manner. The purpose is for absolutely everyone to definitely include the flow and position the scholar for fulfillment. A whole lot is understood approximately the same distance-accomplishing effects of poverty on a scholar's getting to know. Information on those factors offers helpful information to educators in their efforts to assist and educate students who live in poverty. Like HP/HP colleges, every faculty that enrolls such kids have to are trying to find to collect as much know-how as feasible approximately the existing situations of their students.

School lifestyle alert

While children and youngsters understand that their instructors care approximately them and are trying their exceptional to relate to the realities in their lives, they come to be far greater willing to agree with and actively interact in mastering.

Have We Fostered a Bond between students and school?
If my kids do not get via this elegance, they might not graduate, and that means dropping their dreams. We ought to assist them to hold the one's dreams we need to. It is the most vital work we do. It's 6 a.m. and three kids are ready at the door for his or her math teacher to reach. they'd every acquired a name on their mobile telephones the night earlier than reminding them that their work turned overdue and that they had to get in early to finish it earlier than zero hours. Reminders like these are not unusual from their math teacher. The kids recognize he continues near-tune of their development, and while not always performing appreciative of those reminders, they display up.

College culture alert

High-appearing, high-poverty faculties provide "defensive elements" that assist construct a bond between students and faculty. These factors include fostering caring relationships among adults and children in addition to among friends, and placing excessive expectancies, and presenting the guide needed to meet the expectations of the one.

Moreover, these colleges provide opportunities for significant faculty involvement. To try this they use unique techniques such as advisory periods, small learning environments, and student golf equipment, and different extracurricular possibilities.

Uncommon feel

College students at Molalla excessive school, concerned with the boom of college cliques and their bad effect on college students, approached school leaders for aid. Their plan became to release numerous pupil clubs that would foster a more inclusive environment and broaden an experience of belonging for college students, specifically those who have been feeling excluded. They created 4 golf equipment: a leadership membership, a sports activities club, a club led via Latino College students referred to as UNITO, and a gay/ immediately Alliance. Those golf equipment provide opportunities for students to become greater engaged in their school. The success of these golf equipment at Molalla excessive faculty is a mirrored image of the faculty's celebration of diversity and harmony.

Foster caring relationships

"They failed to know my call; they didn't care if I slept in magnificence or maybe if I got here" is an assertion that reflects a common chorus voiced with the aid of students in massive complete high schools of America. Yet this refrain isn't heard in HP/HP colleges, in which a top-class is located on relationships.

School lifestyle alert

The HP/HP colleges that we studied considered "shielding elements" as paramount to their successes. Valuable among these factors is the advertising of worrying relationships among adults and college students as well as among peers. Far too many of our kids, especially at the secondary degree, attend school in large impersonal settings where college students can too easily grow to be lost.

Start scholar advisories

I love my advisory—it offers me a risk to hold track of where I'm and know what's crucial for me to be doing. [My advisor is] also not able to talk to … she cares approximately me.

High quality, productive, and worrying relationships are certainly possible in secondary faculties; but they do not simply appear, as illustrated with the aid of the case of one small college inside the rural western USA even though the faculty served fewer than 400 college students, many of the kids felt disconnected from school. A most important commitment to creating the college extra non-public for children led the team of workers to reorganize the school day to include a well-designed advisory application. All expert team of workers participants, inclusive of the principal, advise a small organization of eighteen to twenty college students four days every week and stay with the one's students for four years, navigating their direction in the direction of commencement and beyond.

Unusual sense

At Tekoa Secondary faculty (grades 7–12) a peer mentoring application helps to come into seventh graders as they acclimate to the "secondary" revel in with the aid of connecting the "sprouts" with older students as publications, mentors, and pals. "Sprouts" is an apt call in this largely agricultural, rural community, where phone calls before the first day of school from their "mentors" both welcome new college students and assure them that some other student can be looking out for them whilst they arrive. Older students help more youthful college students with the myriad of information required upon access to the new school and continue to satisfy with their "sprouts" at some stage in the year.

The college delicate its data system to allow each teacher to get hold of biweekly progress reports for every of his or her advisees for the specific purpose of staying on the pinnacle of each scholar's achievement, which is important to the counselors' credibility and achievement. The college's college agreed to go into daily grades into their college's statistics gadget, permitting advisors to work on the spot wishes with every scholar.

Advisory instructors often evaluation every scholar's progress via school-generated biweekly reports, maintaining students accountable for staying on target. Advisors identify any student who falls in the back of and works with the scholar's instructors to interfere. The simplest advisories meet day by day for at least half-hour a day, offering aid in content material topics, homework, career guidance, and individual needs.

Start by way of supplying every guide with a biweekly progress record for every advisee for the explicit reason of staying on the pinnacle of every student's fulfillment. Agree as a faculty to the well-timed access of grades into the college's database, which in turn tactics and provides accurate biweekly reports for every advisor.

Create smaller mastering environments

We're saving ninety of our children that we used to lose every twelve months after they moved from our middle faculties to the huge one, seven hundred-pupil excessive colleges. Beginning our new ninth-grade Academy is all we needed to do! Many HP/HP colleges provide extra protective factors, consisting of restructuring into small mastering communities. Those faculties create centered gaining knowledge of environments that assist preserve smaller organizations of college students connected in addition to a smaller organization of middle instructors for the duration of the day. In huge or fairly sized high faculties, this approach may be within the shape of ninth-grade academies. In effect, those academies "defend" ninth graders from the impersonal nature of the big, complete high faculty enjoy in which it's far too clean to wander off. Academies are a strategy for relieving the transitions from middle college to school. Creating smaller learning environments and communities of practice has the capability to authentically join students with adults each hour of every day.

Increase the probability of Participation in Extracurricular activities

While we eliminated the prices to take part and provided the clothing, the number of ladies who got here out to join our cheer squad quadrupled! High-acting, excessive-poverty faculties provide a shielding thing once they locate methods to ensure that their students residing in poverty will be in a position to participate in extracurricular sports. The significance of such participation to the introduction of a bond among college students and school has long been regarded. Whereas center-class youngsters have possibilities to develop their capabilities and skills via non-public lessons and participation in network-primarily based sports of their elementary years, children who live in poverty generally do no longer. Poverty poses a spread of limitations to participation for many students, consisting of the price of charges, system or units, uniforms, and transportation domestic after participation.

Further, children who live in poverty often face duties that prevent participation, which includes retaining down activity and worrying for more youthful siblings. Highly competitive "reduce rules," which dramatically reduce the number of children allowed to make the crew, pose some other barrier to participation. Waiving costs, providing device or contraptions, masking the fee of uniforms, providing transportation, partnering with community-primarily based entities to offer scholarships for specialized talent and talent development, and putting off "reduce rules" are the various approaches wherein HP/HP faculties work diligently to ensure that all children have to get entry to the benefits of extracurricular participation.

Will they engage parents, families, and the network?

I was headed to the house of considered one of my second graders to allow the parents to understand that Luis changed into coming to after-school tutoring on time and doing properly, said an educator. Once I knocked at the door, Grandma and pop greeted me warmly in Spanish, inviting me in. Luis's mom become getting ready for dinner. Dad requested me to return immediately to the kitchen to show me what Luis had begun doing at home because he commenced the tuition software. At the cabinets have been taped a mishmash of cereal packing containers, pasta containers, dairy product holders, and simple drawings. All were in English. Dad smiled and explained, "He's teaching all and sundry to read English! We examine five, maybe ten phrases every day!

The story of Luis is a good example of the advantages of enticing mother and father and families. A simple domestic go-to by using the trainer found out how, previously unbeknownst to the school, a younger ESL scholar turned into connecting his tutoring and schoolwork with his own family. On the flip, Luis's family become most appreciative of their son's development in college and welcomed his newly gained English abilities that had been supporting them to learn. His circle of relatives changed into additionally each amazed and pleased that the teacher had come to their home.

College way of life alert

High-performing, excessive-poverty faculties do no longer go it by myself. Alternatively, they construct effective and trusting relationships with college students, their families, and the wider community and community. They realize the achievement of their efforts regularly hinges on the relationships they can foster with and among those corporations. The fulfillment of HP/HP colleges in addressing the getting to know wishes in their underachieving college students who live in poverty does not continually entirely cognizance on lecturers. As a substitute, helping students' families meet their fundamental needs, which include housing, food, scientific attention, and in a few cases safety, can be part of teachers' or directors' jobs. Leaders in HP/HP schools are not naïve about their lack of ability to solve the myriad of problems their children face, but they frequently can help households hook up with the net assets available. They do no longer difficulty themselves with whether or no longer this type of task is of their "task description." If it facilitates kids' study, they do it.

In HP/HP colleges, educators decide to engage different stakeholders, dad and mom, families, community contributors, purchasers, and each person else who holds a hobby in the student or the faculty who can be a potential source of help if engaged finely. Families living in poverty frequently work more than one job might also have confined English language talents, and in a few instances might also have had few positive experiences with their kid's teachers or colleges. These elements frequently work in opposition to a college's attempts to shape relationships with families who stay in poverty and authentically engage them in their children's education. Even in excessive-appearing colleges, this hassle is an ongoing issue. Leaders in HP/HP faculties usually search for methods to provide opportunities for involvement and to gain lower back their consideration.

The critical importance of agree with

In a recent have a look at of the Chicago public colleges, Anthony Bryk, president of the Carnegie basis for the advancement of coaching, and his colleagues concluded, "Relationships are the lifeblood of interest in a school network". Their previous work focused agree with because the vital building block inside the wonderful relationships that foster proper faculty improvement. He concludes, "In short, relational belief is forged in day-to-day social exchanges. Through their actions, school contributors articulate their sense of responsibility towards others, and others in turn begin to reciprocate. Consider grows over the years through exchanges wherein the expectancies held by others are validated with the aid of moves". This pervasive experience of agree with characterizes the relationships found in HP/HP schools amongst educators, college students, households, and different stakeholders.

School tradition alert

Educators in HP/HP colleges' enterprise to set up, and at instances rebuild, agree with among the school and the households it serves. trust develops and the mastering environment of the college improves as parents, families, and network contributors are welcomed, begin to sense "listened to," and connect in significant ways with the gaining knowledge of and achievement in their kids and people of others. In a single HP/HP simple school, a teacher remarked, "without a trusting environment in our study room and with the families of my kids, it's all uphill. We never make the progress we ought to … we by no means can 'click.' trust is what makes all of it occur for us." The development of trusting relationships lies on the coronary heart of efficaciously attractive mother and father, households, and the network. To try this, HP/HP schools appoint a selection of techniques and practices. They function full-service schools, rent faculty/family/community liaisons, provide person mentoring, connect the school and community via service getting to know, behavior home visits, make certain powerful two-manner communique among the school and the family, and use the college as a network middle.

Create complete-provider schools and protection nets
Many HP/HP colleges join needed social and medical offerings with their college students. Those "complete-service colleges" commonly offer services that include social employees, physicians, dentists, vision and listening to specialists, and intellectual fitness and family counselors on web site. Some colleges offer a toddler care center and a family resource middle to help families in assembly their simple needs. pleasure Dryfoos, stated student and longtime endorse of complete-carrier schools, has studied those models for many years and concludes that when a full-provider school works properly, pupil fulfillment will increase, attendance costs move up, suspensions drop, and unique schooling placements decrease.

Another crucial reason for a complete-provider school is to offer wanted safety nets to catch children in disaster and hold them from falling thru the proverbial cracks of life. Leaders in HP/HP colleges increase techniques through which desires can be recognized in a well-timed way. Homelessness, starvation, medical issues, social and emotional distress, imminent bodily risk, and handling infection and death can intrude with learning. High-appearing, high-poverty colleges regularly set up networks inside their school community to live on top of those troubles on behalf of their students. Once challenges are identified, teachers and the body of workers circulate speedy into intervention mode, the use of all of the resources available to them.

Create links among school and domestic

Strengthening the family's capability to aid their children's educational fulfillment and other forms of faculty success is a priority in HP/HP schools. One college organizes a getting to know academy on Saturday mornings to help households of refugee students. Different faculties rent school-own family liaisons who join families with colleges in a diffusion of approaches. Sadowski (2004) identifies six activities a school might don't forget to set up linkages among students' homes and school: (1) dual-language instructions for college students; (2) English as a 2d language, GED, and parenting instructions; (three) home-faculty liaisons (with fluency in the home language); (four) preschool and early literacy applications; (five) early evaluation; and (6) network and faculty sports and occasions.

Taft standard in Boise offers a voluntary (and thoroughly attended) Saturday morning learning academy for all families of refugee students. The building at the success in their summer Tiger delight Orientation Camp for brand spanking new refugee college students, the body of workers desired to preserve connecting with the households for the duration of the faculty twelve months. Diverse topics fill the Saturday morning timetable, including English language classes, ability-building, and trap-up sessions, persisted orientation and assist, and opportunities for refugee students to spend time with their camp friends, all of which necessarily enhance the relationship between these households and their children's college.

The district's "advantage point"

Leading from the broader image: The significance of knowing the students

District leaders are positioned to maximize faculties' efforts to mitigate the sick results of poverty. Inside the same way that educators in high-poverty schools are trying to find to recognize and understand the instances in their students' lives, district-stage leaders need to really recognize the faculties they serve to make knowledgeable decisions and take motion. similarly to thoughtfully deploying resources—in particular federal finances appropriated for the motive of making equity in faculties—district leaders who honestly know the strengths and challenges that represent each faculty can offer to assist with the aid of coordinating efforts among faculties, which includes leveraging network partnerships, providing matching or seed investment for special tasks, and assisting with grant writing.

Provide person mentoring

Mentoring works. Maximum educators have long recognized that meaningful dating with a person is what kids need and need most. Mentors offer one of these courtings. The countrywide Dropout Prevention center identifies mentoring as one of the best techniques to hold kids engaged and in college. The Western regional middle for Drug-free colleges and groups identifies five advantageous effects of mentoring applications: (1) personalized attention and care, (2) access to assets, (3) nice/high expectancies for staff and college students, (4) reciprocity and energetic youth participation, and (5) dedication (Jackson, 2002). Many HP/HP faculties draw from this knowledge to create and perform their personal packages with a nearby team of workers and volunteers; others get entry to the assist of massive Brother/large Sister applications, local YMCA/YWCA offerings, and a host of other community-affiliated programs that provide person mentoring.

Provide a possibility for community-based totally and provider gaining knowledge of our children actively work to assist their community. via clubs and classes, they improve money for families in want, work on a "coats for children" venture, plant trees, construct park benches, help with efforts of the Northwest Blood center, kid's Miracle Network, American Cancer Society, March of Dimes, purple go, and lots of others. They rake leaves in our parks and do backyard work for our elderly parents in need. Our student's sense higher due to those efforts, and our community values the more assist that the faculty gives back to them. While each person is supporting the other, it makes Tekoa a notable vicinity to live and lift youngsters.

At Tekoa high school, all children are predicted to participate in twin networkers. cited for connecting educational gaining knowledge of two real-world troubles past school, network-based getting to know, especially provider getting to know, has become commonplace in HP/HP schools. Many advantages accrue from provider gaining knowledge of, which includes the following: superior instructional achievement, multiplied college attendance, improved scholar motivation to examine, decreased volatile behaviors, expanded interpersonal development and scholar capacity to narrate to culturally numerous companies, and stepped forward school photo and public notion (Billig, 2000a, 2000b). Network-based gaining knowledge also affords a fantastic method to provoke career exploration, internships, shadowing, and in a few instances jobs.

Twenty-five thousand bucks—this is how a good deal cash Molalla high faculty students raised in four weeks in their 2010 percentage the love fundraiser. Every twelve months the budget raised via students is committed to an urgent faculty or network need as recognized by the scholars. The 2010 recipient became a fellow student with overwhelming clinical prices for cancer treatment. Their enthusiasm is contagious as they tackle management roles and organize a couple of tasks to raise cash and request donations. This annual way of life is a month-length attempt for college students to give back to their community. Working together, diverse corporations of college students now not handiest emerge as higher linked with their community, but additionally, grow to be greater unified as a student frame.

Conduct domestic Visits

I used to be worried and very nervous approximately touring my college students' homes, one teacher said. However, I've found out that making that reference to the circle of relatives has made all of the distinction in how nicely my kids are doing at college. I now view them as part of my work, my activity. Many HP/HP schools inspire and conduct some form of home visits. Ten years in the past, check rankings in the Mason County faculty District in Kentucky ranked inside the lowest quartile of all districts within the kingdom. Inspired by a principle of movement that held that to enhance success, educators had to construct closer connections to students' home lives. Therefore, the district, with a cadre of volunteer teachers, launched into a goal of traveling every home of the 2,800 youngsters enrolled. keeping this dedication over the years, together with a nice administrative and collegial guide and the needful professional improvement, has led to each own family's receiving at the least one domestic visit from their baby's trainer annually. Considering that the home visits started, the district has skilled consecutive years of scholar success increase and a fifty percent drop in subject referrals, as well as reduced fulfillment gaps and elevated attendance. Mason County leaders do not forget "getting to know the character talents and pursuits of the scholars" to be the "real advantage" of the house visits. "those visits cross an extended manner toward bridging the barrier created while predominately center-magnificence teachers find themselves coaching in a system in which fifty-seven percent of the scholars qualify at no cost or decreased-priced lunch and a fair more percentage are from single-discern households," defined the assistant superintendent. "Using taking the time to virtually go to the houses to meet the students and their households, we start to build the relationships that studies shows are a basis of scholar achievement".

Now and again these visits have a without a doubt transformational impact on teachers. Here is a descriptive account from a simple college instructor: I stood at the front door of the small clapboard house. Black garbage baggage was stacked beside me. A barking dog turned into chained to a put up inside the naked backyard in the back of me. The weathered door didn't appear to completely latch. I had sent a notice domestic indicating that I should come by way of after school because she had neglected our convention at faculty. As my pupil's mom opened the door and smiled, I puzzled what sort of existence this circle of relatives had. I was invited right into a lounge—greater garbage baggage inside the corner together with a bed on the ground after a TV, which sat on an empty delivery container. We sat at a bare desk with three rickety chairs and had our conference. Three more youthful kids ran via the residence as we mentioned Michael. Mom said she didn't like coming to the school. However, she seemed thrilled that I had come to her domestic and truly cared about her son, and changed into satisfied to pay attention he changed into enhancing. We had a terrific speak. I learned that Michael had no father at home, that his mom had in no way completed essential school, that his older brother changed into in jail, that his own family mother and three different siblings lived on state assistance, and that he had no high-quality relationship with another grownup male in his existence. As I walked down from the front hunch to my vehicle, I realized that I was coaching a child whom I didn't know definitely whatever approximately. I left in an unusual kingdom of unrest, but additionally one of desire. I knew that when I looked at Michael tomorrow I'd see him differently and that by myself would assist us to broaden a higher dating to manual his mastering. I used to be glad I went.

Make sure effective -way communication

We needed to figure out a way to make sure that the own family understood what we have been seeking to do. The telephone was disconnected, translated letters mailed home yielded no response, and notes dispatched thru the scholar didn't work either. Tries to power by way of the rental and knock at the door determined no one domestic. Eventually, we reached them via a community connection one of our paraprofessionals had with the family. We had our convention in the community building at their condominium complicated. It went exceptional! We understand that a "something it takes" mindset prevails in HP/HP colleges. This is specifically genuine in their efforts to speak with the mother and father and families. No matter regularly restrained assets, educators in those colleges do now not make excuses or settle for less than actual connections with college students' dad and mom and families. The purpose of fostering -manner communication among faculty and domestic calls for leaders in HP/HP colleges to be relentless in their insistence that communications be respectful, honest, and well-timed.

Use the school as a network middle

Many HP/HP faculties engage parents, families, and different network contributors with the aid of beginning their doors and increasing their schedules to offer golf equipment, discern assist and training, early adolescence activities, GED applications, advisory groups, network training classes, and a host of different occasions and sports of interest to the community. These HP/HP schools partner with community or town groups, nearby foundations, nation and municipal corporations, carrier golf equipment, universities, and businesses to host these valued endeavors in their homes, as well as provide offerings at instances that higher suit households work schedules.

As an example, in partnership with the town of Saint Paul and the Amherst H. Wilder basis, Dayton's Bluff primary provides college students and families with a recreational facility and the offerings of a nurse practitioner, dentist, and social worker on the school. According to the most important, "The payoff has been large ... our mother and father and children see us as manner greater than a faculty. It helps in so many ways that everyone hooks up with studying."

The predominant's function

Principals, operating with instructor-leaders and group of

workers leaders from various vantage factors in the faculty, are placed to address the extensive spectrum of environmental needs that confront high-poverty schools. Many advocated the moves that principals in HP/HP colleges take to make sure that each pupil is surrounded through the tremendous supports and scaffolds vital to make sure his or her personal achievement. The foremost's function in fostering a healthful, secure, and Supportive getting to know the environment in HP/HP colleges

The most important:

- Relentlessly ensures the school is safe.
- Initiates verbal exchange and supports professionals gaining knowledge of the impact of poverty.
- Organizes collaborative efforts to deal with scholar mobility and different poverty-related factors that negatively impact getting to know.
- Initiates and promotes policies, structures, and practices that link college students and households with scientific, dental, and mental health services, in addition to other resources of support within the network.
- Promotes the development of fine relationships and a bond among college students and college using doing the following:
- Modeling being concerned;
- Facilitating techniques that improve the scholar-grownup connections, consisting of advisories and small gaining knowledge of agencies; and
- Inspecting facts associated with limitations to scholar participation in extracurricular sports and leading collaborative efforts to deal with them.
- Initiates and promotes guidelines, systems, and practices that expand belief among faculty and own family,

inclusive of hiring a school-home liaison and journeying homes.

• Initiates and promotes guidelines, structures, and practices that connect colleges to households and the network, together with providers gaining knowledge of and the usage of the faculty as a community middle.

• Guarantees powerful, common communications among college personnel, students, families, and the community.

High-acting, high-poverty schools do not cross it by myself and they don't reinvent the wheel. They get admission to aid, resources, and steerage on every occasion and wherever they can to foster a healthful, secure, and supportive studying environment. The sources and groups indexed can manual a faculty's efforts to construct sturdy relationships with parents and households.

Assets for connecting with parents, households, and colleges
Boys and ladies clubs of the USA—www.bgca.org
Coalition for community schools—www.communityschools.org
Communities in schools—www.communitiesinschools.org
The countrywide community of Partnership schools—www.csos.jhu.edu/p2000/
YMCA/YWCA packages—www.YMCA.internet, www.ywca.org

Possibly the most broadly respected and accessed of these businesses is the national network of Partnership colleges at Johns Hopkins University. This community of extra than 1,500 colleges originated from the work of the middle on faculty, family, and network Partnerships and its founder and senior student, Joyce Epstein. Guided using more than two many years of research and exercise, the network gives what Epstein calls "a new way" to authentically comprise determine and community involvement right into a college's improvement system. The network enables member schools to prepare and put into effect motion groups inside their school communities, to increase nice partnerships. further to growing new partnerships and helping current ones, the groups—composed of six to twelve volunteers, which include the main, teachers, group of workers, and dad and mom—evaluation school statistics to decide and prioritize needs.

Many HP/HP schools belong to the Johns Hopkins community or other comparable companies to support their work. Any school concerned with furthering efforts to engage parents and families and partner sports at home that guide a baby's mastering might keep in mind Epstein's end concerning the value of those partnerships and undertaking to create something comparable of their faculty. The best effect on scholar achievement comes from family participation in well-designed at-home activities and this is real regardless of the circle of relatives, racial, or cultural history, or the dad and mom's formal education. Fostering healthy, secure, and supportive getting to know surroundings is an essential feature of management in HP/HP colleges. Growing such an environment is inherently connected to its paramount venture—the development of gaining knowledge.

Motion advice

- Relentlessly reveal facts related to making sure a safe getting to know surroundings. Are we making sure every pupil is always secure?
- build a usually held know-how of the impacts of poverty on getting to know a number of the adults inside the faculty. Do we all understand how living in poverty may negatively impact the ability of our underachieving students to trap up?
- Plan for mobility. Are we ready for mobile students' arrival—supplying welcome packets, diagnostic trying out, and suitable placements? Will we develop "seize-up" plans if needed? Do we offer integrated possibilities for brand new friendships with friends? Will we make it an exercise to communicate with dad and mom all through the primary six weeks after enrollment? Do we deal with transportation problems if a pupil is a cell within our district? Have we marshaled schoolwide assist from personnel?
- Ensure all students are connected to a worrying person. Will we understand which college students come to high school without the aid of a caring adult?
- Start scholar advisories. Is each secondary faculty scholar related to a grownup at faculty who regularly video display units his or her development?
- Customize relationships via developing small gaining knowledge of environments and groups of practice. Are the dimensions of our faculty offering issues for a few college students and preventing us from forming being concerning relationships?
- Offer possibilities for all students to take part in extracurricular sports. Do our college students have an

equitable possibility to take part?

• Work to engage each own family with the faculty. Will we have a plan in the region to manual our efforts to build trust and connect with our households?

• Customize the connection among faculty and the scholar's domestic. Who among our personnel visits the houses of our children?

• Initiate an effective person mentoring application. How are we connecting students with worrying adults and positive function fashions?

• Provide network-primarily based learning and provider-learning possibilities to all college students. Are we connecting college students with the community? Are we teaching college students about the cost of giving back? Are we presenting opportunities for college students to discover professional alternatives within the local network?

• Go to every pupil's home. Can we have a plan in the vicinity to manual us in undertaking productive home visits?

• Make sure -way communication among homes and school characterized by the following:

• Language-appropriate written and verbal contacts

• Translation assistance when needed

• Respectful and clean communications

• Frequent contact via the handiest mode

• True requests for comments/reaction

• Willingness to help with requests and circle of relatives needs

• Private invites to take part in college meetings

• Well-timed invites to activities and occasion

• Open the faculty to the community. Have we created a plan to offer welcome and wanted services to our network?

• Join a network to decorate faculty, circle of relatives, and community relationships. Can we enhance our connections with our families and groups?

The district's "advert-vantage factor"

Growing full-provider faculties

Excessive-poverty colleges are normally located in high-poverty neighborhoods in which a complete-carrier model can be especially effective. However, garnering the resources vital to put into effect one of these versions is regularly beyond the purview or capacity of school-stage leaders. District leaders are higher placed to set up partnerships with community-based totally companies and agencies for the provision of offerings at the college website. District-degree leaders in a Midwestern faculty district garnered sources to establish a family resource counselor (FRC) program and staffed every faculty with a counselor assigned to particularly work with the households in highest want. "by no means did they consider the extent of guide wished, and when we started out working with households, in nearly every case the student commenced doing better in college," defined the district coordinator. Family resource counselors assisted families in getting access to offerings for which they had been eligible. As liaisons between home and school, they helped with the whole lot from required immunizations to homework. One FRC truly helped entice a marauding rat that had been terrorizing one among his scholar's families. Each of the district's FRCs provided more than one and sundry help to households. Possibly equally crucial become the deepened knowledge they introduced to educators again at their faculty regarding the precise and substantial challenges their college students confronted. Instructors need to offer students a safe and supportive study room environment that facilitates active participation and engagement of all college students. Growing a supportive and knowledge mastering environment is especially critical while discussion sports address touchy troubles when it comes to intellectual health and wellness. On the way to provide a secure and tasty learning environment for college kids, it is critical for teachers to:

• Collaborate with college students to broaden a group settlement that sets the parameters for sophistication discussions

•Replicate on their own role in discussions - acting as a facilitator of the conversation to assist to generate many viewpoints

• Fee all student contributions and make this acknowledged

• Use more than a few thinking techniques which open up discussion in place of looking to get to a quick proper answer

• Understand that some college students might not sense secure sharing

• Explore approaches of handling this such as the use of think, pair, share activities

• Discover approaches to make sure that all college students get a possibility to speak, together with the usage of communication tickets.

Chapter Ten

Classroom Communities and Personalized Setting

The concept of "personalizing" is not new, nor new to schooling. However, there is a brand new awareness, especially initiated by using the ones involved in schooling coverage. Versions of "personalization" In society at huge, what is personalization about? The largest numbers of mentions on the sector-wide net go to customized range-plates, personalized gifts, and personalized t-shirts. This could usefully offer some kind of cultural warning to educators – that personalized gaining knowledge of could be prompted with the aid of the "add a small identity marker to a mass-produced product and contact it customized" global, or the "been there, were given the

T-shirt" world. In modern-day united kingdom training, personalization is being talked about because of a much broader political context, because New Labour sees it as the new "big concept" for public services (as privatization was within the Nineteen Eighties & Nineteen Nineties). In launching this concept, the Minister of the country for faculty requirements recommended that it "overcomes the limitations of both paternalism a consumerism", and one of the foremost architects of coverage thinking cautioned that personalization was wished due to the fact previous approaches of paperwork and markets have ended in public services turning into "greater gadget- like, greater like a manufacturing line producing standardized items". It is vital to note that personalization is being considered as "a new script for public services". Even as many might also welcome the concept of a new script, a great deal remains to be seen in terms of the way it is going to be interpreted in detail. Researchers have already warned that the DfES view "consists of five core elements supplemented using a huge but loosely defined range of policies". In this context, unanalyzed assumptions about personalization should serve to retain the old script instead of forge a new one.

Exams and tests don't come up with a training

Extraordinary public services can also have one-of-a-kind characteristics that have an impact on their scripts. If a public service has as its point of contact an individual (as in man or woman fitness) then the notion of personal preference can be salient. But education is organized as a collective via the procedure of faculty. So the solution to the "production-line" problem may not be individualization.

Personalized classroom gaining knowledge of

Growing evidence points to the truth that the study room is a good deal extra vital than the faculty for the important thing motive of students' gaining knowledge of. In studies on "school Effectiveness", it's been diagnosed that lecture rooms have the most important effect on the measured performance of scholars, and give an explanation for a lot more of the variation in performance statistics than do faculties: latest studies on the effect of colleges on pupil getting to know leads to the realization that 8-19% of the variation in pupil mastering results lies among colleges with a further amount of as much as 55% of the variation in-person learning consequences among lecture rooms inside faculties"

"Studies of college effectiveness and college improvement indicate that the lecture room effect is more than the entire school effect in explaining college students' progress". So there is the right reason to focus on the study room, additionally in light of the findings that college "leadership explains handiest 3 to five% of the version in scholar take a look at ratings across schools". Research of the influences on pupils gaining knowledge of factor to key classroom variables. One evaluation of studies tested eleven thousand statistical findings7: the two most essential elements were lecture room control and metacognitive processes. Every other confirmed that scholar ideals about their personal attributes, about others, how the world works, and what's critical in existence mixed with the metacognitive as the key drivers of learning in lecture rooms. So we attend the lecture room due to the fact gaining knowledge of its neighborhood and that is the website of most impact. Inside the study room we consciousness of the control and procedures which affect novices' beliefs and inexperienced persons' wondering. A focus on converting the script of the study room affords a huge assignment. The schoolroom is referred to for its constancy inside the face of change. The primary form of classrooms is remarkably comparable internationally and has changed little for the reason that earliest times.

When we come to talk approximately gaining knowledge of, one of the curious things is that we often don't communicate approximately mastering. Alternatively, other issues hijack the conversation. Major among these are 1. coaching. Phrases consisting of "coaching and getting to know rules" or "teaching and mastering techniques" are used more and more, however closer examination indicates that they might higher examine "coaching and teaching" because the actual attention given to getting to know is minimum. This situation signals us to the manner that matters of getting to know are frequently attributed to functions of teaching. 2. Overall performance. "Overall performance" isn't always learning, even though it could increase from studying. In some eyes, the goals of the school had been decreased to measurable consequences of a constrained sort: overall performance tables, overall performance pay, and overall performance control. But high degrees of overall performance aren't achieved using pressurizing performance.

3. Work. that is the dominant discourse of lecture room lifestyles: "get on together with your work", "homework", "Schemes of work", "have you ever completed your work?" but, it can lead to a state of affairs of meaningless work, as when people speak about being "on assignment" without assessing the studying first-rate or engagement. When we come to speak approximately personalized mastering the hijack can be clean. For instance, one author suggests that newcomers "have to be able to inform their personal tale of what they have got found out, how and why, as well as being capable of reel off their qualifications, the formal hurdles they've triumphed over". The first part seems like a brand new customized script for freshmen. By contrast, the DfES introduces customized studying inside the voice of a (fictional?) teacher: "they absolutely stretch

every one of my pupils. They pitched their work carefully to do it but locate it tough. Then they will determine exactly how to tailor the following degree". So the verbal exchange turns into considered one of personalized coaching and personalized work. On different occasions, it turns into personalized performance as when the Minister states that a key technique is "assessment for studying that feeds into lesson making plans and coaching techniques, sets clean objectives, and certainly identifies what pupils want to do to get there". Researchers who recognize these troubles in talking about learning and their implications for study room alternate have warned: "it'll need great clear up to save you dialogue of personalized learning dropping its focus on learners and mastering and slipping returned into over-simplified attention of coaching provision and associated systems".

Given this capacity for distortion far from a focus on gaining knowledge of, what view of customized mastering is beginning to emerge in the UK? Taking as a trademark the 100,000 United Kingdom web pages which use the term, 36% of them are associated with "individual" 35% of them are associated with ICT/internet/e-learning 17% point out the study room, generally in passing. The share mentions individuals and corporations in lecture rooms, without ICT, the internet, and so forth. Is simply 0.3%. So we're liable to the dominant interpretation of personalized getting to know becoming character gaining knowledge of with ICT. And the concept that "personal" = "person" is observed in government statements: "The valuable feature of this kind of new system can be customized - so that the machine fits the person in preference to the character having to fit the system." To enlarge from this as the handiest model of personalization, this paper outlines three exclusive variations of what might be supposed and attracts together studies on each. Every version represents a one of a kind solution to the two key questions on personalized mastering:

• What view of the character is that this?

• What view of learning is that this?

For each version, a demonstration is offered of the study room practices and the studies base. And the research covers several many years. "Personalized gaining knowledge of has been growing as an educational model because the mid- 1970s". The spelling with a z suggests the source is the US, as does the term "instructional version", which extensively approaches teaching.

Telling tailored to the man or woman in this version of the time period "character" equates with "person", however, no in addition knowledge of the man or woman is sought. The concept of getting to know is the dominant considered one of being taught. So the process of personalization is ready making the mode of "transport" (i.e. the coaching – whether or not by using someone or a mechanical alternative) precise to the person (to some diploma). In lecture rooms, there has never been a device wherein one trainer teaches 30 scholars in my opinion, so various appeals to useful resource-primarily based mastering and to sorts of generation are made. An early example, "personalized gadget of preparation" (PSI), can be traced to the handiest view of the man or woman and of learning – behaviorism. Features protected:

"(1) The go-at-your-very own-tempo feature, which

permits a student to transport through the direction at velocity commensurate with his [sic] capacity [sic] and other demands upon his time.

(2) The unit-perfection requirement for enhancing, which we could the pupil cross in advance to new cloth most effective after demonstrating mastery of that which preceded.

(3) the usage of lectures and demonstrations as the car of motivation, instead of assets of critical facts." The message right here seems to be self-training of a traditional type, using texts and obligations designed by way of the teacher. packages of the version were seen in universities for the reason that Nineteen Sixties, and in some cases led to the adoption of huge-scale introductory PSI guides, however, those had been suspended amidst conflicting perceptions from individuals and observers. In an example in which PSI had been used for 8 years student grades, typical delight, and perceived effort have been typically much like the ones from a lecture-based route. In college contexts, there may be parallels to be made with useful resource-based totally schemes which sell individual pathways via them, along with SMILE arithmetic. These schemes regularly find themselves inhibited by the view of coaching which is dominantly held by teachers, policymakers, and others – which the teacher is there to "educate", now not to assist learners through an aid gadget. Most units designed inside a PSI framework have emphasized lower-order knowledge acquisition. As such, they may maintain a depersonalized, decontextualized, generally written technique to understanding that is frequently observed in school rooms and colleges.

The emphasis on trying out that allows you to allow progress through the scheme displays a view of assessment based on conventional perspectives of getting to know. It's far the idea of procedural display: "I show you" and you then are tested through being asked to show: "show me". structures such as PSI recommend that this model of learning and personalization do now not provide responsive environments of the kind that authorities seem to trace at, on account that inexperienced persons adapt to it instead of it adapting to them. Energetic and collaborative additives aren't a characteristic: typically the individual is treated as a detached person, a customer of the program. The research summarized above suggests that the mere addition of some tailoring to what remains a predefined program is not likely to noticeably modify the script of lecture rooms. Such consumerist notions seem to disregard the reality that gaining knowledge is not like shopping. And these notions are ineffective for improving engagement: on occasions while tries to "improve motivation" were derived from this view, as an example by using the addition of financial incentives, those were useless in improving performance. 'As an alternative, we need to study the concept of studying and the conception of the character.

A notice on technology

Given the emphasis which the famous view of personalized learning gives to ICT, it's essential to recall the evidence. Lots of ICT software introduced into school rooms embodies a narrow concept of studying. "Teaching machines" of the 1960s claimed to provide a personalized direction, however, the offer becomes restrained to some alternatives via a prescribed program of pathways. This idea continues today.

The common view of personalization and ICT
But even by the Nineties, ten years' work analyzing the advent of generation into the schoolroom showed that getting to know gains happened while "teachers extended their conventional views of coaching and gaining knowledge of - from instruction to information creation". nowadays the same point is made approximately personalized studying, highlighting "a danger that digital studying Environments can be used to provide personalized technological veneer to modern-day methods of coaching as opposed to making the tough however essential shift from an instructive teaching version to constructivist".

Three variations of personalized classroom learning
- Variations of mastering and personalization
- The personalized Inquiry lecture room
- That means-making with the aid of many

In this model, the character is seen as an active interpreter in their world, and gaining knowledge is seen as a system of actively constructing knowledge. The term 'private' might also emphasize exclusive understandings which one-of-a-kind newcomers assemble, in part reflecting the special meanings they convey. So the procedure of personalization is ready attractive with the style of meanings learners bring and assisting them to assemble new understandings via a method of inquiry and investigation. Social methods may be referred to, but as a course to individual consequences. In a study room, practices might encompass adapting the curriculum to rookies' questions, supporting them in making plans learning, engaging and addressing more than one interpretations, and promoting learner overview of the system. Factors consisting of those are now and then summarized inside the word "preference and voice". In school rooms, students may exercise alternatives affecting what they research, how they examine, how nicely they examine, and why they learn. This will be in assist of enhancing their inquiries in preference to for its personal sake. Even younger kids take delivery of limits of choice: "I want to make my personal picks once in a while". When inexperienced persons are given the possibility for self-route, there is:

• Increased intrinsic motivation
• Better learner engagement
• Advanced performance
• More potent orientation toward gaining knowledge of
• Fewer reports of disruptive behavior

When newcomers aren't given possibilities for self-course:
• Newcomers choose less difficult responsibilities
• Students depend on others for evaluation
• Pupil trouble-solving is less effective

Evaluations of this subject note the exchange in the fashion of the trainer's making plans: "college students may be in school rooms which promote learner-driven gaining knowledge of, scholars might be advocated to expect some responsibility for school studying with less in preference to more educational mediation. This isn't always to indicate that teachers avoid making plans. Instead, it indicates that teachers avoid over-engineering, via regularly released manipulate of positive techniques and targets.

Constructing collective knowledge

In this model, the individual is visible residing on the center of the internet of relationships and contexts, and studying is seen as fundamentally social, the means with the aid of which people join groups and end up who they goal to be. Here the private is necessarily social and the man or woman is seen as growing thru interplay with others. So the manner of personalization is ready constructing participation through belonging and collaboration, so that getting to know advances the collective know-how and, in that manner, supports the increase of person know-how. Key techniques of interpretation, interplay, and interdependence are promoted, and these contribute to turning into completely human.

In a lecture room, practices may consist of:

1. Constructing affiliation getting to know each different telling the story we deliver, appreciatively.

2. Growing a community timetable eliciting the questions added to the theme assisting learners' plan intentional gaining knowledge of.

3. Community sports for learning reciprocal coaching development of dialogue jigsaw responsibilities reviewing how the community is learning organization dreams for evaluation.

4. Network governance study room reviews, "the schoolroom we want"

5. Community weather improvement of considering and pro-social behavior assisting each different to analyze

bridging to different groups. Through those types of tactics, pupils come to be more active and engaged as they create information assets for every different, they analyze greater about collaboration and often are involved in taking the consequential products in their studying beyond the lecture room wall. In summary, college students are groups, no longer passengers. Diverse studies replicate this. Whilst lecture rooms function as getting to know communities. People feel part of a bigger complete

Various contributions are embraced. The engaged inquiry emerges. College students help every other to study. Productive engagement develops, with an orientation to research. Students show better understanding, knowledge, software, and switch. The discourse of the subject develops. Conceptions of getting to know are richer. Studying collectively will become understood. A community study room – from 1894. As in advance variations, there are implications for the function of the instructor, and the way instructors are visible: "The criteria for judging trainer effectiveness shifts from that of handing over correct instructions to that of being able to build or create a classroom studying community." dealing with personalized lecture room getting to know.

Changing the script of lecture rooms depends crucially on teachers, their expert vision, and how they see classrooms suit for the future as opposed to for the beyond. If those factors are not more desirable, the old script will continue to be. As we circulate far from the slender perspectives of personalized study room gaining knowledge of, it facilitates to be clear that the instructor's role will become extra considered one of coping with surroundings and its sources, helping newcomers to build inquiries, selling collaboration and that specialize in gaining knowledge of. While such modifications are made, teachers perform differently about:

• The stability of electricity – from trainer to more shared within the community

• The characteristic of content material – from fabric to be covered to knowledge to be tested

• The role of the teacher – from sage on the level to manual at the aspect

• The responsibility for learning – from the trainer to the newbies

• The reason and system of assessment – from performing and proving to gaining knowledge of and enhancing.

But, alongside such implications for instructors, there are also implications for how instructors are treated:

"All this 'personalization' will come to naught if I and my colleagues who share college students do now not have the authority to act upon our conclusions approximately a person or a set of students. If we must always ask for permission or refer each alternate to higher authorities, there may be no 'personalization." those points lead us back to take into account the feature of the college in building the kind of climate and organizational conditions which might be possible to assist instructors of their position which in flip contributes to a richly customized study room surroundings. If we goal to enhance styles of getting to know each in lecture rooms, the college's style of operating can also affect the procedure of development. So we need to ask what kind of Faculty Corporation could aid customized classroom mastering. This query frequently ends in a focal point on structural functions, as an instance its buildings, its number of pupils, and its mode of funding, and so on. But those structural variables do no longer have an unbiased effect on schoolroom mastering – their impact happens through the human elements of the faculty, mainly its way of life and the extent to which it operates as a network. For example, lots of attention has been given to the issue of college size (i.e. the range of students on roll). While this has been addressed especially for large secondary faculties in the United States of America, there appears to be right proof that secondary colleges of six hundred or even four hundred convey advantages to college students, especially disadvantaged college students, and concrete settings. however the tendencies to construct smaller faculties or to break up massive schools into smaller gadgets are insufficient on their own, without interest in the other elements: "small colleges should facilitate meaningful staff-pupil members of the family, a sense of belonging and attachment, more individualized education which can create most useful stages of a challenge for all college students, and opportunities for both college students and teachers to exercising autonomy. in the absence of those results, we suspect smallness in itself has a little fee." Certainly, one has a look at determining evidence to signify that small colleges have been related to better suicide fees among students.

Length or managing the subculture?

Structural features including faculty size can be associated with unique sorts of business enterprise. For instance, the primary college usually had twelve months-long student connection with an unmarried instructor, whilst the secondary school has the "egg-crate" design of self-contained classrooms, which is related to concern specialization of instructors, departments, and hierarchy. It's far those capabilities that need re-design.

Evidence from massive reforms in the US recommends that what makes small schools work includes:

• Strong ongoing relationships between students and adults, and with parents

• College's company is flat, no longer hierarchical

• Teacher studying is embedded and ongoing

• The faculty develops its very own subculture

So college size may also actually be a problem of the manageability of operating a school in a manner that actions away from the production-line version. This concept can embody findings of large schools showing lasting improvement in personalization whilst giving extra interest to relationships and tactics. Forces against small personalized faculties. Several have been studied:

• The perception that big schools are extra price-effective. Even though small schools may also have slightly higher expenses in keeping with scholars, if budgets are analyzed via the achievement price of college students, no longer simply the wide variety of students, their greater achievement and lower dropout costs indicates a number of the lowest charges in the device.

• The belief that big faculties provide more desire. Greater sources are supposed to permit a much wider variety of provisions, but organizational constraints consisting of timetables typically imply very confined picks for a character student.

• Deeply embedded perspectives of schools. The folk's theories of teaching and mastering are very sluggish to exchange, so orthodoxies of schooling stay. Traditional instructor-targeted photos work in opposition to the idea of personalized relationships for mastering.

• Quick repair reforms. Even as these regularly increase brief-term efforts – especially in the direction of overall performance goals - they will divert attention from wider problems of the social and studying relationships.

Restructuring massive colleges

Several studies have observed that all else identical, faculties have better levels of fulfillment while they create smaller, greater personalized gadgets. In such "communitarian" faculties, students are higher recognized, and staff increases a more collective perspective about the purposes and strategies for their work. It's far the manageability of social touch which is increased here and results in achievement on different dimensions: "Early findings endorse that regardless of difficulties of implementation, while small learning communities are used college weather, protection, and scholar attendance improve observed by way of gains in student fulfillment. Their more customized getting to know environments seem primary to enhancing student results".

Every other manner of understanding is to remember the anonymity that can characterize massive colleges. While that is commonplace college students act to make them greater like small colleges, with the aid of identifying with a set of friends, and, frequently a selected subpopulation of students. However, the tradition of such scholar groups may additionally emerge as indifferent from the aim of mastering, and the undertaking is a way to reconnect the academic and social purposes. For instructors too, the undertaking of developing their approaches to teaching and gaining knowledge is exceptionally supported inside a viable group of co-workers. Verbal exchange and collaboration amongst instructors are vital for improving styles of learning.

The college as a community

Some colleges operate more like communities than do others. This difference makes a difference to more than a few behaviors and capacities as freshmen. Secondary schools that rating high on an index of communal business enterprise "attend to the wishes of college students for affiliation and … provide a wealthy spectrum of grownup roles [that] will have fine results on the ways both college students and instructors view their work. Adults engage college students individually and mission them to engage in the existence of the school". Such colleges show higher instructor efficacy, morale, and leisure, and students in such colleges are more interested in teachers, absent less frequently, and there are fewer behavior problems. A study of 11,794 16 year-olds in 830 secondary colleges found out that scholars' gains in success and engagement were significantly better in colleges with pra ices derived from taking into consideration the school as a network, in place of the commonplace form of considering the school as paperwork. Further for primary faculties: those wherein students trust statements which include 'My college is like a family and 'college students without a doubt care about each other' show "a host of positive consequences. These consist of higher academic expectations and academic overall performance, stronger motivation to research, extra liking for college, less absenteeism, extra social competence, fewer behavior troubles, decreased drug use and delinquency, and greater commitment to democratic values". Whilst students' feel of school membership is excessive, their patterns of behavior outdoor college are also affected, as an instance significantly decrease drug use and delinquency. So schools that can be skilled as communities might also decorate students' resilience. Again, a few parallel methods perform for instructors. The feel of network amongst instructors has been proven to narrate to the fulfillment of students, and this, in turn, pertains to the style of pedagogy which instructors lead in their school rooms. And when teachers take collective responsibility for college students' academic achievement or failure rather than blaming college students for their personal failure, there are huge achievement profits.

Findings imply that the faculty has a great effect on key issues: scholars' association to high school and teachers' beliefs approximately converting their classrooms. While college students feel personally known and instructors experience expert efficacy, many blessings comply with.

The elements of college that have been highlighted right here are the social arrangements and methods. Success schools operate in a related community fashion, not a fragmented bureaucratic fashion. The latter characterizes orthodox corporations because the metaphor of the system and the photo of the manufacturing line imply. The approaches that are vital at the college stage parallel those that are critical at the classroom degree.

Forces against a wealthy view of personalized studying. Various dynamics can serve to make the creation of a wealthy model of customized mastering extra difficult in school rooms. The primary is inertia because to trade the script of lecture rooms is to go in opposition to the dominant fashion and the sample which has existed for a while:

"Customized studying challenges the mutual resorts which frequently grow up in routine instructor-scholar classroom practices and requires high expectations, effective responses and new varieties of learner-aware pedagogy". So instructors themselves may additionally experience past their comfort zone in the beginning. But there are wider forces too. Returning to the factors which inspired my current hobby in personalized

Getting to know if schooling has to turn out to be "more system-like, more like a production line generating standardized goods", what are the forces that create this photo, and consequently what changes need to be made for training to end up greater personalized in its pleasant sense? it would seem a need to study current forces which include:

• Prescription of curriculum and teaching methods

• Emphasis on individual achievement in performance checks

• Making teachers answerable for pupil performance

• Talking of coaching as "shipping"

Even though the forces indicated here do no longer decide

exercise in a person lecture room, they do influence the broader weather of school rooms and the styles of getting to know and non-getting to know we see in them. Though, the improvement of a wealthy model of personalized learning has the capability to make a full-size contribution to converting the script of the classroom for the 21st century.

Turn your study room into personalized studying surroundings using now you've in all likelihood heard of personalized learning, which tailors practice, expression of learning, and evaluation to each scholar's unique desires and possibilities. Even as one-on-one training geared towards the strengths and challenges of each pupil has continually been perfect, handiest in current years have technological advances allowed it to become a truth in public training.

Personalized getting to know capitalizes on students' almost instinctual ability to apply era, but it's so a great deal extra than technology and algorithms. It's the useful layout of combined preparation to mix face-to-face teaching, era-assisted education, and scholar-to-scholar collaboration to leverage each pupil's hobbies for deeper mastering. When finished right, it meets several of the ISTE standards for college students and ISTE requirements for Educators at the same time as main to an extra rigorous, difficult, enticing, and idea-scary curriculum.

During the last four years, they transformed the conventional study room into a blended-mastering environment that gives a greater personalized getting to know enjoy each one in all my students. It hasn't been clean. It's taken a whole lot of studies, trial and error, and adjustments. However, the consequences have truly been really worth it.

Right here are five instructions that they found out that have helped others take their study room from a traditional sage-on-the-degree affair to a tech-assisted customized studying haven.

1. Research from others. The journey from old school to new learning paradigm was bumpy at the start. They tried blended classes that took less time than planned, had technology failures, chose the wrong technique of shipping for diverse forms of content material or capabilities, and generally made every mistake you can believe. But they didn't surrender, and sooner or later they had greater successes than failures. Their college students' enter and in addition pedagogical have a look at helped me refine my lesson planning till I got it proper.

They began by researching personalized and blended getting to know as a member of the Rodel trainer Council (RTC) to create the Blueprint for customized studying in Delaware. I was also a member of the BRINC Consortium, a set shaped to put into effect mixed getting to know in several Delaware districts.

Being capable of work with different teachers additionally implementing blended gaining knowledge was key to my endured growth. We labored with the present-day trainers to apprehend the shifts in pedagogy important to transition to mixing studying. They heard Caitlin Tucker at a BRINC training and have used her books to manual my continued improvement.

All of these studies helped me discover greater effective methods to steer my students while empowering them to take responsibility for his or her very own gaining knowledge. On the pinnacle of that, getting to know from and participating with others is a trademark of the new ISTE Standards for Educators, which suggest we "devote time to collaborate with each colleague and students to improve exercise, find out and proportion sources and ideas, and resolve problems."

2. Use the era you've got.

Although it is not the focus of a scholar-focused school room, technology plays a massive component inside the fulfillment of this technique as it allows the differentiation of coaching, evaluation, and expression of studying in addition to the gathering of scholar data. They don't have a one on one environment at the moment, but the college students — who're their co-inexperienced persons and teachers — have helped me adapt to anything equipment are to be had. The standard hardware in core content material lecture rooms all through my district consists of a fixed of fifteen iPads, a projector, and a document digicam.

Students are allowed to apply their mobile telephones for instructional purposes. We use Schoology as a getting-to-know management machine. They use Google study room and curriculum websites which include CommonLit | Free Fiction & Nonfiction Literacy assets to embed first-rate virtual content material within our LMS. Lots to their wonder, technology itself perform the smallest role in imparting customized studying for my college students.

3. Let students make choices.

When they first launched into this project, they decided to "release" one piece of the venture at a time that allows you to control pupils' pathways via the cloth. Considering that then, they have found out to take a greater personalized technique to assignments, which additionally aligns to the ISTE widespread for Educators that suggest us to "foster a tradition where college students take ownership of their learning dreams and results in each impartial and institution settings." Class regularly starts with a mini-lesson, which then flows into students making selections about what they need to do after fulfill precise gaining knowledge of objectives aligned to the standards. Their units in Schoology offer to steer to the scholars whilst allowing them to pick out their own getting to know pathways and whole the sports within the order that makes the maximum feel to them.

For instance, while analyzing a short tale, they can select among just studying or analyzing along as they pay attention to a tale. They also can determine whether to annotate online or on a printed replica. They can take notes on paper or file their mind verbally as they analyze the story. At the same time as my students are nonetheless required to write down conventional essays on many assignments, they also get the danger to show their mastering in a spread of different approaches. Whilst appropriate, they could put up their analysis through writing a conventional essay, creating a website, growing info photos, writing a script for a video that they then report, or thru a conversation device, they advise.

4. Pick the pleasant content shipping technique.

They had any other a-ha moment when they finally understood the way to pick the right shipping technique for numerous forms of content material. Their first few tries covered locating a video on every topic to offer heritage facts or turning in a face-to-face lecture on a brand new concept, followed by using an internet quiz. Their inaugural online lesson consisted of a folder with a page for my crucial question, a duplicate of my PowerPoint, and a hyperlink for students to put up their notes.

However, they used to be absolutely the usage of generation in the region of my ordinary face-to-face teaching. When requested to explain the "why" behind my alternatives for the duration of expert learning classes, they realized there was extra to growing combined training than certainly including era.

Today, they cautiously assemble my gadgets with specific gaining knowledge of desires that pressure the method of shipping and learning activities. Whilst determining a way to shape my instructions, they have a look at the mastering activities they have used in the past to decide which had been successful and which want to be subtle or changed. As a result, instead of lecturing to college students and displaying them a PowerPoint for the duration of elegance time, they regularly provide them screencasts or films to watch at home.

The screencasts, which I create with Zaption, Screencast-o-Matic, and Video Ant, are higher than PowerPoints because students can listen to my voice in preference to clicking thru a silent slide deck. And videos are better than face-to-face lectures because they can pass ahead, pause or rewind as wished until they get the lesson. They nonetheless get a hazard to ask questions at some stage in our elegance time or online.

This flipped learning setup frees up my college students to use magnificence time to practice their competencies. For instance, they could annotate a short story or poem in Google docs or participate in a Socratic seminar. Throughout our unit on studies into social justice problems, college students acquire a digital review of the research technique and select their studying activities primarily based on their desires. a few may meet with me to check the way to embed quotes while other companies begin making plans for their displays and still others work independently on amassing legitimate studies.

5. Assess as you go

Rather than simply giving a very last exam on the give up of each unit, they attempted to use formative evaluation to permit others to give the college students steering and assistance when they want it. They take advantage of a spread of methods for this. As an example, my video lectures frequently include interactive questions to assess their knowledge of the fabric. Playposit and TED-Ed: instructions worth Sharing are my move-to equipment for this type of assessment. And our school room is regularly noisy and active as we play a spherical of Kahoot, which gives me immediately, actionable comments on what we need to do subsequent, who needs to be pulled into a small organization for reteaching, and who would be better off in a group that pursues extended getting to know whilst I reteach the relaxation of the class.

They also gather formative evaluation information through:

- Dialogue threads.
- Self-grading quizzes, which provide students immediate and actionable remarks on their proficiency in unique abilities.
- Monitoring of college students works in progress on Google doctors.
- Go out tickets, which investigate the elegance' consolation degree with new principles.

I use all of these statistics to inform modifications to learning sports as well as a choice of assets to assist students to meet the standards addressed in the unit. When the tests show a student has mastered a skill, I can offer them coaching to go deeper or study new talents.

6. Pull all of it together.

The authentic goal become to convert my lecture room right into a mixed studying version that might supply my college students with the nice get admission to rigorous, enticing, personalized getting-to-know experiences. Going into the fifth year, they were pleased with the development they've made in the direction of this intention and excited to enforce new thoughts such as extra flexibility in seating and corporations in addition to higher use of formative records. Their study room today is a hugely specific area than it was five years in the past. In place of displaying as much as a class to listen me supply all the content material and train the capabilities, they want to fulfill the requirements for our curriculum, my students are now the masters in their very own learning destinies.

Instead of relying on notes they take at some point of one-time lectures, they can access and even go back to my films and screencasts and different sources when they need them most, as they're operating on an assignment or reviewing for a take a look at. Their position was standing in the front of the room lecturing approximately the studies process, modeling diverse additives, and tracking college students' progress in the direction of a very last, effectively formatted studies paper. Currently, they commenced partnering with the Human Ecology foundation to expose my college students to a range of actual-international problems. The scholars then form groups and choose one to investigate and suggest an answer or way make an effect. Not best are they getting to know to do authentic studies, they'll be volunteering and mastering approximately the issue through the first-hand revel in. students may even win a scholarship for his or her studies and initiatives!

They are to be had to help students, conduct test-ins, and check their personal responsibilities and institution effects during the assignment. But maximum of the time they just live out of the way even as they learn how to effectively research, collaborate and create presentations together. The biggest praise they have acquired for the reason that all this started got here from a scholar in my AP Language and Composition elegance. He informed me, "Your class is easy. They don't suggest simple — They mean it is easy for me to analyze due to the fact they will select assignments that permit me to do my quality work."

They strive to make my training that form of "smooth" for every student they train. Across the board, my students knew that they experience higher organization for college or jobs due to our use of collaborative generation. They've had students who are now in university tell me that our use of digital content made it easier for them to modify to college.

Lecture room control is an important factor in any educational putting. That is because significant mastering takes location when college students are in a safe environment. A mixture of suitable classroom placing, effective preventive measures for behavior problems, and implementation of thrilling and attractive curriculums in addition to actively regarding all college students in studying activities guarantees that student's studying desires are met. In their classroom control plan, the principal purpose is to have the proper environment for all novices.

In their commitment to making the lecture room hard and secure surroundings, I will actively engage my students via the implementation of the curriculum. They can set up precise operating relations with the students with the aid of having one on one interactions in elegance to get to realize them higher because assembly college students' gaining knowledge of needs paperwork and vital a part of my study room. By way of making sure that students effortlessly engage with each other in addition to with the trainer creates significant discussions and interactions that result in better information of content material. College students will consequently be a part of their mastering through group work and open discussions that make certain effective participation for all college students as they study from me and each other. Those steps will lead to an equitable and democratic study room so that it will facilitate powerful gaining knowledge of. They will be calm, patient, and truthful to all students to be able to win their consideration and create a favorable studying environment for them to ask questions and get involved in their getting to know.

Behavioral dreams for students

The most good sized conduct intention for my students is to have mutual respect for each different and the instructor. This may pass a long manner in creating a study room where gaining knowledge of takes location. Moreover, appreciate creates a secure environment where call calling and put-downs aren't allowed. Many assume college students to revel in their rights and freedoms for as long as they do not intervene with studying. They can consequently engage students to draw up a charter so one can govern their conduct in the classroom. They will provide you with guidelines that they experience will make contributions to successful lecture room relationships according to Glassner's preference principle which stipulates that each individual has sufficient energy to modify his existence as he desires. Involving college students in making their personal guidelines will make them be greater inclined to obey them and absorb the effects of disobedience without fighting; on account that they have unanimously agreed on the policies, in addition, to conducting interventions in the event any of the regulations is damaged.

Classroom conditions

One of the classroom situations that they were able to create could be a terrific classroom seating association for college kids. They will have tables organized in a circle, which includes their own desk within the classroom to create a surrounding for rich discussions. This is supported using Browning (2005), who observes that appropriate lecture room seating arrangement facilitates for the least distance and fewest bodily obstacles among college students and the instructor. Circular schoolroom seating arrangement facilitates for student's eye touch and facial expressions of every scholar as they trade and proportion thoughts, therefore, developing expertise. The opposite circumstance can be to actively engage students in studying. Attractive college students in study room discussions will draw and project thoughts from them as they analyze from every other. Kauffman et al (2006) argue that learning needs to actively contain students. They will consequently constantly provoke and project students to suppose significantly to develop excessive order thinking skills to even help them in the choice-making during their lives. Furthermore, they can attempt to create a sense of community inside the schoolroom to ensure that students feel cared approximately and are similarly advocated to care approximately others; as a result, developing a sense of connection amongst students. Moreover, a sense of network will encourage students to be active participants in schoolroom activities.

College students conduct

They can use an intrinsic conduct management plan to assist students to conduct themselves correctly because they need to take possession for his or her conduct and apprehend how it affects the entire lecture room. As accountable teachers, the sense that it is their responsibility to educate college students a way to take responsibility for their moves and the way to in their view evaluate their own actions to avoid making excuses whilst misconduct arises. Browning (2006) advocates for true scholar conduct to keep away from mastering disruptions and have a look at mutual recognize. They can therefore educate students on effective self-evaluation talents for their very own moves to ensure that every student is responsible for his personal moves. Based on agreeable schoolroom behavior and charter drawn in session with the scholars, the students will understand suitable and unwanted behavior as well as the outcomes that comply with in case of unwanted behaviors. To ensure the achievement of true pupil conduct, they can involve their parents in behavior control via introducing a behavioral log that will have a segment for the mother and father to talk with me. The conduct log can be used to acknowledge and encourage desirable conduct. It's going to also be used to factor out misconduct; which must equally be communicated to the pupil's parents.

Misbehavior Interventions

In case of misbehavior, the student in query will take obligation for his misbehavior. They will assist the pupil to discover a connection between his conduct and the outcome in addition to the reasonable outcomes. This offers an opportunity for pupils to pick out their personal conduct. They can assist the student to reflect on his conduct and agree on preventive measures. This could be finished outside the schoolroom if you want to guard pupil's shallowness and avoid gaining knowledge of interruptions. It's also a powerful technique of ensuring that the pupil reaches a long-term answer for his behavior. That is in settlement with Glassner's fact remedy model that allows college students to take responsibility for his or her movements.

Gadget introduction to students

They can introduce the device to college students by discussing with them the policies and approaches, school room routines, disciplinary interventions, and right student-teacher relationships. This may be completed on a primary day to permit students to recognize what is predicted of them on the way to prevent indiscipline. They can also explain for and speak with the scholars about their rights due to the fact they have a proper to know their rights in a democratic mastering society. They will consequently discuss with students about their proper to experience safe, proper to examine and proper to be handled with respect and dignity. Further to discussing their rights, I can additionally discuss what the scholars need to do that allows you to have these rights. This may cross a protracted manner in stopping unacceptable behaviors which includes name-calling, threats, bullying, and poor language in the classroom among others that create an insecure mastering environment and display loss of admiring.

They accept as true with schoolroom control is the key to conducive gaining knowledge of surroundings wherein college students experience safe and get actively concerned in mastering activities. Creating an all-inclusive gaining knowledge of the environment ensures a successful curriculum implementation, in which all college students are actively worried about studying activities. The indispensable part of lecture room control is developing positive files with the scholars, placing high expectations for them, and encouraging them to succeed via the use of an enticing curriculum. They agree that this technique minimizes troubles associated with behavior in the study room.

Seven personalized gaining knowledge of techniques and Examples

It occurs all too regularly: the bell jewelry to signal the stop of sophistication, however, a few youngsters are left with doubts and questions — at the same time as others are bored due to the fact the remaining hour became spent on the cloth they already understood. These variations are frequently right down to college students' mastering styles and are fuelling a surge within the use of personalized getting to know techniques and adaptive getting to know generation within the field of k-12 education. Instructors can't always forestall the whole class simply to assist one or two college students who have fallen at the back of. However, they can also forget about college students who research at a special tempo.

Possibly you're thinking:
- What is personalized studying?
- How does a customized gaining knowledge of program gain teachers and students?
- How can they begin the use of customized learning software in my faculty?

What is customized mastering?

In brief, customized mastering involves an academic environment and curriculum that revolves around every individual pupil's desires and capabilities. When colleges put in force a personalized getting-to-know software, the method, and velocity of learning can vary for each pupil. But, the end purpose and academic requirements don't fluctuate. Every student needs to reach a positive mastery stage of the topic by using the cease of the unit or college year.

Why this form of custom does design studying work?

Due to the fact — generally speaking — the gaining knowledge of the system is non-linear. Teachers can't assume all of the students in their study room to analyze inside the precise equal way or at the exact equal tempo. Customizing the gaining knowledge of enjoying and tailoring that to each scholar means every person gets the proper form of training based on how they learn and what interests them. However, what is the results of such software? The advantages of using customized education software students study abilities that cross past academia and could help them within the future. Customized studying generally entails students deciding their personal getting to know the procedure, as we'll discuss underneath. This teaches the scholars vital skills to serve them in the course of their lives. As an example:

- Sharing in purpose-putting facilitates college students

to increase motivation and reliability

• Accomplishing self-assessment allows college students to increase self-reflective abilities

• Determining their great getting to know sports enables students to increase self-advocacy talented students in a customized gaining knowledge of surroundings improve their knowledge notably

In one have a look at by the Gates foundation, using customized learning to complement math guidance significantly stepped forward students' take a look at scores. The common scores of college students within the observation went from some distance under the countrywide average to exceeding the countrywide common, with researchers staring at that: Students attending [schools using customized mastering] made profits in math and reading during the last two years which can be appreciably extra than a digital control group made up of comparable college students selected from similar faculties.

Whilst the effects are not without delay as a consequence of personalized learning practices, they were "full-size," with two-thirds of colleges worried inside the look at experiencing statistically advantageous effects on pupil performance based totally on using personalized gaining knowledge. Students with particular weaknesses are capable of analyzing without the stigma of 'special-ed. Within the Belmont-Cragin essential college in Chicago, personalized mastering permits all college students to get the records they want, and fill in essential gaps. For instance, one trainer might also notice that a few students apprehend a literacy place at their grade level in Spanish, but struggle in English. Those children can take a seat with the special-schooling instructor and have personalized literacy lessons without receiving a unique-ed repute.

This allows all students to preserve the equal stage, with each individual being handled consistent with his or her character strengths and weaknesses. Teachers are capable of awareness their time extra efficaciously because many customized mastering applications consist of solo or collaborative sports, teachers are loose to deal with smaller companies of college students for greater focused coaching. Permit talk about seven realistic strategies that will help you begin a personalized getting-to-know application in your faculty. Seven techniques to put in force customized learning to your faculty

1. Educate instructors a way to verify college students and customize their experience for that reason the first step in creating a personalized gaining knowledge of the application is instructing your teachers. While teachers absolutely understand the procedure, strategies, tests, tech, and dreams involved, then personalized gaining knowledge can run easily. But, when instructors aren't educated thoroughly, your custom-designed gaining knowledge of application gained characteristic properly. So, before you begin, get collectively with your teachers to speak about thoughts, have a look at personalized mastering methods, and installation steps to implement this kind of application collectively. Then, ship teachers on precise training to make customized studying part of their everyday work existence. That is what the Verona location school District in Verona, Wisconsin did. it all started with courses for instructors and school admins with regards to personalized gaining knowledge. Teachers then went lower back to their faculties and endured conversations, and in the end,

practiced with personalized mastering workshops. As a result, teachers were better prepared to put in force and execute a customized gaining knowledge of plans for college kids. Teachers must understand how to investigate the interests, strengths, and weaknesses of each scholar. Then, they're capable of region them successfully in their very own personalized studying procedure.

2. Use Ed-Tech to create personalized mastering surroundings

Using technology to hook up with and engage students is a super manner to offer customized getting to know. In fact, technology's function may be vital. As educator Mary Ann Wolf observes: Personalized studying calls for no longer handiest a shift in the design of education, however additionally a leveraging of cutting-edge technology. personalized gaining knowledge of is enabled using e-getting to know structures which help dynamically song and control the getting to know needs of all college students…everywhere at any time, but which aren't to be had inside the 4 walls of the conventional lecture room. For example, the usage of recreation-primarily based getting to know systems permit college students to analyze at their own man or woman pace, and have fun while doing it! in a single study, schools the use of a math sport inside the study room noticed an 11.6% improvement on standardized take a look at ratings.

One example is Prodigy recreation — a loose, curriculum-aligned math game utilized by greater than 1,000,000 teachers and thirty million students around the world. Prodigy offers content from every major math topic and covers first to eighth Grade. In case you'd like a customized demo of Prodigy tailor-made for your school or district, fill out the form through the button below: different sorts of typically-used tech also can be beneficial in a personalized lecture room. For instance, some schools inspire college students to apply for Google doctors for easy collaboration. This additionally permits teachers to monitor the works-in-progress in their students.

3. Allow college students to have a component of their studying enjoy

College students who're allowed to have a say in their personal studying revel in increase important talents along with self-advocacy. While given the chance to take part in intention placing within the schoolroom, students are also more encouraged to reach the one's dreams. For instance, the Middletown, big apple, faculty district applied a customized gaining knowledge of the application that helped college students to recognition on their goals. Even younger grades had been worried about setting dreams and, goal artifacts across the classroom helped encourage them to stay with the goals they had set. As a result, this faculty district saw a boom in college students attaining their NWEA MAP boom objectives. After four years of using a personalized gaining knowledge of the program, the percentage of students accomplishing growth targets in reading went from 44% to sixty-five%. In math, the proportion went up to 67%. Personalizing content material delivery and interaction additionally allows students to enhance using giving them manipulate over their own studying surroundings. For instance, supply students the choice between analyzing a brief story or paying attention to an audio version whilst reading. Permit students to pick out whether they'll take notes online, on paper, or report their notes verbally. Allowing this type of customized learning offers college students the ability to choose the system that first-class fits their desires.

4. Deliver college students multiple possibilities to show their understanding

At the same time as widespread test consequences and essays have to in no way be disregarded, giving college students different ways to expose their knowledge of topics allows them to take responsibility for their training. As an instance, one trainer from the Middletown college District, referred to in advance, stated: students use a Google shape, and the paperwork is sent to me routinely so they can right now see how they are self-assessing. It gives them a feeling of accountability and it additionally shall we me be aware of how they think they did… they take advantage of their self-assessment to assist guide my education and to assist group them for math and ELA. Constant evaluation of students as they circulate via route fabric offers instructors a unique insight into the information degree of every student. Knowing that a scholar is suffering from a subject today offers instructors the ability to assist them to apprehend on a one-on-one foundation tomorrow. Teachers can use Google bureaucracy to test the heartbeat of pupil engagement of their elegance. Otherwise, children who are suffering cross ignored till they give up on a unit, and the problem turns more difficult to accurate. To customize a lesson even similarly, instructors can supply college students the possibility to show what they've learned in a sensible setting. As an instance, a math trainer will have his or her students prepare dinner an easy meal, the usage of math in a realistic manner to measure the right quantity of every component.

4. Build customized mastering playlists

Whilst teachers use playlists for self-guided studying activities, students are enabled to select the varieties of learning activities that work nicely for them. This, in turn, facilitates each man or woman student to do their exceptional work each day. So, how does a customized gaining knowledge of playlist work? First, instructors set a rotation of studying sports related to the topic. Those can be people gaining knowledge of activities, virtual content, organization collaboration, or peer-to-peer activities. The choice of interest can be completely up to the student, giving them the freedom to select whichever kind of learning hobby works best for them. To make sure each scholar is doing the proper quantity of labor, assign a factor price to each activity and set a minimum point requirement. In that manner, college students accomplish all the essential learning, however are allowed to achieve this in their very own way and at their personal pace. Finally, instructors can set mastering checkpoints wherein college students are required to illustrate their mastery over a certain issue before moving directly to the following step. Allowing students to have interaction as friends or maybe complete assignments solo offers teachers precious time to spend with college students who need more practice.

6. Make the classroom flexible

Bendy seating preparations have grown to be extra famous in the latest years, and for the proper reason. After rearranging their classrooms for an extra bendy seating arrangement, instructors stated advantages together with:

- Lower in area issues
- Improvements in attendance and grades
- A more nice surroundings in the classroom

• Extra consolation for students, main to better attention (and noticeably, fewer sleepers in elegance!).

Every other manner customized getting to know is visible in a flexible school room is thru rotating stations. Having precise stations that cater to your personalized gaining knowledge of playlists permits students to attend to the right tasks inside the proper area. This encourages collaboration and makes it easier for teachers to work with smaller groups for focused practice. Kayla Delzer, a passionate suggest of bendy seating, argues that changing the bodily space of a schoolroom at once maps to an impact on pupil conduct and gaining knowledge of outcomes, arguing: Our study room environments need to be conducive to open collaboration, verbal exchange, creativity, and essential questioning. This surely can't be achieved when youngsters are sitting in rows of desks all day.

7. Turn instruction so college students can examine at their very own tempo

Flipped instruction is a brand new fashion that has been gaining speed because the early 2000s. The idea behind this method entails inverting the ordinary gaining knowledge of procedure: instead of getting lectures at faculty and sports at domestic, students watch recorded lectures at domestic and interact in activities together throughout elegance time. This allows students to look at video lectures at their very own pace, pausing or rewinding each time they feel vital. College students can also interact and ask questions via online chats with their classmates and teachers. The college of Washington's depiction of the Flipped school room, what are the outcomes of flipped guidance? One survey determined that, of instructors who had tried flipped guidance, 96% said they'd recommend it. Another look at noticed massive results inside the college students while the usage of flipped education. Earlier than the flip, extra than 50% of inexperienced persons failed English, and 44% of novices failed math. But, after enforcing flipped guidance, only 19% of newcomers failed English and 13% failed math.

Like different instructional leadership strategies, it would take some getting used to — however, it's obvious that flipped mastering allows students to personalize their mastering enjoy, giving them the capability to study in a manner that is first-class for them as individuals.

Are you ready to put into effect customized learning for your faculty?

Each toddler in your faculty learns at a distinctive pace. Each one has wishes and hobbies which can be unique to their unique learning fashion. Imposing a custom-designed getting getting-to-knowcation offers all of them the potential to analyze at their personal pace, and within the manner that's fine for them. So, are you geared up to make this a reality for your college?

www.ingramcontent.com/pod-product-compliance
Lightning Source LLC
LaVergne TN
LVHW041449170726
843492LV00005B/1159